UNCONFORMITIES IN SHAKESPEARE'S HISTORY PLAYS

INIURIOUS IMPOSTORS AND *RICHARD III*
MEMORIAL TRANSMISSION AND QUARTO COPY IN
  RICHARD III
THE TRAGEDY OF KING RICHARD THE THIRD:
  PARALLEL TEXTS (ed.)
POETRY AND BELIEF IN THE WORK OF T. S. ELIOT
THE IMPORTANCE OF RECOGNITION: SIX CHAPTERS
  ON T. S. ELIOT
JAMES JOYCE AND THE CULTIC USE OF FICTION
KONSTFUGLEN OG NATTERGALEN: ESSAYS OM
  DIKTNING OG KRITIKK

UNCONFORMITIES IN SHAKESPEARE'S HISTORY PLAYS

Kristian Smidt

Humanities Press
Atlantic Highlands, New Jersey

First published in the United States of America 1982 by
HUMANITIES PRESS INC.
171 First Avenue, Atlantic Highlands, New Jersey 07716

ISBN 0 391 02556 2

Printed in Hong Kong

For Anne and Katinka

Contents

Preface

It would possibly have removed many of the problems which have exercised the ingenuity of explicators for three centuries if Shakespeare himself had lived to set forth his own writings. But we must not delude ourselves into thinking that they would all have been eliminated. It is part of the purpose of this book to show that irregularities of various kinds enter into the very fabric of his plays, and that they are inseparable from the quality of the experience we have when reading or seeing them. Ever since Ben Jonson's inflated praise of his friend and rival in the First Folio, panegyrics have tended to obscure the occasional roughness of Shakespeare's work as well as the resilience which defies it. And sophisticated critics have enhanced the tendency by pretending that every cloud has a silver meaning if we can only discover it. It is hard for the ordinary Shakespeare-lover to escape the ambience of critical conformity. But if we see the plays clearly for the completely and deeply human products they are, we shall probably be in a better position to enjoy them genuinely.

My subject has necessitated a certain amount of controversy, and I shall certainly not please everyone. I have tangled with other critics and scholars, sometimes in agreement, more often perhaps in disagreement, and I am indebted to a great many of them for lights and goads. But I have tried not to burden my text with too much discussion of minor issues. Instead I have added fairly plentiful notes, where it is hoped that specialists may occasionally find points worth considering.

The choice of the English history plays for this study was a natural one in that they are among the earliest expressions of Shakespeare's dramatic genius and that they form a distinct group as far as subject-matter is concerned. They also offer peculiar advantages to an analysis of composition and structure, both because of their special dependence on their sources and because of the sustained forward drive of their plots. I do not think Shakespeare's unconformities are confined to the history plays, however, and there is every indication that a similar study of other groups and periods of plays would yield findings similar to those which are here presented.

My thanks are due to Dame Helen Gardner for her generous encouragement and to Mr Neville Davis and Mrs Joan Rees of the University of Birmingham for valuable comments. I am also grateful to the University of Oslo for a year's leave of absence which saw me through the drafting of the book, and to the Norwegian Research Council for Science and the Humanities for a grant in aid of publication.

The New Arden Shakespeare has been used for reference and quotation wherever available, in other cases the New Penguin.

Oslo   K.S.

1 Introduction

The geological term which appears in the title of this book was first used in a Shakespearean connection by A. P. Rossiter. Writing about *Richard II*, he declared that 'Whether you approach [this play] from the angle of the texture of the verse, the verse-styles, character, plot or theme, you encounter what geologists call "unconformities".'[1] A similar term had already been employed by M. R. Ridley, commenting on theories of composite authorship in *1 Henry VI*: 'any reader who sets himself the exercise [of distinguishing the different hands] will, I think, find himself perpetually aware of sudden changes of tone, sudden dislocations, like geological faults, difficult to account for on the supposition of a single authorship.'[2] I do not share Ridley's view of the causes of these faults. Composite authorship will certainly not account for all of them. But the phenomena described by Rossiter and Ridley are possibly more widespread than anyone has yet realised, not only in *Richard II* and *1 Henry VI*, not only, indeed, in Shakespeare's history plays, but in the entire canon. And the geological image is an apt one because one does have the feeling quite often in reading these plays (stage representations tend to iron out the irregularities or create new ones) of suddenly changing direction or striking on faulted seams. There is no doubt an element of subjectivity in the experience, but it is usually possible on analysis to trace actual discrepancies – whether in 'the texture of the verse, the verse-styles, character, plot or theme' – which give rise to the sense of being unprepared for what happens.

It is in the plot factor that these discrepancies are most easily observable, and I shall be principally concerned with the action of the history plays, though with frequent reference to character and theme and with some attention to verse and verse styles. It is well to remember that however romantic Elizabethan playwrights may have been in their neglect of the unities they were obviously Aristotelian in regarding the *mythos* or fable as the first prerequisite of drama. The prevalence of the word 'history' in play titles, even when the plays had nothing to do with chronicle matter, is an indication of this, as is the use of 'argument' for the narratable contents. In collaborative ventures the playwrights must have agreed on the plot outline before they started filling in. They may have treated time cavalierly, but their actions developed in a time sequence. Also, however dependent they may have been on supernatural agencies and mysterious potencies, they were rationalists to the extent that cause and effect (not always as we would understand them, admittedly) were made to govern their plots. All this is as true of Shakespeare as of anyone else, even though the sweep of his poetry or his thematic patterning may obscure some of the groundwork of his plays. Linear development in time and causal linkage define his normal practice at the basic plot level. The plot, therefore, is where any lack of interrelationship is most significant. This is especially so whenever a piece of action is anticipated or prepared for in some way and fails to materialise, or materialises in a different way from what we have been led to expect.

Expectation and fulfilment are key concepts in the kind of structural analysis which I propose to present. They correspond to such other pairs of concepts as intention and execution and purpose and performance, but the first terms are probably safer in that they concentrate on the effects actually produced, not on those which may merely have been meant. Expectation and fulfilment are aspects of audience participation,[3] and it may be asked, of course, to what extent we actually form definite expectations while watching a play as spectators. Apart from noticing obvious pointers to further developments, do we anticipate future action or just tag along? And how much does preparation of events really matter? Probably not so much as we imagine in the study. We may be largely bounced into accepting what the writer says, to use E. M. Forster's phrase, and Shakespeare may have counted on the ability of his actors to bounce us into concordance with his surprises. But there still has to be an element of anticipation. As it has been aptly said, 'unless we anticipate, however wrongly, there can be no surprise'.[4]

In any case, whether as readers or spectators, we are brought into an imagined setting and await developments. As the action begins to unfold, tensions are set up and conflicts initiated which will need to be resolved in the course of the play. Objectively expectations are created by the prominence of certain characters who are either present or much talked about, by the focus on certain themes discussed in the dialogue, and by the manifestations of incipient conflicts or conflicts already in progress. There may also be distinct signposts pointing to likely developments, either by way of general comment or in the form of specific promises and prophecies. All this has been admirably analysed by Wolfgang Clemen.[5] It is only natural that a good deal of the pointing forward should be found in the opening scenes, but there is nothing to prevent new expectations being created much later; or, for that matter, to prevent fulfilment from occurring early on, though we expect most of it to take place in the closing scenes.

It is hardly necessary to remark that expectations aroused by what is said and done in the play are modified and extended by the knowledge we bring to it from outside: knowledge both of human nature, and of dramatic tradition, theatrical conventions, etc. If the play is built on a literary source we may even be familiar with the material it draws upon, and if it is historical we may know the history. Such information may hamper as well as help, since the dramatist is naturally not obliged to defer to his sources or even to historical accuracy. There is a complication, too, in the possibility that he may have carried a specific source in his mind more completely than appears from his play, so as to leave us at times with a lack of reference unless we know that source quite well. A. P. Rossiter thought that in *Richard II* we may at times be greatly puzzled unless we make mental reference to the anonymous play *Thomas of Woodstock*. Then again gaps between expectation and fulfilment may be due to the author's failure to dramatise enough of the raw material, i.e. to insufficient plotting. The chronicles of the English kings tell of events as they supposedly happened and do not always thread them on an unbroken string of cause and effect with an unchanging selection of characters. And not infrequently there is a lack of clarity and a degree of inconsistency in the sources which are mirrored in the plays to which they contribute. In such cases, and to the extent that we need to make informed guesses as to the dramatist's intentions to guide our own expectations, a study of his literary and dramatic antecedents may be extremely rewarding. Shakespeare's departures from his sources and invention of new material, for instance, are likely to be matters of deliberate choice, and sometimes what he omits from his sources is a better indication of his intention than what he uses. In *King John* he may be supposed to teach that even tyrant kings must not be resisted. But this impression will be modified if we see that he avoids relaying the explicit statement of the doctrine of blind obedience contained in his source play, *The Troublesome Raigne of King John*.

Most expectations are in fact fulfilled in the plays. Not necessarily those of the protagonists, for the protagonists may expect success where we foresee defeat. But in terms of drama the destruction of expectations as well as their realisation counts as fulfilment. There is non-fulfilment only when preparations and promises are ignored and forgotten, as in *Richard II* when Aumerle and his accusers are not brought to the formal trial promised by Bolingbroke, or in *King John* when the theme of bastardy which so much dominates the first two scenes is not developed, or in *Richard III* when Jane Shore does not put in an appearance despite the importance attributed to her influence. It is unpursued possibilities such as these which may indicate the presence of faults in the geological sense, together with apparent dislocations and interpolations of matter revealed by disruptions in the forward movement of the plot and by repetitions or contradictions in the dialogue. Some faults, of course, are completely trivial and probably due either to plain forgetfulness or to a salutary lack of pedantry. Thus when the Duke of Richmond summons the Earl of Pembroke to come to his tent at two o'clock in the morning and the latter apparently fails to keep the appointment the summons may be taken as an example of Richmond's good organisation before the battle and Pembroke's non-appearance conveniently ignored, as it probably is by all readers and spectators. There are pointers to future action which may merely serve the purpose of rounding off a scene, or adjusting character portrayal, or leaving the playwright a chance of following them up if it proves expedient, but which do not necessitate further development. One such instance is King Henry's decision at the end of the opening scene of *3 Henry VI* to send Exeter as a messenger to the northern lords in order to reconcile them. We hear nothing further of this mission and it hardly matters. It has served to illustrate the king's conciliatory attitude. In other cases, however, the dramatic implications seem too serious for the issue to be dropped. There is the promise of a major clash at the end of the opening scene of *1 Henry VI*, when both Exeter and the Bishop of Winchester seem about to hurry to Eltham, one to protect the young king, the other to abduct him.[6] When next we see Winchester, in the third scene, he is in cardinal's robes engaged in a fray with the Duke of Gloucester, and Exeter is not seen again till the third act, when he assumes the choric role which is his chief assignment in the play. Inevitably in discovering such inconsistencies one tries to decide how significant they are and to explain why and how they have come about. It may even be possible to hypothesise the form in which the dramatist originally thought of presenting his play. We may find signs of revision and adaptation, sometimes of extensive changes in the plotting, and they all call for examination.

To illustrate more fully the kind of problem involved when the reliability of the text comes under suspicion, as it does in a number of these cases, we may consider a scene from *Henry VIII*, a play which has often been held to be non-Shakespearean, in parts or *in toto*, but which I shall treat as being to all intents and purposes entirely Shakespeare's. It is a play, it should be noted, which is not on the whole remarkable for its unconformities. But in Act II, Scene i something curious happens. When Buckingham is led to execution he makes two different speeches, one in the presence of Sir Thomas Lovell who conducts him 'from his arraignment', the other in the presence of Sir Nicholas Vaux, who takes over the custody of Buckingham at the waterside. The first of these speeches is an expansion by Shakespeare of the words spoken by Buckingham to the Duke of Norfolk on receiving sentence of death, as reported in Holinshed. The other was largely invented by Shakespeare. In the first speech Buckingham addresses 'all good people' and swears that although he has 'receiv'd a traitor's judgment' he has been faithful to the king:

> And if I have a conscience, let it sink me,
> Even as the axe falls, if I be not faithful.   (ii.i.60–1)

He continues:

> The law I bear no malice for my death,
> 'T has done upon the premisses but justice:
> But those that sought it I could wish more Christians:
> Be what they will, I heartily forgive 'em;
> Yet let 'em look they glory not in mischief,
> Nor build their evils on the graves of great men.
> For then my guiltless blood must cry against 'em.

The duke then turns to the 'few that lov'd [him]' and begs them:

> Make of your prayers one sweet sacrifice
> And lift my soul to heaven.

Then at Lovell's entreaty he specifically forgives him, too, and magnanimously declares:

> There cannot be those numberless offences
> 'Gainst me that I cannot take peace with: no black envy
> Shall make my grave.

He concludes this part of the scene with six lines of earnest blessings for the king.

When Vaux takes over, however, Buckingham is no longer in a forgiving mood:

> Yet I am richer than my base accusers,
> That never knew what truth meant: I now seal it,
> And with that blood will make 'em one day groan for't.

He admits, virtually as he did to Lovell, that his trial was 'a noble one'. But he speaks bitterly of his sovereign and earnestly warns his listeners against trusting their friends too much, for they

> When they once perceive
> The least rub in your fortunes, fall away
> Like water from ye, never found again
> But where they mean to sink ye.

And finally, once more addressing 'all good people', he asks them to pray for him.

If we compare these two speeches we find not only a number of repetitions ('all good people', the fair trial, his innocent blood rising to accuse his enemies, appeals for prayers, the image of being sunk) but above all basic and striking contradictions. Speaking to Lovell, the duke insists that he forgives everybody. He only warns his accusers that if they continue in wickedness his blood 'must cry against 'em'. And he blesses the king. Speaking to Vaux, he says nothing about forgiveness but threatens his 'base accusers': his blood 'will make 'em one day groan for't'. He speaks reproachfully of the king and ends his speech in a bitter and cynical mood.

The two speeches occur in a continuous sequence, interrupted and divided only by a few lines spoken by Lovell and Vaux. But clearly they were not written with the same picture of Buckingham and the same conception of his end in the author's mind. There is nothing to disprove conclusively that Shakespeare wrote them in one stretch of composition, but if we think he did we must be ready to admit that his ideas changed while he was writing. For no amount of sophistication can make the repetitions and contradictions seem functional. And it may be just as natural to assume that Shakespeare first wrote one of Buckingham's speeches for a relatively short scene and later returned to revise and possibly expand the scene. However we tackle this problem we are still faced with the more important and difficult one of assessing whether both speeches were finally passed for inclusion and, if not, which was meant for excision. The repetitions may help to decide, if no good reason can be found to suppose them intentional. But the whole tenor of the play must be considered in an attempt to judge the appropriateness of either or both of the speeches.

In general there is no way of knowing for certain to what extent the various play manuscripts which must have been in existence in Shakespeare's day preserved alternative readings or readings actually discarded by the author, leaving them still legible to an editor or printer.

But we can hardly recognise the presence of basically illegitimate readings in printed texts in cases where they seem easily demonstrable – as most scholars occasionally do – without allowing for the possibility that they may also occur in cases where they are harder to prove. Besides, unconformities may have come about in the author's mind rather than on paper. It would indeed be strange if a dramatist in the heat of composition should not at times overlook connections and change his ground. J. W. Lever speaks of 'the oversights, hesitations, and changes of plan normal to a writer in the course of composition'.[7] Whatever the causes and origins, the signs of contradiction and discontinuity are often evident.

There has been nothing like a thorough investigation of the unconformities in the plays, and the reason is probably the excessive veneration with which the Bard has been approached since textual scholarship began, and the mistaken assumption that to find fault with Shakespeare is to deny his genius. Coleridge must take some of the blame for this. His lofty view of the unifying power of the imagination to effect 'a balance or reconcilement of opposite or discordant qualities' and his application of this view to Shakespeare, sincerely as we may respond to both the view and the application, still no doubt hold a good deal of criticism in thrall.[8] There has been an understandable reaction, too, against the work of the 'disintegrators' of the early part of our century, who rode on the wave of a theory no longer much in favour, that of Shakespeare's extensive participation in joint play-writing projects. Adventurous scholars like Dover Wilson no doubt went too far in portioning out some of the Shakespeare canon among different collaborators. No doubt, too, there has been much irresponsible guesswork as to what Shakespeare really intended to write, causing fears of anarchy in conservative quarters. But such fears hardly warrant general condemnation of all speculative enquiries, still less a refusal to recognise faults as faults (I use the word with deliberate ambiguity, as I shall probably do again). The adulation which accepts the formula that 'Shakespeare doesn't commit an inconsistency, he achieves one', or that 'Shakespeare is Shakespeare, the master-craftsman who knows what he's doing',[9] would be all very well if it were reserved for the works that might have come from Shakespeare's hand supposing (a) he had had the leisure to tidy them up at the time when they were written and (b) 'the Author himselfe had liu'd to haue set forth, and ouerseen his owne writings'. As it is, the response which assumes guaranteed infallibility takes no account either of the haste and improvisation which must have often attended the birth of the plays or the accidents which beset them during up to three decades of handling.[10] The guessing game, if it comes to that, is as actively conducted by the fundamentalists as by the more critically minded. Since we can never be absolutely certain that what we have received in print is in every respect what Shakespeare would have wanted us (or his contemporaries) to see and hear, the attempts of rigidly conservative scholars to explain problematic readings and apparent inconsistencies on the assumption that the text is always inspired sometimes lead to quite extravagant conjectures. Add to this the superstition that the master-craftsman always knew what he was doing, and the conditions are favourable for a great deal of very alexandrian exegesis. The result is a general subtilising of Shakespeare's intentions which is in most cases likely to be more arbitrary and to represent a more insidious intentionalism than the serious attempts which have been made to look into the genesis of the plays for causes of obscurity or lack of coherence. Thus when Emrys Jones, in a book on Shakespeare's cultural background, wishes to defend the received order of the *Henry VI* trilogy as the order of composition, he offers suppositions involving Shakespeare's mental processes which are ultimately far less convincing than the straightforwardly sceptical views of Dover Wilson which he rebuts.[11]

One of the commonest temptations in modern Shakespeare criticism is to find psychological explanations for inconsistent behaviour on the part of *dramatis personae*, even when the inconsistency is not apparent to anyone but the explicator. One critic finds it odd that the conspirators in the Southampton scene of *Henry V* 'accept without demur the repeated implication that they had acted on the basest of motives – the greed for money' and that the king remains silent on this point. This is inconsistent, he thinks, with the fact that 'two of the plotters were men of authority as well as rank in the kingdom' and with the assumption that the audience must be quite familiar with the Earl of Cambridge's real motive for the conspiracy (not greed but the reinstatement of the Mortimers on the throne) and must have known that King Henry was aware of it. He then proceeds to thought-reading and explains that the conspirators are trying to save their families by their silence about their political motive and that Henry wants to avoid 'drawing attention gratuitously to the weak legality of his own claim to the crown'.[12] But there is nothing whatever in the text to suggest concern for the traitors' families, and though Shakespeare the author may have wished to avoid 'drawing attention gratuitously to the weak legality' of Henry's claim, there is no basis for ascribing a sense of insecurity to his creature King Henry at this point. The chorus introducing Act II insists, anyway, that the lords have been corrupted by French gold, the charge of corruption is repeated by Exeter at the beginning of II.ii and amplified by the king, and Shakespeare's main intention, I would think, was to use the conspiracy for additional denigration of the perfidious French and to demonstrate God's providential care for King Henry. Another critic, worried by Hal's political irresponsibility in the tavern scene of *1 Henry IV* when he turns away the king's messenger who has come to summon him to the palace, gives a completely unfounded reading of the prince's mind at the crucial moment: 'when Falstaff reenters with word of the rebellion,' he says, 'Hal, now aware of his error, makes no verbal note of it because ready adaptability to circumstances, not egocentric brooding, is natural to him.' The critic, in other words, would have us believe that Hal at this moment learns the chief lesson of his holiday life without breathing a word to make us conscious of the fact.[13] A third critic, discussing Shakespeare's inconsistent characters in *King John*, seeks a justification which seems all too fashionably modern. Shakespeare, he says, 'has deliberately moved in the direction of provocative ambiguity'.[14]

Perhaps the worst of it is that all this subtilising gets in the way of real understanding: especially for the 'general' reader, who would be better served by an assurance that a tangle is a tangle, a fracture a fracture, than with verbal sophistications and dubious casebooks purporting to explain the mental processes of imaginary characters. How does one offend Shakespeare most – by recognising that he and his associates occasionally made mistakes or by supposing that when he called a spade an xyz it was an ingenious way of calling it a mattock?

In the year of the quatercentenary of Shakespeare's birth Professor Alfred Harbage exposed the superstition of authorial and textual infallibility in a brilliant essay, 'Shakespeare and the Myth of Perfection'.[15] He showed how critics since the eighteenth century have been so blinded by the perfection imputed to the dramatist that they have gone to any lengths to justify his seeming aberrations. In a revealing and amusing example Harbage finds that 'A blemish has been rationalized into a beauty, a discrepancy into a subtlety, a numerical error into a "touch of nature".' I shall not rehearse Harbage's critique, which should be read by anyone interested in textual interpretation, but there is plenty of material to illustrate his contention that in the twentieth century we can no longer 'say that the scent of incense is strongest in the vicinity of the least able. A really ominous progression has occurred. It is now the major Shakespearian critics who serve the myth of perfection.'

Fortunately, since Harbage wrote his essay there have been signs of a growing critical attitude to the textual tradition. E. A. J. Honigmann's book *The Stability of Shakespeare's Text* (1965) questions the all but absolute authority of the First Folio and suggests that many variant readings should be considered as tentative or alternative, since the author obviously hesitated occasionally, and since his manuscripts often passed through many hands before they (or copies of them) found their way into print. Joan Rees, in *Shakespeare and the Story* (1978), stresses the living and leaping quality of Shakespeare's continuous invention. She bases her discussion, she says, on 'the linear development of the plays and their narrative techniques'. She realises that Shakespeare, like all artists, sometimes ran into difficulties with his material or stumbled on new paths as he went along. She allows for improvisations and is willing to see the remains of abandoned intentions exposed to view. She also clearly demonstrates the triumph of Shakespeare's creative faculty in compensating for defects in the story line. At the International Shakespeare Association's congress in Washington in 1976 there was a session on Shakespeare's artistic lapses.[16]

It is being realised more and more that the discussion of anomalies is not dependent merely on 'conjectures about Shakespeare's "original" intentions and methods of composition', as it has been alleged.[17] There is a considerable amount of objective evidence to enable us to locate and describe disturbances, whether accidental or intentional. Some of the evidence, such as the kind of loops in the dialogue which are brought about by the repetition of the same or similar speeches before and after an interpolated passage, has not been much drawn upon before. Much of it is well known but needs to be uncovered more completely. How we go on to explain the disturbances may be another matter, but it is intimately linked with the nature of the evidence. And if some intentionalism is involved it is an intentionalism made necessary by the circumstances attending the transmission of Elizabethan play-texts. We often have to peer behind the heads of scribes, editors, compositors, actors, and prompters to discover the author. And even then we may find him in two minds.

In considering the unconformities of Shakespeare's plays my main concern is not evaluation but analysis. Thus when I find the choruses of *Henry V* awkwardly fitted in place and partly in disagreement with the plot I am not saying that the play would be better without them or disparaging their stirring poetry but trying to explain how, and to some extent why, *Henry V* became the play it is. Interest in 'faults' of structure may still expose one to the suspicion of lacking admiration and respect for the greatest dramatic poet of all time, whereas it ought to be seen as quite the opposite. I do think faults are sometimes faults in the common sense, but I would also agree with Dr Rees that very often they are more than compensated for by corresponding beauties, and that faults themselves may be turned to advantage. Or they may be gloriously surmounted and made to appear insignificant. I certainly have no wish to deny the frequency of subtlety and intentional ambiguity in Shakespeare or his mastery in using them. But so much has been written, and well written, about Shakespeare's genius by singleminded critics that the balance needs to be readjusted for a fuller understanding of the complex and dynamic nature of that genius. I would like to imagine a three-dimensional understanding, since it should take into account the depth perspective provided by an awareness of the creative process which went to the making of the dramatic artefacts.

I hope at least for agreement that any analysis of Shakespeare's plays must begin with textual analysis, that is to say it must be based on a considered opinion of the nature of the text. One cannot, for instance, safely discuss character and motivation and what really goes on without being reasonably certain that what has been transmitted is what was intended. The literary scholar who enthuses on ironies which may be accidental and the modern critic who is delighted with absurdities which are probably unintentional have little excuse for their innocence in an age when so much information is readily available concerning the provenance and relationship of various editions, printing-house procedures, etc. A theatrical director is free to interpret according to his unaided judgment, though even he would probably benefit from a geological study of his chosen play. The scholar-critic is not free in the same sense.

It will perhaps be said at this point that history plays are a genre apart and cannot be approached with the same preconceptions about unity of interest, conservation of character, and continuous plot development that we would bring to the analysis of a tragedy, a problem play, or a comedy of intrigue; that structure in the history plays is determined by the mere succession of events as recorded in the chronicles; and that their first concern is not to shape artistically but to instruct. This means that unconformities in the sense in which we have considered them would be only normal in history plays and could not be used to deduce anything about their genesis and early life. But do these plays in fact form a separate and identifiable genre?

The Elizabethans themselves cannot help us much in deciding this question. Heminges and Condell grouped the plays we are concerned with as histories, but Meres called them tragedies – at least those he mentioned: 'for Tragedy [witnes] his *Richard the 2. Richard the 3. Henry the 4. King Iohn, Titus Andronicus* and his *Romeo* and *Iuliet.*' If we look at the title pages or head-titles of the early quartos and the First Folio we shall find that only three of the plays under discussion are anywhere called histories, whereas three are presented as tragedies. The Folio often avoids the problem, especially in the Catalogue and running titles, by using the formula 'The

Life . . .' or 'The Life and Death of . . .'. On the other hand, some of the
plays not included among the 'Histories' in the Folio and some we would
never think of as histories were originally classified as such in the
Stationers' Register or quarto editions, viz. *Titus Andronicus* (SR), *The
taming of a Shrew* (SR and Q), *The Merchant of Venice* (Q), *Hamlet* (Q), *King
Lear* (SR and Q), and *Troilus and Cressida* (Q). There were refinements such
as *The true Tragedie of Richard Duke of York* (i.e. Q *3 Henry VI*) and *The
Chronicle History of Henry the fift* which might be taken as vouchers for
historicity, but then what of *The Tragicall Historie of Hamlet* (Q) or the *True
Chronicle Historie of the life and death of King Lear and his three daughters* (Q)?
Clearly the titles show no feeling for precise distinctions, in fact the words
'tragedy' and 'history', as I have said, seem practically interchangeable.
Shakespeare was hardly thinking of a genre distinction when he wrote in
3 Henry VI:

> Why stand we like soft-hearted women here,
> Wailing our losses, whiles the foe doth rage;
> And look upon, as if the tragedy
> Were play'd in jest by counterfeiting actors?   (II.iii.25–8)

It may not be entirely irrelevant to this discussion to remember that the
three parts of *Henry VI* were not always 'king' plays. *1 Henry VI* could be
the 'harey the vj' recorded by Henslowe as 'ne' in 1592, but *2* and *3 Henry
VI* were the two parts of *The Contention* till an entry in the Stationers'
Register changed the titles in 1602, and the Folio confirmed the change. I
shall argue in later chapters that Shakespeare wrote a Talbot play which
became the backbone of *1 Henry VI*, and that the *Contention* plays may have
been planned as the tragedy of the Duke of York. This may indicate that
the 'histories' are somewhat less uniform as a group than is commonly supposed, but hardly settles the question of genre, and we must turn to
modern critics for further enlightenment.

E. M. W. Tillyard and Lily B. Campbell taught a generation of scholars
that Shakespeare's history plays were didactic in intention, Tillyard
emphasising the providential view of history embodied in what he called
'the Tudor myth' and Campbell especially the reflection of topical events
and problems in the depiction of similar events and problems in the past.[18]
The Tudor myth, which according to Tillyard linked the eight plays from
Richard II to *Richard III* into one cycle, preconceived as such,[19] was derived,
again according to Tillyard, chiefly from Edward Hall's *The Union of the
Two Noble and Illustre Famelies of Lancastre and Yorke*, which chronicles
events from the end of Richard II's reign to that of Henry VIII. The myth,

as everyone now knows, is based on the idea that Henry Bolingbroke in deposing the rightful king, Richard II, and causing him to be murdered, brought a curse on the country which resulted in civil wars and untold deaths and was renewed by the crimes of the Yorkists until time completed its revenges against Lancaster and York alike, and Henry Tudor 'providentially heal[ed] the old division by marrying the heiress of York'.[20] This didactic view has had great success in the world and has been upheld with minor reservations by prominent scholars like Irving Ribner and M. M. Reese.[21] In 1957, however, Derek Traversi demurred,[22] and in the sixties the whole Tillyard/Campbell orthodoxy came under fire from many quarters. One of its most assiduous opponents was A. L. French, who in a number of articles emphasised the blindness of the forces which lead to 'retribution' in Shakespeare's histories and saw this tendency as pointing forward to the great tragedies rather than back to the morality plays.[23] A full-scale attack was launched by Robert Ornstein in *A Kingdom for a Stage: The Achievement of Shakespeare's History Plays*, published in 1972.[24] Ornstein not only denied that Shakespeare was at all concerned with the Tudor myth, or indeed with any kind of political didacticism, but asserted that the myth was not even formulated, let alone endorsed, by Edward Hall. He has been followed more recently by John Wilders in another important book, *The Lost Garden* (1978), where the key concept for the understanding of Shakespeare's view of history is that of a fallen humanity which struggles without supernatural guidance for aims which are neither unequivocally good nor unmitigatedly bad. These and other contentions have left scholars today divided between the view of Shakespeare as defender of the Tudor monarchy with its claim to absolute obedience and the picture of him as radically independent thinker, more interested in man than in political principles.

With regard to form, Tillyard found a flourishing tradition of chronicle plays before the time of Shakespeare and thought that it was characterised by looseness of construction:

> it can be stated dogmatically that Shakespeare grew up along with an increasing trend to write plays of this kind, [. . .] Just as Holinshed seizes on the factual side of Hall and ignores his philosophy, so most of the English Chronicle Plays ignore the steady moral bent of *Gorboduc* and exploit the mere accident of successive events.[25]

But Shakespeare, says Tillyard further on,

> turned the Chronicle Play into an independent and authentic type of drama, and no mere ancillary to the form of tragedy. He did this largely

because he grasped the potentialities of the old Morality form, never allowing the personalities of his kings to trespass on the fundamental Morality subject of Respublica.

Tillyard finds considerable variety in the actual plotting of the plays but in general thinks the plots are firmly handled, even when, as in *Richard II* and *Henry IV*, the epic element becomes prominent:

> Shakespeare in *Richard II* and *1* and *2 Henry IV* gave us his version, which I have called epic, of what life was like in the Middle Ages as he conceived them and in his own day. This version was entirely successful and presents not even a parallel to the form of tragedy. It is one of Shakespeare's vast achievements.[26]

Ribner and Reese avoid setting up a distinct division between history and tragedy but on the whole support Tillyard's views. Ribner in particular gives a detailed and in fact extremely useful exposée of the complex influences leading up to the history plays and concludes by describing them as a new genre, though capable of great formal variety and characterised more by subject matter and purpose than by any fixed structural pecularities. By 1594, says Ribner,

> we can already see two general lines which the history play is to follow. On the one hand there is to be the line stemming from *Gorboduc* and continuing the scheme of the morality drama; on the other there is to be the tradition of the heroic drama, with its secular tone and romantic hero, but carrying on the episodic structure of the miracle play. The two lines are both to continue separately and to combine.[27]

Whereas Tillyard sees the Yorkist and Lancastrian tetralogies not only as two firmly organised sequences but as one carefully planned history cycle, Ribner holds that the tetralogies are distinct and self-contained units, and that Shakespeare wrote the later group 'entirely independently of his earlier compositions, although it too was seen in the large framework of the "Tudor Myth"'.[28]

Robert Ornstein, on the other hand, strongly denies that there was any dramatic tradition which Shakespeare could use as a basis for his histories. The handful of chronicle plays produced before he began to write were worthless as models, and the morality influence in Elizabethan history plays reduces itself on examination to mere echoes − 'tags, epithets, reminiscences of themes and character types, conventions transmuted and adapted to new artistic purposes.' Shakespeare is 'the artist as historian' (the title of Ornstein's opening chapter). Ornstein, like Ribner for once, sees the two tetralogies as separate architectural units, but he is chiefly intent on the great variety of form in the individual history plays and regards each play as an independent work of art with its 'own artistic integrity and individuality of theme, style and structure'.[29]

Here, too, Ornstein is largely supported by Wilders, who thinks of the history play as 'a very recent form devised almost single-handed by Shakespeare himself', closely resembling tragedy in that it incorporates the lives and deaths of great men, the real bearers of history as Shakespeare sees it; but distinguished from pure tragedy by an additional concern 'to portray the continuing life of a nation'. The histories are not necessarily tragic, but in Wilders's view most of Shakespeare's tragedies are in a sense history plays, so that there is no great difference.[30]

I find myself in close agreement with Wilders in seeing the lives of individuals – often tragic lives – as a main concern of the history plays, and the acts of individuals in these plays as events in the larger life of the nation. I am also prepared to see the tragic form subsumed in the histories. Where I would chiefly dissociate myself from Wilders is in his view of the inconclusive or ironical endings of the history plays. Such endings he thinks entirely intentional and designed to emphasise the continuity of history, whereas I sometimes find other explanations more plausible. Wilders is in no doubt as to the formal excellence of these plays, however: 'They emerged chiefly as brilliantly constructed works for the theatre.'[31]

There is another way of looking at the problems of historical philosophy and dramatic genre which is attractive in that it represents a compromise between extreme views. A. P. Rossiter, like Ornstein, sees Shakespeare as the untrammelled artist, but also as a man with a lively awareness both of the society he lived in and of the past which had shaped it. He was influenced by myths and orthodoxies but countered them with subversive opposites. Thus in *Richard III* Rossiter finds the orthodox Tudor myth offset by another myth, that of 'Richard the Devil-King'; and 'The outcome of this conflict of myths was Shakespeare's display of constant inversions of meaning'. 'Had he entirely accepted the Tudor myth, the frame and pattern of order, his way would have led', Rossiter supposes, 'towards writing *moral history*. . . . Instead, his way led him towards writing *comic history*.'[32] In a thought-provoking essay on 'Ambivalence: The Dialectic of Histories', Rossiter develops this idea in more general terms showing how Shakespeare's imagination took advantage of received ideas and attitudes. And, as he demonstrates in some detail in a number of essays, that imagination was extremely sensitive to pattern and shape.

We must probably be content to leave it at that. Shakespeare's history play was neither a dramatised epic nor an adapted morality, even if it absorbed features from both epic and morality play. It had no identity to cut it off from tragedy, and it had some affinities with comedy. It comprised considerable variety in the working-out of the individual plays. Above all, as most commentators agree, those plays have organised shape and were plotted to present something more meaningful than mere happenings in a more or less haphazard order. And indeed if we go afresh to the plays themselves it is not hard to see that they are powerfully organised around central characters and concerns.

The variety is certainly there. Probably there is no such amount of variety in any comparable group of plays. Shakespeare, it is recognised, 'was an inveterate dramaturgic experimenter from the beginning to the end of his career'.[33] And in the histories it looks as if he was trying to write a different kind of play each time. *1 Henry VI*, as we shall see, is basically a heroic drama with a neatly constructed conflict, heightened by the quasi-supernatural character of the two main antagonists, with an added action on the political level. *2 Henry VI* has a direct, forward drive through all its profusion of intrigue, shedding victim after victim in a complex but realistic power struggle until it ends with a simple confrontation of two main contenders. *3 Henry VI* is in Andrew Cairncross's words 'a study in anarchy'. It has a murky, chaotic action involving cruelty, betrayal, and perjury. It abounds in rhetorical speeches and makes open use of moral allegory and symbolic action. But there is a seesaw of victory and defeat which provides a kind of structural rhythm not unlike that which governs *1 Henry VI*. In *Richard III* Shakespeare fully adopts unrealistic methods, presenting the titular hero as an avowed villain, an ironical humorist who completely dominates the action, and using prophecies, choruses, and ghosts extensively. *Richard II* is again 'an attempt to do something different', 'it is deliberately a play of character, thought, and emotion rather than action' (Stanley Wells). It is the most poetic and tragic of the history plays and the most ironical in structure, with a plot equally divided between a falling and a rising ruler and a pensive treatment of the divine right of kings. The two *Henry IV* plays are mainly comedies and the two most similar in kind, though there is a darkening of mood in the second part. In both there is a marked division of interest between a number of disparate characters and settings. The last play of the sequence returns to foreign wars and heroic drama but reveals the distance which Shakespeare has travelled since his first history play in the irony with which the central character is portrayed and in the generous admixture of comedy in the martial glamour. *King John* and *Henry VIII*, outside the two tetralogies, are different again. It would be hard to extract a formula for a new genre of history play out of so much diversity.

But the organisation is also there. Drama was drama whatever it was called and required a minimum of planning. And a gifted dramatist would hardly be content with a mere stringing together of picturesque and anecdotal material. There were limits, of course, to what he could do with history. Henry VI would have to be murdered in the Tower and not killed at St Albans if he was to remain recognisably historical. But Margaret could be made to haunt the court of Edward IV, and the French Dauphin to fight at Agincourt. I have already discussed the gaps between expectation and fulfilment which may be introduced by the author's reliance on his sources, sometimes leading off in wrong directions, sometimes neglecting to provide sufficient explanation, and sometimes allowing narrative looseness and occasional confusion to influence his own treatment. But I also pointed out the significance of his departures from his sources. And it is interesting to notice that scholars have become more and more inclined since Dover Wilson's day to stress the wideranging character of Shakespeare's reading and the multiplicity of the source materials he utilised.[34] In any case he selected, modified, and adapted to his own needs and purposes. He characteristically concentrated events in time to bring about not only a sequential but a consequential development. And he paid ample attention to exposition, action, and dénouement, though the linkage of the history plays in twos and threes sometimes obscures one or other of these elements. *1 Henry VI* and *2 Henry VI* have no proper ending, *2 Henry IV* no separate beginning, and *3 Henry VI* no middle. But there is a fossil ending embedded in *1 Henry VI*, *2 Henry VI* fulfils itself in *3 Henry VI*, and *2 Henry IV* continues from *1 Henry IV*. They are all informed and shaped by conscious workmanship. This is not always equally successful and could hardly be expected to be. It is sometimes marred by accident or carelessness. Plots may be fractured by alterations of arrangement or overall design. There is sometimes a failure to achieve complete integration, leading some critics to the backward conclusion that complete integration was not aimed at. But the architecture is there to justify the intentions.

It is an architecture which is primarily to be seen in the individual plays and in one case in a double or two-part play, *2–3 Henry VI*. Only secondarily is there a connection of a more than sequential kind between the plays of the two tetralogies or of the whole Plantagenet cycle. This connection is not to be found in the providential scheme represented by the Tudor myth, which is itself something of a myth. The theme of guilt and penance indeed is present in the Lancastrian plays and helps to knit them together, but it has nothing to do with the Tudors; and the theme of retributive justice in *Richard III* is largely limited to that play. Nowhere is there much sense of a supernatural direction of events except by occult influences in *Richard III* and superficially in *Henry V*. But the plays of the first tetralogy (including the English scenes of *1 Henry VI*) are powerfully organised to depict the stages in the rise and fall of the house of York. There is a gradual progression as the Yorkist claim changes from being based on legitimacy to being motivated by pure lust for power, with Richard of Gloucester actually defying legitimacy. The influence of Marlowe is perceptible. And the lust-for-power theme which runs through all these plays is qualified by increasing savagery as we move from wars in France through the Wars of the Roses to the internecine struggles of the climactic phase. The plays of the second tetralogy similarly pursue a unifying theme, that of establishing and legitimising the house of Lancaster and of rooting it in the affections of the people. It may be said, and has been said,[35] that England, or Respublica, is the real subject of all these plays and in a sense this is true. It is also true of *King John* and *Henry VIII*. They all have to do with good government and the basis of authority. But unless we make them unduly allegorical and unduly sentimentalise the rural and popular scenes it is impossible to see England as more than a background and chorus to the violent conflicts between its rulers and their rivals. This is not saying that background is unimportant. It is a frequently underestimated aspect of drama. But it means that the nation as such does not often enter significantly into the structure of the plays.

I have to some extent anticipated my conclusions as to the structural rationality of Shakespeare's history plays in order to confirm the critical consensus that they were plotted with some care and to provide a point of departure for an examination of the instances when care for progression and consistency seems to have yielded to other impulses or exigencies. The history plays are not amorphous. We may expect them to have unity of design, consistency of motivation and theme, logical development in a time sequence, and stability of characters and of character portrayal. We may further expect a correlationship of preparation and fulfilment. When these things are wanting we may legitimately ask why, and to both the hows and whys we may now proceed.

2 The Whole Contention – One Play into Two

The order in which the First Folio of 1623 printed Shakespeare's plays gives us very little help in determining the chronology of their composition, and even their titles are sometimes misleading. Thus everything points to the likelihood that Shakespeare began his series of plays about English kings with what the Folio called *The second Part of Henry the Sixt*. This is a firmly plotted drama which has a natural sequel in *The third Part of Henry the Sixt* but which presupposes no antecedent history play and indeed ignores or contradicts a great deal that we find in the so-called *first Part*. The two earliest instalments in what the author seems to have *eventually* intended as a trilogy were originally published in quarto and octavo in 1594 and 1595 respectively, in mutilated versions carrying the following titles:

> The First part of the Contention betwixt the two famous Houses of Yorke and Lancaster, with the death of the good Duke Humphrey: And the banishment and death of the Duke of *Suffolke*, and the Tragicall end of the proud Cardinall of *Winchester*, with the notable Rebellion of *Iacke Cade: And the Duke of Yorkes first claime vnto the Crowne*.

> The true Tragedie of Richard *Duke of Yorke, and the death of* good King Henrie the Sixt, *with the whole contention betweene* the two Houses Lancaster and Yorke,

It is these two plays which the Stationers' Register called 'The firste and Second parte of Henry VIt' when in 1602 Thomas Millington assigned his rights in them to Thomas Pavier, and which were published together in 1619 as *The Whole Contention*. Only four years before the appearance of the Folio they were still isolated from the as yet unprinted *1 Henry VI*.

This is merely the external evidence for the priority of *The First part of the Contention*, alias *2 Henry VI*.[1] The internal evidence is equally telling, particularly some of the details of plot.

The treaty negotiated by Suffolk which causes such consternation to all but the king and the cardinal in the beginning of *2 Henry VI* is not that subscribed to after much persuasion by the King of France at the end of *1 Henry VI*. The last-mentioned treaty knows nothing of Margaret or of Anjou and Maine. Conversely, the broken marriage arrangement between the King of England and the Earl of Armagnac's daughter in *1 Henry VI* has seemingly been forgotten in *2 Henry VI*. Nor is there in York's scornful reminder, in the latter play, of Somerset's treachery –

> Last time I danc'd attendance on his will
> Till Paris was besieg'd, famish'd, and lost.   (I.ii.171–2)

– any reference to the siege of Bordeaux, where Talbot lost his life on account of that treachery. In fact, as others have pointed out, neither Talbot, nor Joan of Arc, nor, for that matter, Sir John Falstaff, is ever mentioned in the two plays that make up *The Whole Contention*. An Earl of Salisbury appears prominently in *2 Henry VI* without any sense of the need for a distinction between him and his father-in-law bearing the same title who was killed at Orleans. Bedford is mentioned as a politician (in I.i) but not as one who fought and died in France. Suffolk is an earl at the end of *1 Henry VI* and a marquess at the beginning of *2 Henry VI*, before being made a duke. In the latter play the Duke of York carefully explains his claim to the crown to Salisbury and Warwick (II.ii), but says nothing of his interview with Edmund Mortimer in the Tower of London which occurs in *1 Henry VI* – Salisbury actually now declares that Mortimer was kept in captivity by Owen Glendower till he died. In *1 Henry VI* the king is a young man when he is crowned in Paris, whereas both *The Whole Contention* and *Richard III* insist that he was only nine months old.[2]

Some scholars, particularly E. M. W. Tillyard and Andrew Cairncross, have argued with great conviction for the priority of *1 Henry VI* and the organic nature of the whole trilogy, indeed of the tetralogy which also includes *Richard III*;[3] but they largely choose to ignore these discrepancies between the first and second parts, which surely are too many and some of them too important to be lightly disregarded. We may no doubt have an impression of continuity as we proceed from the first to the second part, reading them for enjoyment or even more watching a theatrical performance, but continuity is not unity, and the struggle for the possession of France, which is the main theme of *1 Henry IV*, has little to do with the internal feuds and battles of the *Contention* plays. As I shall argue more fully in my next chapter, there may have been a Talbot play by Shakespeare before *2 Henry VI*, but not an earlier dynastic play.

It also seems likely that *The First Part of the Contention* and *The True Tragedy of Richard Duke of York*[4] were not at first envisaged as two separate plays. *The First Part* has no such distinct ending as we have come to expect in an Elizabethan drama, except for a perfunctory five concluding lines. On the contrary, we are told by Salisbury in the third speech from the end that the Yorkist victory is not yet secure: 'Well, lords, we have not got that which we have.' So obviously there is more to follow as the rebels decide to race the king to London. If we were to see the play as being largely the tragic love story of Margaret and Suffolk (Gwyn Williams practically does this in an interesting essay in the Summer 1974 *Shakespeare Quarterly*) we would find a conclusion in the queen's grief at the death of Suffolk, but this is too early an ending for the other business which has been prepared: the rising of Cade and York's rebellion. If on the other hand we see it as the tragedy of the Duke of York the ending comes after the play, in the sequel: *The True Tragedy* begins with an act, featuring the agreement between York and Henry and the death of York, which might well have formed the conclusion of the earlier play, and follows it with a second act[5] which might have been a fitting beginning for a new history.

The earliest quarto titles provide interesting clues to the genesis of *2* and *3 Henry VI*. 'The First Part of the Contention' calls for no comment, assuming that 'The Contention [etc.]' was at first intended as the name of the whole play. But 'The True Tragedy of Richard Duke of York', even with the additional mention of the death of Henry, is hardly very appropriate for the second part *per se*, seeing that the hero apparent of the title dies in the first act. It seems natural to infer that the one play which Shakespeare originally planned was to be predominantly the tragedy of the Duke of York. In the opening scene of *The First Part* it is York who remains behind after the other nobles have slipped away, to soliloquise at length about his secret aspirations; and though the presence of York is overshadowed in the three middle acts of the play by the figures of Gloucester, Margaret, and Suffolk, as well as the king, we are never allowed to forget his importance. The incidents involving the armourer's man and the award of the regency of France, and the whole rebellion of Jack Cade, have to do with the position and prospects of York. And the last act of *The First Part* together with the first act of *The True Tragedy* are mainly his.

The plot of the two plays is continuous and in the main coherent up to and including the battle of Wakefield. By that time the author may have complicated it too much for a single showing and filled it with too many characters and incidents before he reached the tragic dénouement. Besides, there was obviously more matter for drama in the material he was using, even after the death of York. Above all, Henry and Margaret were still interesting, and two of York's sons, the historical successors of Henry VI on the throne of England, had already been introduced. It would have been natural and tempting to adjust his plans to comprise a double play, fitting the first instalment to the duration of an afternoon's performance by removing the final catastrophe to the beginning of the second part and pro-longing the action by an additional two hours' worth.

With the appearance of Edward and Richard in the Marches of Wales after their flight from Wakefield the plot consequently makes a new start. It even opens with a line similar to the first line of Act I:[6]

> I.i.1: *War.* I wonder how the King escap'd our hands!
> II.i.1: *Edw.* I wonder how our princely father scap'd.

The scene is leisurely and largely narrative. It includes the vision of the three suns, a messenger's account of the death of York (which we have seen) and Warwick's account of his own defeat in the second battle of St Albans (which we have not seen). (It is also somewhat awkward in that its two halves seem to be placed at different removes in time from the battle of Wakefield: the brothers have apparently just escaped from it, whereas Warwick heard of it ten days ago.)[7] But in the following scene the dialogue and action once more become truly dramatic, and after the moral interlude in which Henry, seated on a molehill at Towton, witnesses the horrors of war, the plot mounts to another climax with the death of young Clifford and the virtually decisive victory of the Yorkists. This climax, in fact, has all the appearance of another ending. 'And now to London with triumphant march,' cries Warwick. Edward is to be crowned and seek an alliance with France by marriage, and Richard is to be Duke of Gloucester. Shakespeare may have contemplated stopping there, except that he leaves the word 'ominous' worrying our ears as Richard expresses his dislike of his new title. And except, of course, for the fact that King Henry, Queen Margaret, and Prince Edward are still alive, and the play is still short of its two or three hours' traffic.[8] So now a third beginning is made and entirely new business is introduced. The last three acts of *The True Tragedy* do indeed include the death of Warwick and the final defeat of the Lancastrians, with the murder of Prince Edward at Tewkesbury and of King Henry in the Tower. But they might have been a 'King Edward IV' play.[9] They are basically concerned with Edward's hasty marriage to Lady Elizabeth Grey in despite of his proposal to Princess Bona of France, and the consequences of this marriage in alienating Richard, Clarence, Warwick, and King Lewis, and in eventually providing Edward with an heir. (We are strongly reminded of King Henry's breach of promise to another French lady and the consequences of his rash marriage to Margaret at the beginning of *The First Part of the Contention*.) A number of new persons are introduced in addition to Lady Grey and the French royal household, while others have disappeared. Of the three 'northern lords' whose disaffection troubled King Henry at the end of the opening scene Westmoreland has not been heard of again, Northumberland vanished before the battle of Towton (to be eventually reported killed at the end of the play)[10] and Clifford fell at Towton. In Acts III–V we hear no more of the northern lords, or of Norfolk. Instead, new leaders, Oxford and Somerset, join Warwick to command the armies of the queen. Montague may at first have been a newcomer in this part of the play, too (see below, p. 31). Others who make their first appearance in the last three acts are Stanley, Hastings, Rivers, Montgomery, and the mute characters Pembroke and Stafford. The changeover in personnel is to a large extent due to Shakespeare's following Hall, but not entirely. Thus Somerset is one of Margaret's commanders at Wakefield in the chronicle, but does not appear till Act IV of the play. In any case the recasting helps to demonstrate the break between the first two acts and the last three. At a deeper level, so does the bolder, more emphatic character drawing which we encounter after the second act, and which we will consider more closely in its place. This particularly applies to the transformation of Richard of Gloucester.

To sum up this part of my discussion, it looks as if Shakespeare expanded his original Henry VI/Duke of York play by stages so as to create an effect not so much of the episodic structure which many critics have found in it as of a series of new starts. There is something to be said for regarding *The Whole Contention* as a single long play, a ten-act play, perhaps, if Shakespeare had divided it into acts. But this would mean overlooking, or tolerating, a number of structural 'faults' which break up the action at three points at least: after the fifth, sixth, and seventh acts of the complete sequence.[11] It would also mean treating *The First Part* on a level with *The True Tragedy* and ignoring its superior quality as an independent play. The signs indicate that Shakespeare wrote as far as to the death of the Duke of York before deciding to divide his history into two plays, and then went on so as to make his parts roughly equal in length. He then added *1 Henry VI* to the two-part play after it was finished. The most natural division between the two *Contention* plays is undoubtedly still after the first act of *The True Tragedy*. But I shall proceed with my analysis of the two parts on the basis of the received texts, recognising that in certain important respects they are distinct dramatic entities. There are developments of temper and theme, for instance, which help to give them a difference of character.

The opening scene of *The First Part* sets the action on foot. There is no undramatic exposition of earlier events, but the situation is perfectly clear nevertheless. The ceremonial occasion of welcoming England's new queen provides an excellent opportunity for the presentation of all the main characters, the reading of the treaty with France causes the major conflict to explode almost immediately, and the departure of the nobles from the stage in ones, twos, and threes makes it possible to reveal the multiple stratifications of passions and tensions which will direct ensuing events, focusing at the end of the scene on the Duke of York as he remains alone and soliloquises in the first piece of extended rhetoric in the play. At this point expectations will have been aroused as to two important issues: the fate of the Lord Protector and the outcome of York's pretension to the throne. We will have realised that the king is politically weak – his mindless remark about the terms of the treaty, 'They please us well', could hardly be more revealing – and that the peers are divided into at least five factions governed by individual or party interests: Suffolk with the queen; Gloucester, Salisbury, and Warwick; the cardinal; Somerset and Buckingham; and York. To these may be added Eleanor of Gloucester, whose ambition for greatness is shown in the following scene. They are all contenders for power, except Duke Humphrey, who can only lose it. But most of them are ready to gang up for immediate ends, and as the plot unfolds our expectations are fully rewarded. The alliances and counter-alliances are handled with great deftness, and there is a sense of inevitability about the development of the action. As Cairncross puts it, 'Shakespeare was, in 1590–1, an adept in the art of planning, and in this respect *2 Henry VI* will bear comparison with almost any other of his plays.'[12]

Of course even here Shakespeare did not plan ahead in every detail before committing his ideas to paper. That this is so may be indicated by the unexplained postponement of the hawking excursion to St Albans for which Gloucester is summoned and on which his wife agrees to join him before her spirit-raising session (I.ii.57, 83–4): the excursion does not take place till after four intervening episodes (the armourer's man, the conversation of Suffolk and the queen, the appointment of the regent of France, and the conjuring). This is as clear an example as any of a reordering of scenes where the author did not bother to remove the traces of his original intention. And there are other irregularities. The Parliament scene in Act III, for instance, has a number of puzzling elements. Salisbury and Warwick are obviously present,[13] and one would expect them to speak up in defence of Gloucester, but they are oddly silent. More surprisingly, York openly attacks the Protector twice over, after having previously assured his friends that he believes in Gloucester's virtue (II.ii.73). He even gives his voice for the murder of Gloucester,[14] although he has led us confidently to expect that he will leave it to the Protector's declared enemies to do away with him (i.i.254; ii.ii.68–75). Dover Wilson, speaking of York's surprising participation in the arrest of the Duchess of Gloucester, suggests that Shakespeare decided to give more prominence to York than was contemplated at first.[15] This is quite conceivable. On the other hand, Buckingham's part looks as if it may have been reduced. In the beginning of the play, Buckingham is an active conspirer against Gloucester and Eleanor, but he fades completely into the background immediately after the Duke's arrest, until he re-emerges in a virtually new role as the king's most trusted friend during the Cade rebellion (along with Clifford, who now makes his first appearance). One suspects that some of the activity at first attributed to Buckingham may have been transferred to York.[16] There is also a minor irregularity in iv.i, where the lieutenant who captures Suffolk seems to have knowledge of York's rising before it occurs. With regard to larger issues it may be said, perhaps, that the loss of France is treated very perfunctorily for such an important matter and that Warwick's promise concerning Maine in the first scene, 'Which I will win from France, or else be slain', is never followed up. But since it is Somerset and not York who is sent as regent to France we can hardly be surprised at his poor success. And when he brings news of ultimate defeat the listless response of the king, 'Cold news, Lord Somerset: but God's will be done!' is part of the characterisation of this anaemic ruler. As for Warwick, he is kept too busy making kings to have time for France, and his promise need not be considered a prophecy. There are other prophetic utterances, however, which look more serious and which are not, in the event, taken seriously. At the end of ii.ii Warwick and York make the following declarations:

> *War.* My heart assures me that the Earl of Warwick
>   Shall one day make the Duke of York a king.
> *York.* And, Nevil, this I do assure myself:
>   Richard shall live to make the Earl of Warwick
>   The greatest man in England but the king.

These are the kind of assurances that can usually be relied upon to foretell the outcome of events, but as it happens the Duke of York does not live either to be king or to fulfil his promise to Warwick. When he penned those lines Shakespeare cannot have fully known the shape he would give to his Henry VI plays. They may be one sign among others that he read, or rather reread, his chronicle sources piecemeal as he wrote, and that he did not carry a complete record of historical developments in his head.

Be that as it may, the dramatic urgency of events in *The First Part of the Contention* gives little opportunity for reflection on departures from a posted course. Nor is the episodic matter, of which there is plenty in the play, unduly digressive. The Hume and his conjurers, the armourer and his man Peter, Saunder Simpcox and his wife do figure in episodes which are not in themselves of primary importance. Even Cade's rebellion is only a tributary to the mainstream of the action. But apart from adding variety and comic relief, as well as epic breadth as is often suggested, all these episodes are tied in with the central concerns of the play. The conjuring scene includes a forecast of future events, and the fall of Eleanor of Gloucester, though it is not made the direct cause of Duke Humphrey's fall, clearly prepares for it. The armourer not only compromises the reliability of the Duke of York and prevents his getting the regency of France but, like the lieutenant in the scene of Suffolk's death, helps to show that there is a widespread popular recognition of the Yorkist claim. Simpcox has a thematic function in that he demonstrates the readiness of the king to be imposed on and the clearsightedness of Gloucester. And Cade's rebellion has its chief significance as a rising for the reinstatement of a Mortimer – at least that is how it is represented by Cade on York's instructions – and as a test of York's chances of support.

Altogether, the plot of *The First Part* is relatively simple, indeed astonishingly so considering its exceptionally large number of characters, all with their own aims to pursue. There are more than seventy speaking parts, far exceeding those of any other Shakespeare play, not to mention the 'infinite numbers' which the Folio recklessly instructs to enter with Jack Cade in IV.ii. The plot gathers up the various intrigues and surges forward in two great waves, one breaking at the death of Gloucester exactly midway in the play as we have it, the other at the defeat of King Henry at St Albans. From beginning to end the fortunes of the Duke of York are kept in view, and at the end of the play a whole set of characters has been wiped out, including most of York's rivals for power. The elimination of Suffolk and Cardinal Beaufort follows hard upon the death of Gloucester, while Somerset and Old Clifford are killed at St Albans. Queen Margaret is ready to play a new role and already begins to rehearse it. And the sons of York begin to emerge from the background to take an active part on their father's side. The stage is set for the bloody encounters of *The True Tragedy*.

Not only is the plot firmly handled in *The First Part of the Contention*, but it is also distinguished by the depth and variety of its character drawing as compared to most of *The True Tragedy*. And this applies to quick sketches like that of the impostor Simpcox as well as to intimate studies like that of the king. The portraits of Henry, York, Gloucester, and Margaret, in particular, already reveal much of the power of penetration and expression which was to result later in the creation of a Hamlet or a Macbeth. In the case of King Henry, Shakespeare even goes some way towards achieving the dramatisation of an internal conflict which so much fascinates us in the creatures of his maturity. Henry wants to reign, yet he wants to be a subject. He continues to dote on Margaret though he is afraid of her and sees her unfaithfulness. He is too timorous or lethargic to act according to his conscience when Gloucester is accused of treason, but rouses himself to assert his authority when it is too late to save his uncle's life. His 'bookish rule' is amply commented on by others, but Shakespeare makes Henry's own speech and behaviour provide the most telling epiphanies of his political immaturity. 'They please us well', 'Or Somerset or York, all's one to me', 'Cold news, Lord Somerset: but God's will be done!' – these are typical responses of one whose heart may be in heaven but whose head is in the clouds.

Gloucester, too, is distinctly individualised. The 'good' Duke Humphrey is no simpleton though he fondly imagines that his innocence will protect him even against Machiavellian onslaughts. His detractors accuse him of inventing strange punishments for small offences, but we are more inclined to believe his own words when he declares that 'Pity was all the fault that was in me'. His affection for Eleanor seems deep and genuine in spite of her 'bedlam brain-sick' ambition, and his solicitude for her is as touching as his loyalty to the young king.

York on the whole makes a favourable impression, and again we are inclined to trust the speaker's own words, even when he boasts

> I am far better born than is the King,
> More like a king, more kingly in my thoughts;
>
> (v.i.28–9)

His kingly thoughts are certainly for his own preferment but still for England's good, and they have a quaint, visionary beauty beyond the range of the other characters:

> Then will I raise aloft the milk-white rose,
> With whose sweet smell the air shall be perfum'd,
> And in my standard bear the arms of York,
> To grapple with the house of Lancaster;
> And force perforce I'll make him yield the crown,
> Whose bookish rule hath pull'd fair England down.
>
> (i.i.255–60)

One feels that York is perhaps the only person in the play who still believes in ideals of chivalry.[17] He is ready enough, it is true, to profit by the wicked machinations of others, biding his time

> Till they have snar'd the shepherd of the flock,
> That virtuous prince, the good Duke Humphrey:
>
> (II.ii.72–3)

As we have the play, he even has a large share of responsibility for the murder of the Duke. But he is not the man to plot against Humphrey by underhand means, and perhaps we are meant to see him partly as the dupe of Suffolk and the cardinal in the arrest of Eleanor. Holy Henry and chivalrous York might have made a lasting truce if there had not been fanatics on either side. And if there had not been Marlovian stirrings of an amoral and irrational kind in York himself. Coming from Ireland to proclaim his right he muses in soliloquy: 'Ah! sancta majestas, who'd not buy thee dear?' Surprised in these thoughts by the arrival of Buckingham, he mutters 'I must dissemble'. These are touches which prepare us for his son Richard.

Of Margaret it is perhaps enough to say that she changes roles twice in the course of *The First Part of the Contention*, but that there is nothing unconvincing in the changes. The eager bride of the first scene who expected King Henry to resemble Suffolk 'in courage, courtship, and proportion' (I.iii.54) quickly becomes the disappointed queen and the conspiring mistress of Suffolk and continues in this part until, after an interval in the fourth act in which she makes only two brief appearances, one silent, she is transformed in the last act into the fierce Amazon which is to be her role in the sequel. ·

The realism of the portraiture is restricted but not contradicted by two elements which feature strongly in both the *Contention* plays but which are perhaps most noticeable in *The First Part* because of the contrast they set up between factualness and artifice. One is the allegorical element. Without going quite so far as M. M. Reese, who opines that *2 Henry VI* 'adopts in the main the structure of the morality, with *Respublica* threatened by the various personifications of Lust, Pride and Ambition',[18] one cannot overlook the tendency to represent the characters at times as abstract qualities in a pageant where Ambition and Goodness play for mastery. In the second scene the Duchess of Gloucester declares that 'being a woman, [she] will not be slack / To play [her] part in Fortune's pageant'. No one, in fact, is slack to assume a part in the moral spectacle. 'Pride went before, Ambition follows him,' says Salisbury in the first scene, referring by the former appellation to Suffolk and the cardinal and by the latter to Somerset and Buckingham. These attributions stick with remarkable consistency. In II.ii.70, for instance, the Duke of York again speaks of 'Beaufort's pride' and 'Somerset's ambition' and in I.iii.176 Warwick addresses Suffolk as 'Image of Pride'. In a number of speeches, however, personifications abound though there are not always distinct personal correlatives. Gloucester's last long speech in III.i is a good example, and especially significant in that it returns to the theatrical metaphor introduced by the duchess. He is addressing the king:

> Ah! gracious lord, these days are dangerous.
> Virtue is chok'd with foul Ambition,
> And Charity chas'd hence by Rancour's hand;
> Foul Subornation is predominant.
> And Equity exil'd your Highness' land.
> I know their complot is to have my life;
> And if my death might make this island happy,
> And prove the period of their tyranny,
> I would expend it with all willingness.
> But mine is made the prologue to their play;
> For thousands more, that yet suspect no peril,
> Will not conclude their plotted tragedy.   (III.i.142–53)

Ambition, Rancour, and Subornation have to be fitted to Beaufort, Suffolk, Buckingham, York, and the queen, who are Gloucester's accusers and named by him in the continuation of this speech, and there might well be looks and gestures to make the connections specific. But there is no need for close identification. Certainly in Margaret's violent outburst against the king on the banishment of Suffolk, the first in her succession of elaborate curses, the personifications do not refer to actual persons, unless by stretching probability somewhat we take 'threefold Vengeance' to apply prophetically to York's three sons and the Devil to Richard:

> Mischance and Sorrow go along with you!
> Heart's Discontent and sour Affliction
> Be playfellows to keep you company!
> There's two of you, the Devil make a third!
> And threefold Vengeance tend upon your steps!
> (III.ii.299–303)

The arithmetic of this speech is problematic and might make one suspect corruption, but the way of thinking is characteristic of the play.

So is the Senecan rhetoric expended in numerous long speeches, and this is the other element which limits the realism of the portraiture. It begins with the release of Gloucester's pent-up indignation, or 'grief', as he calls it, after the king's departure in I.i, in a passionate diatribe which is nevertheless dramatically appropriate and effective in its context, and which is given its full impetus by the clever device of forestalling our criticism,[19] prompting the cardinal to remark:

> Nephew, what means this passionate discourse,
> This peroration with such circumstance?   (I.i.103–4)

Shakespeare was still writing in a highly conscious way, and the perorations with much circumstance are part of the artificiality which he inherited, along with allegory, from an earlier theatrical tradition. But even in the *Contention* plays he was beginning to write fully dramatic dialogue, and many of the rhetorical speeches are both functional and in character. This is true, for instance, of the Duke of York's soliloquies at the end of I.i, and III.i. It is not true of Margaret's complaint in III.ii.73–120, which may be in character but which becomes dramatically irrelevant as she unfolds the whole romantic story of her Channel crossing while we are waiting for further revelations concerning the death of Gloucester. The lieutenant who captures Suffolk improbably turns out to be his former groom and he also speaks some of the most highfalutin verse in the whole play. Nor can we be easily moved by Young Clifford's oratorically embellished fury on finding his father killed in v.ii. It is an added tribute to the vividness of characterisation if we feel that it carries us safely over such passages.

I have dwelt a little on the portrayal and presentation of the characters in *The First Part of the Contention* because these features contribute to the general impression of consistency. Shakespeare evidently composed this play with a good deal of care. By comparison *The True Tragedy* seems very loosely organised, and in fact it lacks the powerfully simple structure of the initial play. In the first place, since it comes to a climax in Act I with the death of the Duke of York, practically a new start has to be made in Act II and a great deal of tension worked up before there can be another major discharge. Then, as we have seen, there is a new climax and another new start in Act III. In the second place, the events depicted are chaotic, and the plot mirrors the chaos, whether functionally or not is hard to decide.[20]

There is something quite odd about the inception of *The True Tragedy*. We must be still on the battlefield of St Albans where *The First Part* ended and where the Yorkists now display the blood of their defeated enemies on their swords, while Richard makes grotesque play with the severed head of Somerset. Then after twenty-four lines we are suddenly transported to Westminster in the middle of one of Warwick's speeches, for a confrontation between Henry and the Duke of York. Editors, following Theobald and Capell, tend to locate the whole scene at Westminster to avoid this jump, but there can be no doubt that the jump occurs. And the best explanation I can suggest, apart from untraceable accidents of transmission or revision, is that Shakespeare inserted the first twenty-four lines by way of introduction when he found it necessary to divide his play into two. That these lines were not written immediately after the last act of *The First Part* is indicated by the discrepancy between their account of St Albans and the events we have actually witnessed. The names of the defeated Lancastrians in the opening of *The True Tragedy* are taken from Hall, but neither Northumberland, Stafford, Buckingham, or Wiltshire figures in the battle as represented in the earlier play. And as regards Old Clifford in particular, now said to have been 'by the swords of common soldiers slain', this report of his death is at variance with both *The First Part* and the remainder of *The True Tragedy*, where York is both shown and spoken of as the slayer of Clifford. We may also wonder what has become of the Earl of Salisbury, whose safety is of such concern to York at the end of the first play that he declares, 'This happy day / Is not itself, nor have we won one foot, / If Salisbury be lost.' (v.iii.5–7). Instead of Salisbury, two new characters now appear on York's side, Salisbury's son Montague and the Duke of Norfolk. Here, however, there is a definite clue to the mystery. Montague incorrectly calls York 'brother', a form of address which would have been natural in the mouth of Salisbury, who was York's brother-in-law, but is improper in that of Salisbury's son. It seems clear that at some stage of revision or adjustment Montague replaced the Salisbury of Shakespeare's original version, whether for actor-economy or for other purposes.[21] Salisbury was removed from the play altogether, but he left traces in some of the speeches of the first two scenes. (In the copy which was used for the Folio presumably only the stage directions and speech headings had been revised.)

The latter part of the play, however, is that which seems particularly confusing, and not only on account of new characters. Warwick and Clarence separately change sides, and Clarence defects again to rejoin his brother. Montague remains with Edward but reappears with Henry. Henry is captured and delivered and captured again, while Warwick, having just left the palace, is said to be already at Coventry. Edward is captured at one moment and rescued the next, only to escape, we are told, to Burgundy and return while we are still digesting the information. Warwick is to fight Pembroke and proceed to York, but we next find him at Westminster, with no further news of Pembroke.[22] And the final battles of Barnet and Tewkesbury, coming after the series of St Albans, Wakefield, St Albans, Towton, practically merge one with the other. Throughout all these surprises and entanglements one hardly knows at any point who is wearing the crown. In *The First Part* and the first two acts of *The True Tragedy* it may be hard to tell what individuals are most central to the plot; in the last three acts of the latter play it is sometimes difficult to know what is really going on, except that the struggle between York and Lancaster continues. We may complain with some justification that both readers and audiences can only be mystified by the continual reversals of fortune and changes of allegiance, often thinly motivated or poorly prepared for, which make up the action. For it is both the plot and the reality it mirrors which are chaotic. And the argument which is sometimes put forward that there is a connection between artistic disorder and political disorder is of doubtful validity. Shakespeare might have simplified his plot considerably and still conveyed the impression of political chaos. The cloak-and-dagger capture and rescue of Edward, for instance, is hardly necessary for his purpose. He may have been writing against time to finish his play, and he may have needed all the incidents he could lay his hands on to make it long enough, but one would be glad to find better excuses than these for the structural carelessness of the last three acts.

There is, of course, a structural pattern of sorts, one of alternating victory and defeat on either side as one might expect, though the pitched battles, apart from Wakefield and the second battle of St Albans, are all Yorkist victories. A. S. Cairncross has traced this pattern in his introduction to the Arden edition of *3 Henry VI* and shown that there are five main movements roughly corresponding to act divisions. Cairncross perhaps makes it all look a little too neat, but the rhythm of alternation does help to shape our general impression of the play and gives some sense of control. The same may be said of the relative simplicity of the character drawing as it emerges from Act III on. In Act I the finely shaded presentations of *The First Part* are continued and, in a sense, consummated, when Henry's authority and York's courtesy are given a last chance to assert themselves against their owners' more insistent impulses. In Act II the fine shading remains. But then a bolder delineation takes over. Margaret has already become the 'she-wolf of France' and the active marshal of the king's forces, and her son Edward, whom we do not hear of before he appears as an adolescent in *The True Tragedy*, is her care and supporter.[23] It is because of their intransigence and that of York's sons on the other side that the bitter struggle continues. Henry becomes a mere drop-out except for moments of prophecy and his hour of passionate dignity at the end. Edward of York is a womaniser, Clarence a waverer. Warwick remains simply the kingmaker, even after his change of sides. As for Richard, he now becomes a scheming murderer lusting for revenge.

This treatment of Richard is actually rather surprising.[24] He first appears at the end of *The First Part of the Contention*, where he distinguishes himself in battle by killing Somerset and three times saving the life of Salisbury. Prior to this he is abused by Clifford both for his deformity and his crooked 'manners':

> Hence, heap of wrath, foul indigested lump,
> As crooked in thy manners as thy shape!   (v.i.157–8)

He repeatedly has to hear similar abuse in *The True Tragedy*. Yet the impression we have of Richard in the first half of that play is mainly of a brave soldier and a man of honour, who admires and loves his father ('Methinks 'tis prize enough to be his son'), is capable of respecting an enemy ('Northumberland, I hold thee reverently'), and on occasion uses a religious oath with sincerity ('By Him that made us all, I am resolv'd / That Clifford's manhood lies upon his tongue'). He is already a humorist and already ambitious, but with a saving grace, and he occasionally reveals a poetic sensibility one might not have expected in him, as when he persuades his father to break his oath to King Henry and enthuses on the joys of kingship:

> And, father, do but think
> How sweet a thing it is to wear a crown,
> Within whose circuit is Elysium
> And all that poets feign of bliss and joy.   (i.ii.28–31)

Or when he and Edward see the three suns:

> Three glorious suns, each one a perfect sun;
> Not separated with the racking clouds,
> But sever'd in a pale clear-shining sky.
> See, see! they join, embrace, and seem to kiss,
> As if they vow'd some league inviolable:
> Now are they but one lamp, one light, one sun.
> In this the heaven figures some event.   (ii.i.26–32)

If we expect to see a Tamburlaine emerge from the youthful Richard, however, we are disappointed. Instead he develops into a Machiavelli of the blackest Elizabethan dye. A change of personality seems to occur after the arrival of Lady Grey and the beginning of Edward's impolitic infatuation. His loyalty to his brother and his kin crumbles all at once, though he continues to pretend it. In the long soliloquy of III.ii we see Richard moving from mere dreams of sovereignty beset with conscientious scruples to a fanatical resolve to obtain it. He will

> Change shapes with Proteus for advantages
> And set the murderous Machiavel to school.   (III.ii.192–3)

From now on he is being prepared for his role in *Richard III* and his characteristic attitudes in that play are developed. There is no longer either poetry or humanity in the ambition which rides him. He is himself alone. At the end of the play he stabs Prince Edward and murders the king.

The *dramatis personae* stand out in clear outline against the lurid background. But it was obviously not the study of individuals that interested the playwright when he wrote *The True Tragedy*. As J. P. Brockbank remarks:

> For the greater part of the third play [*3H6*] Shakespeare is content to follow Holinshed in making his characters public masks, without intimately felt life, and therefore hardly seeming responsible for what they do. He tightens the sequence of atrocities, telescopes time, and eliminates all rituals of government, until the stage action and reaction appear yet more savagely mechanical than in the chronicle.[25]

Instead of character study there is a strong insistence on thematic as distinct from more purely dramatic elements, most clearly exemplified in the episode of the king's meditations during the battle of Towton. They provide a unity which may be wanting in the action, and the centre of interest lies in following up the study of ambition and power-striving that was begun in *The First Part of the Contention*. In that first play pride and ambition were a disease from which almost everyone suffered, and the play must be more saturated with words like 'proud', 'ambitious', 'haughty', 'presumptuous', 'aspiring', 'imperious', and 'insolent' than any other. The women suffer from the disease as much as the men, or even more. But the disease is offset and, in a sense, contained by the presence of two central characters who are the opposite of ambitious and by the fact that the

Duke of York, though ambitious, is also civilised. Since the plot turns mainly upon the aspirations of York his motives are of decisive importance in determining the temper of the play. And York throughout *The First Part* is careful to justify his actions by reference to his legitimate title to the crown. He rehearses his genealogy to Salisbury and Warwick (or in effect to the audience) and instigates Jack Cade to prepare the way for his rebellion by pretending he is a Mortimer. Apparently the common people are aware of York's title since both the armourer and the lieutenant speak of it. He may therefore be seen as fighting in the cause of justice. And King Henry, being just, is forced to admit in the beginning of *The True Tragedy* that his own title is weak. But the discussion in the Parliament House in fact concludes the treatment of the legitimacy theme as far as the main interests of the plays are concerned. By bringing the question as to whether a king may adopt an heir into the open and answering it by a 'No', it not only does away once and for all with Henry's reliance on legality but ironically puts the Duke of York, who is now the adopted heir, in the same questionable position that Henry Bolingbroke was in.[26] If Richard II could not disinherit his next in succession, as Exeter maintains on behalf of York, then neither can Henry VI. From now on the assertion of legitimacy serves only as an excuse and is not taken seriously even by Warwick, witness his betrayal of the cause he has so long believed in only minutes after he has pleaded it to King Lewis of France. Holy Henry himself is goaded once, in the Parliament House scene, to assert might above right. Addressing his adversary he declares:

> Suppose by right and equity thou be king,
> Think'st thou that I will leave my kingly throne,
> Wherein my grandsire and my father sat?
> No: first shall war unpeople this my realm;   (I.i.127–30)[27]

And he is seconded by Young Clifford:

> King Henry, be thy title right or wrong,
> Lord Clifford vows to fight in thy defence: (I.i.163–4)

The main driving forces after the Parliament House meeting are ambition and revenge, and Clifford helps to set the tone by his vindictive madness in the encounter with Rutland:

> The sight of any of the house of York
> Is as a Fury to torment my soul;
> And till I root out their accursed line
> And leave not one alive, I live in hell.   (I.iii.30–3)

York and his sons do not fight again for justice but for power. We have already seen that the duke has a secret craving for greatness which has nothing to do with his title: 'Ah! sancta majestas, who'd not buy thee dear?' In *The True Tragedy* his sons Edward and Richard make their appeal to this desire in the duke and are rewarded with an immediate response. Edward declares he 'would break a thousand oaths to reign one year', and Richard echoes Tamburlaine in his description of the bliss of sovereignty. After the death of York, and especially after the newly-created Duke of Gloucester has begun to favour us with his confidence, the question of legitimacy is blown to the winds. Lust for power is all that remains.

It is interesting to notice in all this that the Tudor myth, so often invoked by critics as a unifying element, is very little in evidence in the *Contention* plays.[28] The murder of Richard II is mentioned twice in *The First Part*, once by York (II.ii.26) and once by the lieutenant (IV.i.94), but the issue that is debated is not whether Richard was deposed and murdered but whether Clarence or Gaunt was next in succession. In *The True Tragedy* the matter of the forceful deposition of Richard comes out in the Parliament House meeting, and Henry on one occasion, rebutting Clifford's argument of right by conquest[29] and admonishing his son, shows something like a guilty conscience on account of his inheritance:

> But Clifford, tell me, didst thou never hear
> That things evil got had ever bad success?
> And happy always was it for that son
> Whose father for his hoarding went to hell?
> I'll leave my son my virtuous deeds behind;
> And would my father had left me no more!   (II.ii.45–50)

There is no explanation of the 'things evil got', however, beyond the reference to the getting of England and France by force, and the application is of a general moral nature. Certainly Margaret and her son do not know the meaning of guilt. (Ironically enough it is Margaret who speaks of heavenly justice against usurpation in III.iii.76–7.) Had Shakespeare intended to make the process of divine retribution for ancestral sin a unifying theme, he would no doubt have made this much clearer. As it is, there is very little sense of metaphysical influences at work in the *Contention* plays, or even of divine wrath being stored up for the day of vengeance, as in *Richard III*.[30] The one exception may be the death of Cardinal Beaufort in *The First Part*, but that is a piece of theatricality rather than an event with philosophical implications.

The Whole Contention does show a continuous process of moral corruption and political disintegration in which justice gives way to ambition and
oathbreaking becomes an infection.[31] The process involves increasing
cruelty, and the theme of violence becomes another unifying element in
The True Tragedy. The savagery released by Clifford in avenging his father
on the innocent Rutland is stepped up by Margaret in the taunting and
butchering of the Duke of York, and this in turn is avenged by the brutal
stabbing of the young Prince Edward and the murder of the defenceless
Henry. The heartless absurdity of the carnage is epitomised in the quasi-
sacrificial scenes witnessed by Henry during the battle of Towton. *Richard
III* will complete the process.

The last scene of *The True Tragedy* fittingly opens with a roll-call of all
the 'valiant foemen' that the Yorkists have 'mow'd down in tops of all
their pride'. A touch of tenderness is added by the spectacle of the fond
father kissing the baby prince and asking his brothers to do likewise. And
in the concluding lines Edward promises 'stately triumphs, mirthful comic
shows, / Such as befits the pleasure of the court'. The plot has come to an
end as far as King Henry VI and, seemingly, Queen Margaret are concerned, and established the house of York firmly on the throne with a new-
born heir. But we have already heard Richard of Gloucester secretly
plotting to 'sort a pitchy day' for his brother Clarence and to 'blast [the]
harvest' of the young prince. There are worse things to follow.

The True Tragedy, then, is unified within itself by its concentration on
the struggle for power. It must further be seen as part of a grand design
comprising also *The First Part of the Contention* and *King Richard III* and
depicting a decline from civilised and Christian government through
brutal confusion to the rule of evil. In that larger design the middle play
will seem more orchestrated than it may appear when experienced in isola-
tion. But whereas *The First Part* will stand performance on it own, *The
True Tragedy*, or *3 Henry VI* as we may now revert to calling it, is definitely
a link play.[32]

3   Treachery and Dissension – Two Plays into One

Whatever view we take of the genesis of *The First Part of King Henry the Sixth*, no one will dispute the fact that there are two major and clearly distinguishable plot components in the play: the war in France and the 'jarrings' in England. There is monumental disagreement, however, as to whether these components do, or do not, compose one play. Most modern scholars of repute, including Tillyard, Alexander, Price, Kirschbaum, Bullough, Brockbank, and Cairncross – a formidable enough array – have declared in favour of the view that the complete play was conceived and written as a dramatic unity, whilst at the other extreme Pollard, Greg, Chambers, and Dover Wilson – an older generation on the whole – have argued strongly not only for disjointed conception but for composite authorship.[1] My view, which I shall try to substantiate, is that by any but the laxest standards of dramatic unity the two major strands of the action are separate and remain distinct, though I am willing to consider the whole play as essentially William Shakespeare's.

It is regrettable that the discussion of this play has been biased for some time by the distinction between plot and design popularised by Hereward T. Price. In his frequently quoted essay *Construction in Shakespeare* published in 1951, Price singles out *1 Henry VI* for particular attention and attempts to show how all its separate parts and aspects are patterned around a central idea, that of 'the responsibility of those that govern, especially the effects arising from the strength or weakness, competence or incompetence of the King'. The result, in Price's view, is a masterpiece of carefully planned construction; one only has to recognise Shakespeare's intentions. 'Critics who cannot follow Shakespeare's intentions pick holes in the construction of these [the historical] plays. Looking for plot, they ignore design.' '*Henry VI* may have no plot, but it certainly has a severely controlled design.'[2]

Now it seems to me pretty obvious and amply demonstrated by countless critics and scholars that all of Shakespeare's plays have design in the sense of thematic focus, linkage of scenes, ironical or incremental near-repetition of incidents, pattern of imagery, etc. The fact that design may be less than 'severely controlled' and that a particular critic's view of design in a given play can be stretched to accommodate almost anything that happens to be contained in the play, these things do not invalidate the concept of design itself. But it is highly misleading to suggest that there is an inherent opposition between design and plot. And how it can be maintained that *1 Henry VI* has no plot is, to say the least, incomprehensible.

Price in fact imposes his own sense of unified design on *1 Henry VI* by ignoring the play's discontinuities. If 'the responsibility of those that govern' is the unifying theme, how often and how clearly is it found in the Talbot scenes? And how can it be said that the French, unlike the English, 'have a leader who unites them and in whom they never lose confidence'?[3] Where, then, is Talbot, 'the Scourge of France', who has reclaimed 'fifty fortresses, / Twelve cities, and seven walled towns of strength' to obedience to King Henry (III.iv.5–7)? Unfortunately, Price's uncritical praise of this play's unity of design has been echoed by influential scholars like Leo Kirschbaum.[4] A younger disciple paradoxically asserts that 'The flexibility allowed by design is also illustrated in *1 Henry VI*, a play constructed of five separate strands of action which bear directly upon each other at scattered points only'.[5] Or consider this by the same author:

> There is still another method used to give the impression of progressive action in *1 Henry IV*, and it is perhaps the *tour de force* of the play's construction. The procedure is really quite simple. Shakespeare created an elaborate structure of dramatic suspense by continually prefiguring events which, it turns out, never occur.[6]

Thus, indeed, may deficiencies be turned into beauties. There are surely better ways of defending the poet.

To return to my opening paragraph, I would not deny that there is a connection between the two major plot components of *1 Henry VI*. Quarrels at home are repeatedly said to be the cause of the reverses in France. The messenger who brings the first news of disaster in Scene i takes it upon himself to berate the assembled lords for maintaining 'several factions' and for consequently failing to provide the men and money needed to hold England's French possessions. Later Exeter becomes the main spokesman for this complaint, notably at the end of III.i:

> This late dissension grown betwixt the peers
> Burns under feigned ashes of forg'd love,
> And will at last break out into a flame;
>
> · · · · ·

> And now I fear that fatal prophecy
> Which in the time of Henry nam'd the Fifth
> Was in the mouth of every sucking babe:
> That Henry born at Monmouth should win all,
> And Henry born at Windsor should lose all:

We here undoubtedly have a central ideological theme embedded in the play. J. P. Brockbank, like Price, thinks it integral to the action:

> While 'martiall feates, and daily skirmishes' continue in France, the play returns in four scenes to England and conveys the essential Holinshed by keeping the civil causes coincident with the military effects. Thus the dramatic concurrence of the siege of Orleans and the brawl outside the Tower of London (I.iii) directly expresses the chronicle point, 'Through dissention at home, all lost abroad' (*Hol.*, p. 288).[7]

If we ask, however, whether this ideological explanation of the military collapse of the English is borne out by the actual events depicted in the play, the answer must be an almost unqualified no. The conflict between Gloucester and Winchester, which is the most violent of the domestic dissensions and potentially the most disruptive, has no demonstrable bearing on developments in France. York has a personal interest in the fate of the French dominions, but for most of the play both he and his opponent Somerset remain outside the French plot, and only towards the end is their quarrel linked with the conduct of the war. By that time they are both commanders in the theatre of operations. They are responsible for the death of Talbot, but York subsequently brings final victory to the English arms. Civil dissensions, then, are only asserted, not shown, to be the cause of defeat.

What the military leaders themselves, especially Talbot, blame for their setbacks is not lack of support from home but treachery. Words like 'treachery', 'treacherous', 'traitor', and 'betray' abound in the play. The second messenger in the opening scene has a long story to tell of Sir John Falstaff's cowardice at Orleans leading to the 'general wrack and massacre' of the English force and in particular to the capture of Talbot. And when Talbot himself appears in Scene iv he bitterly reviles 'the treacherous Falstaff'. We briefly catch sight of Falstaff as he flies from the fighting at Rouen, and he appears once more during the coronation in Paris, when he is charged with cowardice in the battle of Poitiers, stripped of his Garter, and banished on pain of death. After his portentous presentation by the messenger in the first scene and by Talbot we rather expect to see more of him, and it may be legitimate to wonder whether a scene or two representing him more fully may have been lost or excised. Falstaff, however, is not the only person to betray the English. The master-gunner of Orleans is a kind of traitor, and when Salisbury is killed by a ball from his cunningly pointed cannon Talbot speaks of 'The treacherous manner of his mournful death'. The Countess of Auvergne is another.[8] And above all Joan of Arc is a traitor, allying herself with the powers of evil against the rightful masters of France. When she deceitfully enters into Rouen and drives out the English. Talbot exclaims:

> France, thou shalt rue this treason with thy tears,
> If Talbot but survive thy treachery.
> Pucelle, that witch, that damned sorceress,
> Hath wrought this hellish mischief unawares, (III.ii.36–9)

Burgundy is a renegade, and King Henry denounces his 'monstrous treachery'. Even the part played by York and Somerset in the defeat of Talbot is regarded as another example of betrayal. York four times in twenty-one lines calls Somerset a traitor, and Lucy declares that Talbot has been betrayed by both the wrangling dukes:

> The fraud of England, not the force of France,
> Hath now entrapp'd the noble-minded Talbot:
> Never to England shall he bear his life,
> But dies betray'd to fortune by your strife. (IV.iv.36–9)

To offset these instances of treachery and betrayal there are conspicuous examples of loyalty and courage. In addition to Talbot himself the most obvious ones are the Duke of Bedford, who, though sick to death, remains to 'revive the soldiers' hearts' during the fighting at Rouen, while Falstaff flies, and Talbot's son John, who refuses to leave his father in his hopeless last stand at Bordeaux to fly to safety. Altogether, treachery and loyalty rather than political ineffectiveness are what the war plot hinges on. If Holinshed's explanation of defeat. 'Through dissention at home, all lost abroad', is sometimes echoed in the play, its action is more clearly inspired by passages such as the following which Shakespeare would have read in Hall:

> euen as Englishmen valiantlye wonne, and victoriously cõquered tounes and castles wyth open warre and apparant conquest: so the Frenchmen fraudulently stale & couertly obtayned diuers fortresses and holdes appertainyng to thenglishe faccion (1550, fo.v).

The war plot itself is neatly constructed and provides all the completed action we find in the play. It begins with news of losses in France coinciding with the death of the conqueror king, Henry V. Then there is a rhythm of defeat and victory three times repeated, at Orleans, Rouen, and Bordeaux, the last defeat being followed by victory at Angiers.[9] Including exposition and dénouement this makes a distinct five-part structure. It all ends with a peace in which the French king has to reaffirm English supremacy. There is no reason to call it 'a rotten peace' as H. T. Price does.[10] The treaty is a compromise, and this word is actually used, but it is honourable for the English. York's military victory is frustrated by Henry's concessions but not cancelled. And the chief terror of the English, Joan the sorceress, has been captured and put to death. Peter Bilton rightly remarks, 'the pessimism about the French campaigns is left unjustified by this play, which ends on a victorious note.'[11] The whole movement of the play, in fact, is from defeat to victory, contrary to a widespread notion which sees it as dealing with the loss of France.[12] It should be noticed in this connection that Margaret is taken prisoner at the end, not just casually encountered, and that only a private infatuation makes Suffolk forgo the political advantage of capturing her.

The structural rhythm of the play is emphasised by the deaths of Salisbury, Bedford, and Talbot in the three main engagements. There is also a remarkable symmetry in the roles of Talbot and Joan, as if they were made to feature in equal balance in some of the more striking episodes. Consider the following encounters tabulated by their order in the play:

	Joan and Charles
Talbot and Salisbury	
Talbot and Countess of A.	
	Joan and Burgundy
Talbot and Falstaff	
Talbot and his son	
	Joan and spirits
	Joan and her father

Especially the contrasting parallelism of the father-and-son and father-and-daughter scenes points to a deliberate attempt at symmetry. And nothing could be more conclusive than the deaths of the main protagonist and the main antagonist and the signing of a peace treaty leaving the English finally victorious. There is a conventionally natural ending in York's last lines in v.iv:

So, now dismiss your army when ye please;
Hang up your ensigns, let your drums be still,
For here we entertain a solemn peace.

If anything can be objected against this structural plan it would have to be that it is perhaps *too* neat. Or the neatness is not, it may be said, fully supported and justified by an equally confident handling of incident, character, and dialogue. Most of the military activity is rendered in a primitive technique which even the Chorus of *Henry V* would hardly think worth an apology. Cities change hands like dice and a few leaders do the work of armies. Joan the holy maid and heroic patriot and Joan the witch are two persons rather than one. And the dialogue, while mostly composed of short and dramatic speeches, becomes long-winded and repetitive in the Bordeaux scenes, long stretches of which are in rhymed verse and look like remains from an earlier, more declamatory play.[13] Bits of the action may be missing here and there, too. I have already suggested that Falstaff is strangely insignificant as far as his participation in the plot is concerned, compared to the importance attributed to him by report. And even Talbot is not seen to perform all that we are led to expect. At the end of the coronation scene he is commanded by the king to march against the Duke of Burgundy, but we next find him on an expedition against Bordeaux, plotted, as Somerset alleges, in conjunction with York, who 'set him on'. There could conceivably have been a scene here in which Burgundy escapes from Talbot's pursuit and another in which York plans a diversion and promises Talbot reinforcements. But whatever may hypothetically have been left out the omissions are relatively immaterial. And no objections or suspicions can detract from the impression that *1 Henry VI* is a unified and well-shaped play as far as the war/treachery plot is concerned.

The jarring nobles are an altogether different proposition. On this plot level major expectations are created, even at the very end of the play, which are not fulfilled till we get to the sequel. Neither of the two main quarrels between the peers in England comes to a conclusion in *1 Henry VI*, but they both point to a continuation beyond the play and in fact link up with the plot of *The Whole Contention*. Gloucester is not yet defined as 'the good Duke Humphrey', but his honesty is manifest, while Winchester's asides reveal his duplicity and unscrupulous ambition. After the violent clashes between their retainers they are outwardly reconciled in the Parliament scene, but Winchester's last words, apart from his final appearance at the peace conference, are full of threats for the future:

Humphrey of Gloucester, thou shalt well perceive
That neither in birth nor for authority

> The Bishop will be overborne by thee;
> I'll either make thee stoop and bend thy knee,
> Or sack this country with a mutiny.   (v.i.58–62)

Similarly, York and Somerset only begin their quarrel in *1 Henry VI* and it is not yet connected explicitly with York's claim to the succession, though the white and red roses emblematically herald the dynastic contention. York's right to the throne is established in the interview with Mortimer but not yet made a cause of rebellion. As for Suffolk and Margaret, this intrigue, too, trails a loose end, since Henry is left at the end of the play affianced to two women, and Margaret has not yet arrived in England. Suffolk's concluding lines are in fact no conclusion but indicate the beginning of a new conflict:

> Margaret shall now be Queen, and rule the King;
> But I will rule both her, the King, and realm.

The theory which is naturally suggested by all this is one that has been frequently enough canvassed, though it is still far from commanding general assent: that Shakespeare used an old Talbot play and turned it into the first part of a trilogy on the reign of Henry VI by adding or expanding the plot components which centre around York, Gloucester, and Margaret. That the Talbot play was an old one, or at least earlier than *The Whole Contention* in date of composition, I think is the right inference to be drawn from the primitive features which I have touched upon and some of which I shall return to. Chambers takes these features to point to another hand or other hands than Shakespeare's,[14] and in fact the question of dating has long been bedevilled by that of multiple authorship. Now that the trend in scholarship is towards the recognition of Shakespeare's hand in the whole of *1 Henry VI* there is no need in the present connection to discuss the theories involving Greene, Peele, Nashe and other collaborators. There are certainly bad verses and scenes in the play which, one might suppose, could have been written only by a lesser playwright, but then Shakespeare may well have retouched one of his own more or less juvenile efforts, leaving traces of immaturity in the lines which remained unaltered. There is at least nothing to disprove the possibility that he himself was the sole author of the Talbot part, having written it perhaps when he was quite young and drawn to a romantic and patriotic subject. Tillyard sensibly remarks that 'In the nature of things so fluent an author as Shakespeare probably wrote in his youth much that has perished'.[15] The Talbot play may be one that did not perish completely. My main point, however, is not to prove Shakespeare's authorship of it but to establish its separate origin.

It furthermore seems likely – and here Irving Ribner among more recent scholars concurs with Pollard, Chambers, and Wilson against the school of Tillyard and Price[16] – that the first part of *Henry VI* was put together after the *Contention* plays had been on the boards. This is borne out by the independence of that pair of plays of anything contained in *1 Henry VI*. As Dover Wilson says, 'whereas *1 Henry VI* was written by a person or persons who knew all about *2 Henry VI*, and I think *3 Henry VI* also, those two plays display complete ignorance of the drama which ostensibly precedes them.'[17] This assertion cannot be lightly dismissed and I have given reasons for supporting it in my previous chapter. Conversely, the intrigues begun in *1 Henry VI* and continued in the *Contention* plays are no proof that Shakespeare began his story at the beginning, so to speak. To take just one detail. Andrew Cairncross regards the reference to Gloucester's wife in the first part (i.i.39–40) as 'an indication of Shakespeare's overall plan for the *H6–R3* tetralogy, and of the priority of *1H6*'.[18] But surely it is rather the other way about: Shakespeare could hardly have referred to the duchess so casually and so early in the play if he was foreshadowing her role in a drama yet to be written. This may well be the kind of reference to Gloucester's political and moral liabilities which he would have found in his sources and which is also exemplified in the slanting allusion to Gloucester's bygone peccadilloes in Henry's appeal to 'what you were. / Not what you are' (v.v.97–8). These references could have gone into a Talbot play without thought of future developments. Alternatively, if the reference to Eleanor is a detail added to an existing play to link it up with *The Contention*, this would explain why the verses in question have a rather patchwork quality:

> Thy wife is proud; she holdeth thee in awe
> More than God or religious churchmen may.

Those who favour a relatively late date for *1 Henry VI* generally accept Henslowe's mention of a 'harey the vj' which was 'ne' on 3 March 1592 as a reference to that play, and I can see no compelling reason why this identification should be doubted. But that does not mean that *1 Henry VI* was all composed at one time as some scholars have contended.[19] It is indeed surprising how few have contemplated the possibility that Shakespeare wrote it all but wrote it as two plays, so to speak, one part preceding and the other part following upon *The Whole Contention*. Geoffrey Bullough approaches some such theory but refuses to commit himself to it.[20] By and large scholars have tended either to agree with Pollard that there was an early Talbot (or Joan of Arc) play by one or more other playwrights which

Shakespeare refashioned after the success of the *Contention* plays, or to maintain that *1 Henry VI* was composed all in one piece. Yet what more natural than that Shakespeare, if he was himself the author of an early Talbot play, should go back to it after finishing *The Whole Contention* and wish to turn it into the first part of a trilogy on the reign of Henry VI? Not only could he make it a prelude to the later plays by adding to it material which would help to explain such things as the rapid development of Margaret's affair with Suffolk and the reasons for York's quarrel with Somerset, but he may also have hoped to improve the Talbot play by providing a more interesting and sophisticated explanation than that of treachery in the field for the disasters which punctuate it. The best way of achieving his double purpose would be to write some supplementary passages and scenes about dissensions among the nobility, a subject which cannot have been absent from the early play but which was not central there.[21] He also may have rewritten and expanded some of the original scenes while probably omitting others. In the process he may well have introduced a more understanding treatment of Joan of Arc than that of crude vituperation, but without entirely remodelling the character and therefore leaving it somewhat inconsistent.[22]

Of course he may have revised an old Talbot play in the light of increased theatrical experience and in the assurance of growing dramaturgic and stylistic skill even before he thought of adapting it for a subsidiary purpose; in which case there must be at least three layers of composition in the play as we have it: the original Talbot play, the revised play, and the additional matter.[23] But most of the revision could have taken place simultaneously with the writing of the supplementary parts and so have constituted one process with it. At any rate, the result is a play which is not entirely self-contained. *1 Henry VI* is dependent on *The First Part of the Contention* as the latter play is not dependent on *1 Henry VI*.

The plausibility of this theory of revision and adaptation is confirmed by signs of interpolation in several places. Thus in the first scene of the play three messengers bring news from France to the lords who are gathered for the funeral of Henry V. The first two essentially tell the same story, though in different words: the first messenger (and I here quote direct from the Folio) that

> Guyen, Champaigne, Rheimes, Orleance,
> Paris, Guysors, Poictiers, are all quite lost.   (i.i.60–1)

and the second messenger that

> France is revolted from the English quite,
> Except some petty towns of no import: (i.i.90–1)

As it happens neither messenger speaks the truth, even in terms of the play, since, as M. M. Reese points out, 'the spectator will be surprised to find, later in the play, Henry being crowned in Paris [. . .]; Orleans still under siege; and Rouen still in possession of the English'.[24] The second messenger is less specific than the first about the lost towns, but he adds the news that 'The Dauphin Charles is crowned king in Rheims'. This information is completely ignored in the remainder of the play as far as to the last act. Charles obstinately remains the Dauphin throughout the dialogue of Acts i–iv. At i.ii.46 the Bastard asks for 'the Prince Dauphin' and at iii.iii.38 Joan calls him 'the princely Charles of France'. Not till v.ii.4 does he appear as 'royal Charles of France', and in the treaty scene he has obviously assumed the royal title.[25] A separate messenger, therefore, was hardly needed for the news of Charles's coronation. But was the *first* messenger there originally? The pattern of three messengers is not common in Shakespeare's plays.[26] It certainly has roots in folklore, and it helps to create a sense of urgency. But in this case the first messenger is not only misinformed and superfluous but he actually produces several inconsistencies. When Exeter asks him 'What treachery was us'd?' he answers, 'No treachery, but want of men and money' (i.i.68–9), virtually contradicting the report of the third messenger, who declares that Talbot would have won a victory at Orleans 'If Sir John Falstaff had not play'd the coward'. Then, too, the effect on Bedford of the first messenger's report, making him immediately call for his 'steeled coat' so that he may go and fight for France makes nonsense of Gloucester's taunting (or is it just challenging?) remark, 'Bedford, if thou be slack, I'll fight it out', which comes after the second messenger's news. This taunt (or challenge) can only refer back to Bedford's despondent words before they have had any news from France at all:

> Instead of gold, we'll offer up our arms,
> Since arms avail not, now that Henry's dead.   (i.i.46–7)[27]

The main function of the first messenger is obviously to reproach the lords for their factions and disputes which, as the soldiers are now muttering, are the real cause of their troubles. Shakespeare may here have elaborated on an idea contained in the old Talbot play, where the person who is now the third messenger presumably described the plight of the English besiegers at Orleans more or less in the words of the present play:

> The English army is grown weak and faint;
> The Earl of Salisbury craveth supply

> And hardly keeps his men from mutiny,
> Since they, so few, watch such a multitude.   (i.i.158–61)

In the following scene the French nobles speak contemptuously of 'the famish'd English' and Reignier has a speech the last line of which may have provided the author with a direct cue for the first messenger:

> Let's raise the siege: why live we idly here?
> Talbot is taken, whom we wont to fear;
> Remaineth none but mad-brain'd Salisbury,
> And he may well in fretting spend his gall –
> Nor men nor money hath he to make war.   (i.ii.13–17)

Not only is the first messenger superfluous as a bringer of news but he disturbs the logical development of the dialogue. If the passage from 'Enter a Messenger' (l.57) to 'Enter to them another Messenger' (l.88) is left out the inconsistencies disappear and nothing is lost which matters to the war plot. The passage might well be an interpolation in the original Talbot play. And this may also explain why it is preceded by an imperfect line of verse: 'Than Julius Cæsar or bright – '. The word or words represented by a dash in the Folio could have been obscured when the additional passage was written or pasted into the manuscript.

The part of Talbot's messenger in iv.iii seems at one time to have belonged to Sir William Lucy, since York once addresses him by Lucy's name. Shortly afterwards Lucy appears again with Somerset under his full name. If Lucy was to appeal to both the dukes in quick succession, either he would need seven-league boots, or York and Somerset must be supposed to be more or less in the same place, which they apparently were not. The original play probably had an interview between Lucy and York only, and it may be noticed in support of this view that Talbot in iv.vi blames only the Regent, i.e. York, and not Somerset, for breaking his word. The interview with Somerset, unlike the one with York, is in unrhymed verse and on the whole in a style superior to that of the York scene.[28] It also contains ideas characteristic of the dissensions plot, and Lucy speaks in the same vein as the first messenger of the opening scene:

> You, his false hopes, the trust of England's honour,
> Keep off aloof with worthless emulation.
> Let not your private discord keep away
> The levied succours that should lend him aid.   (iv.iv.20–3)

It seems extremely likely that this scene is another addition to the Talbot play and that the author to avoid absurdity substituted an anonymous messenger for Lucy in the preceding York scene but inadvertently left Lucy's name unaltered at one point in the dialogue.

Some of the quarrel between Gloucester and Winchester may have featured in the old play, but hardly the part contained in the Parliament scene and certainly not Winchester's final threat to Humphrey of Gloucester. There are two brawls between the duke's and the bishop's men where one would have been enough, and it seems probable that the first one was meant to be omitted when the second one was added. That was why Shakespeare did not bother to degrade the cardinal of the Tower scene, where his title and scarlet hat and robes are so emphatically insisted on: the whole scene had become superfluous; whereas he may have revised the title elsewhere if Winchester appeared as a cardinal throughout the old Talbot play. In the revised and expanded play Winchester definitely is not elevated to a cardinalship till the beginning of the fifth act, and it is important to see him as a man thirsting for greater power than that of a mere bishop and finally achieving it by means of bribery in high places. Exeter's expression of surprised dismay at the news of Winchester's installation in v.i is entirely incompatible with any appearance of the bishop as a cardinal in an earlier scene, and the inconsistency of the Tower scene with the rest of the play cannot, as Andrew Cairncross seems to think,[29] have passed unnoticed by Shakespeare, much less have been carelessly tolerated by him. Winchester's hypocritical defence of his humility in the Parliament scene reveals to what extent his rank is a matter of importance to himself and to his part in the plot:

> Gloucester, I do defy thee. Lords, vouchsafe
> To give me hearing what I shall reply.
> If covetous, ambitious, or perverse,
> As he will have me, how am I so poor?
> Or how haps it I seek not to advance
> Or raise myself, but keep my wonted calling?
>
> (III.i.27–32)

This is clearly no cardinal speaking.

Just as Winchester rises in the ecclesiastical hierarchy, so York advances in the course of the play from plain Richard Plantagenet to Duke of York and Regent of France. It is reasonable to suppose that the Temple Garden scene, the Mortimer scene, and the Parliament scene (i.e. II.iv, II.v, III.i) were added *en bloc* to the Talbot play, possibly replacing omitted matter.

The second half of IV.i, the quarrel between Vernon and Basset, York and Somerset, in Paris, would also be additional. The greater part of all this concerns the status and prospects of York and serves a double purpose in illustrating the dissensions theme and providing an introduction to *The First Part of the Contention*. It is interesting to notice that Exeter's role as we have it belongs almost wholly to the additional passages of the play.[30] As I pointed out at first he is the main spokesman for the complaint which forms the central ideological theme of the revised version. But he seems to have been contemplated at one time for a more active part. At the end of the opening scene of *1 Henry VI* we are made to expect a clash between Exeter and Winchester, who both determine to go, or send, to Eltham, one to protect the boy king, the other to steal him away. Nothing, in terms of the play, comes of either project. By contrast we do see both Gloucester and Bedford following up their stated intentions, the former to proceed to the Tower 'To view th'artillery and munition', the latter to prepare for France.

The last major additions to the old play are the two scenes containing Suffolk's wooing of Margaret and his seduction of King Henry on her behalf. This is entirely new business, and there is only a tenuous connection with the war plot in that Margaret's father has appeared in the company of the Dauphin and that Margaret is taken prisoner by Suffolk near her father's castle.[31] Dover Wilson thinks that 'The prominence right from the beginning given to her father Reignier seems a sufficient confutation of [the] notion' that the Margaret scenes are 'an afterthought added later than the rest of the play'.[32] But Reignier is not particularly prominent. He is absent from the French scenes which precede the wooing, and he nowhere so much as mentions his daughter before we see her promenading on the battlefield. What is more significant, Suffolk is not very prominent either before he suddenly takes the centre of the stage almost at the end of the play, and we certainly have not been prepared for his ambitious speech with which the present play closes.

Altogether, the Margaret scenes have little connection with anything else in *1 Henry VI* but are obviously a prelude to *The First Part of the Contention*, which begins with Margaret's arrival at Westminster.

The difference in stylistic levels between parts which belong to the old Talbot play and parts which belong to the additional matter should be evident to the most casual reader, though in a number of places revision may have obliterated the distinction between new and old. The greatest concentration of third-rate verse is probably found in the rhymed scenes in which Talbot's final tragedy is enacted.[33] There is here, too, an unusual amount of archaism and sloppy English. For a sample, here are two couplets, one from IV.iii, the other from IV.vi:

We mourn, France smiles; we lose, they daily get –
All long of this vile traitor Somerset.

If I to-day die not with Frenchmen's rage,
To-morrow I shall die with mickle age:

It is simple enough, too, to set passages from different parts of the play
side by side for contrast, and here are two pairs of examples, first from the
beginning of the Tower scene and the near-ending of the Temple Garden
scene:

I am come to survey the Tower this day;
Since Henry's death, I fear, there is conveyance.
Where be these warders that they wait not here?
Open the gates; 'tis Gloucester that calls.   (I.iii.1–4)

And, by my soul, this pale and angry rose,
As cognizance of my blood-drinking hate,
Will I for ever, and my faction, wear,
Until it wither with me to my grave,
Or flourish to the height of my degree.   (II.iv.107–11)

Next, from the answers of York and Suffolk respectively to Talbot's
appeals for help in IV.iii and iv:

Alas, what joy shall noble Talbot have
To bid his young son welcome to his grave?
Away, vexation almost stops my breath,
That sunder'd friends greet in the hour of death.
Lucy, farewell; no more my fortune can
But curse the cause I cannot aid the man.

It is too late; I cannot send them now:
This expedition was by York and Talbot
Too rashly plotted: all our general force
Might with a sally of the very town
Be buckled with: the over-daring Talbot
Hath sullied all his gloss of former honour
By this unheedful, desperate, wild adventure:

Clumsy exposition, faulty metre, poor phrasing, and needless alliteration
are some of the blemishes which abound in the earlier-written portions of
the play but are far less frequent in the later ones. In fact the style of the
later portions is closely similar to that of *The Contention*.

Of the discrepancies of a substantial kind between *1 Henry VI* and *The First Part of the Contention* I have already said something in my previous chapter. It all goes to prove the priority in time of the *Contention* plays. As I have indicated I cannot agree with those who think that the whole of *1 Henry VI* was written after what became the second and third parts. The Talbot play was of an earlier date, but it was provided with new passages and scenes and a new thematic emphasis to fit it for a novel function as the opening section of a trilogy. And since that is what Shakespeare ultimately wanted it to be, as far as we can judge, it is only fair to reserve our final appreciation of it for its place in this larger context. Taking a genetic view and analysing the play on its own merits, I have necessarily emphasised the heterogeneous nature of the materials that went to its making and explained them on the basis of a one-way traffic of relations with the *Contention* plays. On an overall aesthetic view the succession of plays on the reign of Henry VI assumes an epic as well as a dramatic character and the traffic of relations runs both backwards and forwards; not, that is to say, only from the Temple Garden to St Albans and from the wooing of Margaret to the death of Suffolk, but back from the Wars of the Roses to the plucking of the roses and from the loss of France to a private infatuation. In spite of all that can be said of lacking cohesion Shakespeare did manage to make his Talbot play a prelude to his more mature historical dramas and to turn *The Whole Contention* into what the Folio calls them, *The second* and *The third Part of Henry the Sixt*.

4 Plots and Prophecies – *The Tragedy of King Richard the Third*

In dramatic method *Richard III* is the most non-realistic of Shakespeare's history plays, not excepting *Richard II*. It has even been called 'the most stridently theatrical' of all his plays.[1] In a sense it is a metadrama in which a self-styled villain conspires with the spectators to produce a black comedy and himself plays a variety of roles in order to deceive and discomfit the other members of the cast. This actor-villain speaks a total of 166 lines (i.e. about 4.5 per cent of the play's dialogue) in soliloquy or in direct address to the audience. He is seconded in his histrionics by one (Buckingham) who 'can counterfeit the deep tragedian'; and he does, in fact, deceive everyone else, including his coadjutor when it comes to the point. Everyone, that is to say, except two old women. One is his mother.

> Ah, that deceit should steal such gentle shape
> And with a virtuous visor hide deep vice!   (II.ii.27–8)

exclaims the Duchess of York in answer to her grandson's innocent description of Richard. The other woman, who is not quite so elderly (though Richard calls her a 'withered hag') is the spirit of Revenge, Queen Margaret. For Margaret, like Richard, is an unrealistic character. She appears from nowhere, or France, to darken the dialogue with her mutterings and curses but has no physical business with the happenings of the play. In addition to her there are supernatural omens and apparitions, a bleeding corpse, a stumbling horse, a sun which apparently shines on one army and not on the other, and a procession of ghosts. There is a chorus of lamenting women and children, a repeated matching of griefs and grievances, a conspicuous use of stichomythia. There are two parallel wooing scenes and a number of parallel execution scenes. There are also attempts to render simultaneous action in two places, twice by interrupting almost continuous events at Westminster with scenes of death elsewhere (Clarence and the lords at Pomfret) and once, more remarkably, by pitching the tents of the opposing army leaders on the stage both at once and watching them alternately.

Much has been written about the formal patterning of *Richard III*. Irving Ribner has emphasised its indebtedness to Seneca and to the morality tradition, as well as to Shakespeare's more immediate forerunner, Christopher Marlowe. After enumerating the Senecan elements of the play – 'the villain-hero with his self-revealing soliloquies, the revenge motif, the ghosts, the stichomythic dialogue, and not least, the abundant echoes of Seneca's own plays' – Ribner declares: 'The dominating figure of the Senecan villain-hero gives to *Richard III* a unity which the *Henry VI* plays lacked.' The morality tradition, he says, 'is carried on in the ritual technique with which *Richard III* abounds'. And he instances the wooing of Anne and the murder of Clarence as acts which are 'handled in ritual fashion'. With Schelling he sees 'the great choral scene of lamentation' in IV.iv as 'reproducing . . . the nature and function of the Greek choric ode', while 'the parallel orations of Richmond and Richard before the final battle' also 'serve a ritualistic function'.[2]

Ribner does not exaggerate. Ritual formalism pervades the play from beginning to end. It is apparent, too, as M. M. Reese has pointed out, in 'its controlling pattern of Nemesis and revenge', in the way in which 'each successive blow of fate is the fulfilment of a curse, until at last the bleeding country is rescued by its foreordained deliverer'.[3] In fact the most significant departure from realistic convention, with its frequent stress on the role of accident, is the extent to which everything that happens is exactly foretold before it happens. Shakespeare made liberal use of prediction in all his history plays, but never as much as in *Richard III*. This play is a web of stated intentions, curses, prophecies, and dreams, and practically all expectations are punctually fulfilled. A. P. Rossiter and Wolfgang Clemen have both admirably explored this aspect of the play,[4] but it will still bear further scrutiny.

Only two minutes after Richard, Duke of Gloucester, has entered solus he informs us that he is 'determined to prove a villain', and, he goes on,

> Plots have I laid, inductions dangerous,
> By drunken prophecies, libels, and dreams,
> To set my brother Clarence and the King
> In deadly hate the one against the other;   (I.i.32–5)

Richard's 'plots', 'prophecies', and 'dreams' in themselves foreshadow the mode of the remainder of the play. His pretended prophecy that a certain

'G' will be the murderer of King Edward's heirs proves more true than the victims of the deceit, Clarence and Edward, suspect, but Richard knows already, and we know, that the G stands for Gloucester and not for George. He speaks the truth though with forked tongue. And he never keeps his audience in the dark.[5]

Richard is himself no prophet. But he is a man of iron will and unscrupulous performance coupled with exceptional gifts of persuasion and dissimulation. What he resolves to do he does, and his confidence in telling us of his intentions leaves no room for doubt that they will be carried out successfully. We know before the event that Clarence will be imprisoned and murdered (i.i.32–40, 119–20), that Richard will marry Anne (i.i.153), that he will have his revenge on Rivers, Vaughan, and Grey (i.iii.332),[6] that something will be done 'To draw the brats of Clarence out of sight' and to get rid of the princes in the Tower (iii.v.106–8, iv.ii.61), that he will do away with Anne and woo Elizabeth (iv.ii.57–61). All this is revealed in soliloquies, and Richard further confides in us about the success of his undertakings (iv.iii.36–43). In addition, of course, he conspires with Buckingham and his more inferior associates and gives instructions to his hired assassins on two occasions. We know what will happen to Hastings if he does not fall in with Richard's plans, and we know exactly what lies and pretences Richard will use to gain the support of the citizens of London for his coronation. Practically all the plot of the play until near the end of the fourth act is contained in Richard's stated intentions.

These intentions are for the most part reinforced by Margaret's curses and prophecies, since Richard turns on those of his own side and consequently his enemies are hers. In the great cursing scene of Act i, Margaret predicts no fewer than thirteen misfortunes relating to King Edward, his son, Queen Elizabeth, her children, Rivers, Hastings, Richard, and Buckingham. There is even a certain amount of detail in her curses: King Edward is to die 'by surfeit' and the Prince of Wales by 'untimely violence', the queen is to outlive her glory and her children and see another 'decked in [her] rights'. 'The day will come', Margaret warns Elizabeth,

> that thou shalt wish for me
> To help thee curse this poisonous bunch-backed toad.
>
> (i.iii.244–5)

As for Richard, she is unsparing in her depiction of punishments for him, especially, as Tillyard points out, the curse of insomnia:

> If heaven have any grievous plague in store
> Exceeding those that I can wish upon thee,

> O let them keep it till thy sins be ripe,
> And then hurl down their indignation
> On thee, the troubler of the poor world's peace!
> The worm of conscience still begnaw thy soul!
> Thy friends suspect for traitors while thou liv'st,
> And take deep traitors for thy dearest friends!
> No sleep close up that deadly eye of thine,
> Unless it be while some tormenting dream
> Affrights thee with a hell of ugly devils!   (i.iii.216–26)

Margaret's curses are no mere displays of clairvoyance but obviously potent agents in bringing about the events which she prophesies, and as they come to pass this is recognised in turn by the victims – all but Richard. As Grey goes to his execution at Pomfret he remarks to Rivers,

> Now Margaret's curse is fallen upon our heads,
> When she exclaimed on Hastings, you, and I,
> For standing by when Richard stabbed her son.
>
> (iii.iii.14–16)

Similarly Hastings, Queen Elizabeth, and Buckingham[7] all remember her words in their hour of distress, and Margaret herself tots up the score of her victories in the great lamenting scene of Act iv.

   Margaret is the chief and most vociferous but by no means the only prophet and author of curses in the play. She herself is first prompted by Richard's reminder of his father's curse denounced against Margaret at the time of his death (i.iii.173–95). If 'York's dread curse prevail[ed] so much with heaven', then she must try the same means of revenge. The Duchess of York and Elizabeth take a lesson from Margaret, and the duchess utters violent imprecations against Richard to which Elizabeth says amen (iv.iv.188–98). Anne in the second scene of the tragedy curses the murderer of her husband and father-in-law and prays to God to revenge King Henry's death. Unwittingly she involves herself in her baneful wishes by hypothetically including the wife of the murderer. She remembers this when her misery is complete, just as Buckingham in the reconciliation scene swears an oath which recoils on himself and remembers it on the day of his execution.[8] Even Richard, in the second wooing scene, swears against himself and is probably too sceptical to realise that his maledictions will be most precisely honoured:

> Myself myself confound!
> Heaven and fortune bar me happy hours!
> Day, yield me not thy light, nor, night, thy rest!
>
> (iv.iv.399–401)

After his night of agony and confused awakening, the sun 'disdains to shine' on him on the day of battle. Vaughan and Hastings before being beheaded foretell the downfall of their judges. The ghosts, of course, add their full share of cursing. And Richmond, on Bosworth field, prays that he and his forces may be God's 'ministers of chastisement'.

Prayers are mostly for chastisement and revenge, and blessings are as rare in *Richard III* as imprecations are plentiful. Clarence prays for his wife and children, the hoodwinked mayor invokes God's blessing on Richard when the latter agrees to accept the crown, Dorset exits to Brittany with the Duchess of York's benediction (she also rather futilely sends her good wishes with Anne and Elizabeth), Stanley blesses Richmond 'by attorney' from his mother, and of course the ghosts whisper encouragements to Richmond in his sleep. But the only time Richard talks of blessings is when he hypocritically craves one of his mother and makes fun of her admonishments (ii.ii.106–11).

Dreams are almost as important as curses and prayers and equally prophetic. Richard uses invented dreams to set Edward against Clarence, Clarence appropriately dreams of drowning and of being tormented in hell, Stanley dreams symbolically of being executed by Richard along with Hastings, and Richard and Richmond dream on the eve of battle of defeat and victory. Hastings sceptically laughs at Stanley's being so simple as 'to trust the mockery of unquiet slumbers' (iii.ii.27) but learns to his cost that Stanley was right. And Richard, who is outwardly the least superstitious of all the characters in the play, is plagued nightly after Margaret's curse by the phantom horrors it promises. As Clemen remarks, 'There is the feeling of fear and uncertainty running like a keynote through almost all the scenes of the play and finding expression in various characters and ways.'[9] So general is the mood of fearsome divination that even the anonymous citizens in ii.iii, commenting on the death of King Edward, are inspired with prophetic forebodings.

Two prophecies originating in a time prior to the action of the play have to do with its decisive events. One is Henry's intuition, referred to by Richard in iv.ii.94–5, 'that Richmond should be king', the other the vision of 'a bard of Ireland' mentioned by Richard almost in the same breath that he (Richard) 'should not live long after [he] saw Richmond'. Like these last two, all the prophecies in the play come true with only a few, mostly questionable, exceptions.[10] Dorset, if he was ever meant to be included in Richard's revenge and in Margaret's curse, completely escapes them both, and Queen Elizabeth saves at least two of her children and will be the mother of a new queen.[11] Stanley, too, escapes in spite of his ominous dream, though he is long kept on tenterhooks both for his own safety and his son's. But the most interesting case of non-fulfilment relates to the despair invoked on their destroyer by the ghosts of Richard's victims. The word 'despair' (and 'despairing') is uttered no fewer than twelve times in their maledictions, and we cannot forget that it had a very definite implication. To die in despair was to die without hope of salvation, especially by one's own hand.[12] In his anguished soliloquy after the spectral visitation, Richard cries out, 'I shall despair. There is no creature loves me;' but there is no hint of despair in the last words he speaks in the tragedy, just before his death is reported; in fact his courage is unabated as long as we see him:

> Slave, I have set my life upon a cast,
> And I will stand the hazard of the die.
> I think there be six Richmonds in the field;
> Five have I slain today instead of him.
> A horse! A horse! My kingdom for a horse!   (v.iv.9–13)

Perhaps he should be understood to be desperately minded though he does not betray the fact or perhaps even realise it himself. But the ghosts are quite specific in referring their curses to the moment of his defeat and summoning fear and guilt to unman him:

> Tomorrow in the battle think on me,
> And fall thy edgeless sword; despair and die!   (v.iii.135–6)

> Think upon Vaughan and with guilty fear
> Let fall thy lance; despair, and die!   (v.iii.143–4)

> O, in the battle think on Buckingham,
> And die in terror of thy guiltiness!
> Dream on, dream on, of bloody deeds and death.
> Fainting, despair; despairing, yield thy breath!
> (v.iii.170–3)

It would be in keeping with the pattern of *anagnorisis* which pervades the play if Richard, too, had his moment of recognition. In *The True Tragedie of Richard the third* we see considerably more of Richard's despair, and though he is courageous to the end as in Shakespeare's play, he recognises in his very last words that he will be 'among the damned soules'. Since so many prophecies are so exactly fulfilled in *Richard III* one must necessarily wonder why this one is not. Could it be that the ghosts were not in the author's first draft, or else that that draft had a scene in which Richard's despair was actually shown? Strong arguments can be advanced for at least the former explanation.

In Shakespeare's main source, Hall's chronicle, the ghosts are only anonymous 'ymages lyke terrible develles' and Hall puts no words in their mouths. In *The True Tragedie* Richard's dreams are troubled by the ghosts of Clarence, the young princes, and 'the headlesse Peeres' which come 'gaping for revenge', but they make no visible appearance in the play, except for Clarence's ghost in the Prologue. It would be only natural if Shakespeare's initial impulse was to follow his sources. And there are indications in the texts of *Richard III* pointing to an early state in which the apparitions were not actually staged. Thus both Richard and Richmond adequately (from a dramatic point of view) describe their dreams after awaking, in passages which were obviously meant to be parallel and contrasting. The parallelism becomes particularly evident if Richard's lines, instead of awkwardly concluding his terrified soliloquy, as they do in the extant texts (v.iii.205–7), are transferred a few lines down to his dialogue with Ratcliffe, thus:[13]

> O Ratcliffe, I have dreamed a fearful dream!
> Methought the souls of all that I had murdered
> Came to my tent, and every one did threat
> Tomorrow's vengeance on the head of Richard.

Similarly Richmond tells his friends:

> The sweetest sleep, and fairest-boding dreams
> That ever entered in a drowsy head
> Have I since your departure had, my lords.
> Methought their souls whose bodies Richard murdered
> Came to my tent and cried on victory.   (v.iii.228–32)

Whether or not the ghosts were in fact added at a later stage of composition, it at least seems reasonably certain that they were not all included at once. A number of peculiarities point to this conclusion: 1. The ghosts of Anne and Buckingham tell the sleepers to dream on *after* they have been called on by the ghosts of the 'headless peers' to awake. 2. Prior to the dream scene there are preparatory invocations of all the ghosts *except* those of Clarence, Anne, and Buckingham.[14] 3. The order in which the ghosts of the princes appear in the first quarto differs from that of the third quarto and subsequent editions, including the Folio. 4. Clarence speaks not only for himself but for 'the wronged heirs of York', which would include the princes. 5. Anne is made to repeat the exact wording of Clarence's curse: 'Tomorrow in the battle think on me, / And fall thy edgeless sword; despair and die! (v.iii.163–4). There are no other comparable repetitions in the string of curses.[15]

What would seem to have happened is that Shakespeare first introduced the ghosts of Prince Edward, King Henry VI, Clarence, the Pomfret peers, and Hastings, in the order in which their deaths occurred in his own plays. Then he, or someone else, added the remainder – the two princes, Anne, and Buckingham – for good measure. And I am inclined to think 'someone else', since the placing of the princes was somehow bungled, since the contradiction between the injunctions to awake and to sleep on went unnoticed, and since Anne's curse is a mere repetition of Clarence's. In any case, and this of course is what I have been leading up to, if some or even all of the ghosts were not part of the original plan for this scene, the forecast of Richard's despair in the battle scene would not be nearly as marked as it eventually became.

The alternative explanation of the non-fulfilment of the ghosts' curses, viz. that the original version contained a scene in which Richard was actually shown to die in despair, is perhaps less likely, but it is strange in any case that the extant texts do not contain a single verbal exchange between the two antagonists Richard and Richmond. As in *The True Tragedie*, if we can trust the surviving version of that play, the defeat and death of Richard is given merely in dumb show. Shakespeare's tragedy has the brief stage direction: 'Alarum, Enter Richard and Richmond, they fight, Richard is slaine.' Obviously there is opportunity here for a variety of theatrical interpretations consonant with the curses. Nothing is actually said about Richard being supernaturally overtaken by impotence at the end, and it rather looks as if Richmond was meant to show his prowess by overcoming the tyrant in physical combat. But it seems just possible that a different solution was once intended.

We are still free to reject both these explanations, and in any other play there would be nothing very unusual in finding anticipations created only to be ignored. In the majority of such cases most readers and spectators will hardly notice that there has been a deception. And this may be the one instance in *Richard III* where Shakespeare allowed an important prophecy to lapse in order to have it both ways: we are made to think of Richard as desperate, but we actually see him fighting courageously to his last gasp.

The plot of Richard's rise and fall is extremely simple. Step by step and according to plan he climbs towards his goal, securing the supports he needs and removing the obstacles in his path ruthlessly and systematically. Anne is a mere object to mount on, Clarence, Clarence's children, and Edward's sons are swept from the line of succession, the queen's kinsmen and friends and Edward's loyal Lord Chamberlain are likewise eliminated. Only once is he dependent on fortune rather than on his own will: in the death of Edward. But even this event is made to seem part of his scheming, as it is part of Margaret's witchcraft. Richard is on the Wheel of Fortune and while it rises on his side he turns it, directing all events. It reaches the top and slows down at his coronation and the murder of the princes. The downward movement is signalised by the first mention of Richmond, which puts Richard in mind of the prophecies of Henry VI and the Irish bard, and by the defection of Buckingham. For a while he is able to stave off disaster. He even shows some of his old spirit in the wooing of Elizabeth. He captures Buckingham and has him executed. But as the descending wheel gathers momentum he loses control, and his fall is rapid: there is not a word spoken between him and Richmond as they fight and 'the bloody dog' is slain.

Seen in this way, the plot has a figurative and emblematic dimension. And Richard's great antagonist in this dimension is Margaret, who long plays his game for him in the external conflict but secretly torments him and finally drives him to destruction. She is mainly activated by personal revenge, but in her own way she prolongs the Wars of the Roses, which are temporarily over after the death of Henry VI but of which there are frequent reminders and which still have a symbolical importance, as both the beginning and the ending of the play testify. Two Lancastrian widows are the only remnants of opposition to York, until Richmond steps in. Poor Anne is quickly overcome, but Margaret fights on till she gets her revenge, constantly reminding us of past battles and crimes and claiming to be the rightful queen. Richmond wins the last battle of the Roses, but not till the conclusion of the play is he called 'the true succeeder' of his house, and it is never made clear how he is the succeeder except that he was designated by Henry VI. In any case he is more a concept than a character and comes to deliver England from a tyrant rather than to claim his own right. 'In its context,' says Reese, 'the lifelessness of the character shows how seriously Shakespeare took him.'[16]

It is interesting to notice that the hired murderers of Clarence would have been taken for Lancastrians in a realistic context. Clarence is the object of God's vengeance, they tell him,

> [*Sec. Mur.*] For false forswearing and for murder too:
> Thou didst receive the sacrament to fight

In quarrel of the house of Lancaster.
[*First Mur.*] And like a traitor to the name of God
Didst break that vow, and with thy treacherous blade
Unrip'st the bowels of thy sovereign's son.   (I.iv.205–10)

The murderers, however, are obviously to be understood not just as
Richard's hirelings but as ministers of the heavenly vengeance they invoke.
We must allow for a certain amount of artificiality in their attitudes.
Similarly with the wooing of Anne. The artificial convention established
by Richard's soliloquy in the opening scene makes it unnecessary, even
absurd, to look for psychological probability in her submission.[17] This
scene, too, has a strong element of symbolical conflict and resolution.

To what extent the figurative dimension of *Richard III* is also a religious
dimension has been a matter of disagreement and extreme opinions. In
1944 – and it is perhaps not irrelevant to observe that this was the year of
the Normandy landings – E. M. W. Tillyard asserted that '*Richard III* is a
very religious play'. 'For the purposes of the tetralogy and most obviously
for this play,' he said, 'Shakespeare accepted the prevalent belief that God
had guided England into her haven of Tudor prosperity.' This view was
endorsed by Irving Ribner in the following decade, quoting Tillyard to the
effect that 'the primary purpose of the play . . . is to "display the working
of God's plan to restore England to prosperity" '. And towards the end of
the sixties it was amplified by E. A. J. Honigmann in his Penguin redaction
of *Richard III*.[18] Discussing what he calls 'the play's two-phase movement',
Honigmann remarked:

> We thus see that the gradual unfolding of a providential design against
> the individualist who set himself up against God's order necessitated
> emphasis upon *character* in the first part of the play, . . . and then upon
> *plot* in the second, where the author's design mirrors that of God. We
> see, further, that Richard's fake piety is not simply a delightful comic
> touch but prepares us for the central conflict of the play, in which
> Richard's mighty opposite is not the puppet Richmond but the King of
> kings.

On the other side of the debate M. M. Reese has maintained that '*Richard
III* is an unremittingly earthy play' and that 'True recognition of a higher
power is found only in Richmond, who is a visitant from another world'.
And in a very anti-Tillyardian piece, 'The World of Richard III', A. L.
French has not only rejected 'the notion that the play is the climactic lesson
taught by the Tudor Myth' but has argued in some detail to prove that
'The world of *Richard III* . . . is by and large the reverse of religious'.[19]

Faced with such contrary opinions it is tempting to take refuge in the usual compromise and declare with the immortal Sir Roger that much might be said on both sides. But in fact I find French's arguments most convincing. There can be no doubt that the idea of heavenly vengeance is central to both the main conflict and to the fates of individual characters like Clarence, Hastings, and Buckingham, but it does not touch anyone deeply and is in fact chiefly a means of energising prayers and curses. The chief minister of heavenly vengeance does not appear till near the end, and in the meantime Margaret represents heaven in a completely pagan spirit. The central conflict involves not so much Richard and God, as Honigmann has it, as Richard and Margaret.

This is on the symbolical level. But of course the play is enacted on a realistic level as well. And Richard is not just 'the formal Vice, Iniquity' of the morality tradition, there is a great deal of realistic detail in his portraiture. In the first place we are given a sound psychological explanation of his villainy, and though Elizabethans may not have known about inferiority complexes they would certainly understand the mechanisms of compensation:

> And therefore, since I cannot prove a lover
> To entertain these fair well-spoken days,
> I am determined to prove a villain
> And hate the idle pleasures of these days.   (I.i.28–31)

In the second place there are hints that Richard does not, after all, tell us everything that goes on in his mind. He does not, for instance, reveal the 'secret close intent' which he must 'reach unto' by marrying Lady Anne (I.i.158–9) or the 'divers unknown reasons' why Anne should grant the 'boon' he asks of her (I.ii.217). Perhaps we are expected to realise that marrying Henry VI's daughter-in-law would put him in a stronger position to reach for the crown, perhaps we are meant to be mystified, or perhaps Shakespeare simply forgot to clear up the mystery.[20] Whatever the explanation, this bit of secretiveness on Richard's part adds a touch of humanity. He does not immediately tell us, either, later on, why his 'kingdom stands on brittle glass' unless he is married to his brother's daughter (IV.ii.59–60), and once more we sense an opaqueness which makes him all the more lifelike. But in this case an explanation is given shortly afterwards: he has learnt that 'the Britain Richmond aims / At young Elizabeth' and has to forestall him. One thing he really suppresses for a long time: his nightly torments. Only his wife Anne is able to bring them to our knowledge:

> For never yet one hour in his bed
> Did I enjoy the golden dew of sleep,
> But with his timorous dreams was still awaked.
>
> (IV.i.82–4; see also V.iii.161)

It is as if a mask of levity is whipped away and we suddenly see an agonised face behind it. There is another brief glimpse of that face as Richard commissions Tyrrel to dispose of his 'Two deep enemies, / Foes to my rest and my sweet sleep's disturbers' (IV.ii.71–2). And when we see Richard after the visitation of the spirits struggling to shake off the impression of his nightmare which has now fully invaded his consciousness we realise that he is not as entirely devoid of moral feeling as he is about to pretend at the commencement of the battle:

> Let not our babbling dreams affright our souls;
> Conscience is but a word that cowards use.   (V.iii.309–10)

Richard has reached a point where he is not even sure of his villain's role. He confounds himself according to the conditional oath he swore to Queen Elizabeth: 'I am a villain. Yet I lie, I am not.' This is psychological realism at Shakespeare's best. And it is supported by general behavioral attributes. Richard is always in a hurry, for instance. 'Clarence hath not another day to live', 'go we to determine / Who . . . straight shall post to Ludlow', 'Then fiery expedition be my wing', 'And brief, good mother, for I am in haste', 'Come, bustle, bustle! Caparison my horse!' The examples could be multiplied, and Shakespeare must have consciously endowed Richard with this urge for haste. He may even have associated it with the saying quoted after Gloucester by the young Duke of York: 'Small herbs have grace; great weeds do grow apace' (II.iv.13).[21]

On the realistic plot level Richard's chief antagonist is neither God nor Margaret but Queen Elizabeth and her 'allies', at least until Richmond takes over. Richard and Clarence in the first scene of the play speak of Elizabeth as the person who really rules the land: 'We are the Queen's abjects, and must obey.' Actually her role is fairly passive, as all but Richard's are. Since the initiative for action always comes from him until he is deserted by Buckingham, there is little conflict in the usual sense. We often see Elizabeth plaintive and in tears, and well she may complain, but she does stand up to Richard both at first and at the end, and is the last person to succumb to his force or persuasion. That she does genuinely succumb I see no reason to doubt, especially since both she and her daughter give their consent to Richard in *The True Tragedie*.[22] But the capitulation is undeniably sudden after her long resistance. And the whole wooing scene is inordinately long, coming as it does just before the concluding phase of the action and having no influence on the plot as such. It includes the longest speech in the entire play, spoken by Richard and ending with a resounding climax which when it was first written may well have been meant to reduce Queen Elizabeth to submission:

> Bound with triumphant garlands will I come
> And lead thy daughter to a conqueror's bed;
> To whom I will retail my conquest won,
> And she shall be sole victoress, Cæsar's Cæsar.
>
> (IV.iv.333–6)

The queen's ironical answer and the ensuing return to stichomythia are hardly what we expect after Richard's great display of eloquence. His long speech is omitted without trace in the quartos, probably as the result of abridgment, though it is tempting to think that the wooing scene as we have it in the Folio contains a conflation of alternative passages. I will not venture to suggest which parts of the scene were the author's first thoughts and which second, or which were meant for excision and which for retention, or whether indeed Shakespeare ever decided what to keep and reject, but the signs of complex composition are sufficiently clear. In a play as long as *Richard III* (it is almost as long as *Hamlet*, and the quarto version is not much shorter than the Folio) there may have been considerable indecision on the author's part as to what and how much to include. Some matter may have been discarded and some added in his efforts to arrive at a satisfactory structure and a suitable length; and the surviving texts may reflect a complicated process of drafting and revision, both substantive texts incorporating more than was eventually intended for stage performance.[23] But, not to digress too much, we may in any case be reasonably certain that Queen Elizabeth disappoints our expectations in the end and proves momentarily to be what Richard calls her, a 'relenting fool, and shallow, changing woman'.

Richard's dealings with the Grey faction are internecine in that the Yorkists now fight among themselves. The chaos of civil war during the last phase of Henry VI's reign has degenerated further into a brutal struggle between brothers and relations in which all idealism has disappeared. The 'glorious summer' of York has been short, and York's widow grieves for her sons:

> And being seated, and domestic broils
> Clean overblown, themselves the conquerors

> Make war upon themselves, brother to brother,
> Blood to blood, self against self. O preposterous
> And frantic outrage, end thy damned spleen.   (II.iv.60–4)

There is now no question of title to the crown, in fact Richard deliberately defies legitimacy and denies the rightful succession. Having ostensibly got Edward to do away with Clarence and then been favoured by the death of Edward, he fabricates stories of bastardy concerning both Edward and his children to prove himself next in line.

The plot is equally simple whether seen from a realistic or an emblematic point of view. But one tends to look more at the details, and there are more questions to be asked, in a realistic analysis. Why, for instance, do we never see Jane Shore? Or the Duchess of Clarence? Or Princess Elizabeth? Obviously there were limits to the number of women who could be put on the stage and there is a large number in *Richard III* as it is – four important characters, in addition to four children. But was Margaret strictly necessary?[24] Or the Duchess of York? Or (one could go on) even Lady Anne? Shakespeare must at least have faced a difficult choice in selecting his women.

In the case of Mistress Shore it does look as if he may have contemplated using her. At the very outset of the play she is spoken of as a person of great influence. Clarence remarks:

> By heaven, I think there is no man secure
> But the Queen's kindred, and night-walking heralds
> That trudge betwixt the King and Mistress Shore.
> Heard you not what an humble suppliant
> Lord Hastings was to her for his delivery?   (I.i.71–5)[25]

And Richard replies:

> Humbly complaining to her deity
> Got my Lord Chamberlain his liberty.
> I'll tell you what, I think it is our way,
> If we will keep in favour with the King,
> To be her men and wear her livery.
> The jealous o'erworn widow and herself,
> Since that our brother dubbed them gentlewomen,
> Are mighty gossips in this monarchy.

There is further bantering about Mistress Shore between Richard and Brakenbury. After the death of the king she is referred to as Hastings's mistress (III.i.185). And in the crucial council scene at the Tower (III.iv), Richard accuses the queen, 'consorted with that harlot, strumpet Shore,' of having withered up his arm by witchcraft. Clearly one who was both so influential and so crafty might have defended a place beside Richard's other enemies. In *The True Tragedie of Richard the third*, which, *pace* Honigmann,[26] was probably written before Shakespeare's play, Jane Shore has a not insignificant part and is even mentioned by way of advertisement on the title page, in a moralistic appendage ('With a lamentable ende of Shores wife, an example for all wicked women'), which does not do justice to the sympathetic treatment of Jane in the actual tragedy. Geoffrey Bullough has suggested that Shakespeare wished to avoid dramatising incidents which had already been on the boards in the earlier play, but he offers no objective support for this view.[27] It seems more likely that Shakespeare jettisoned Jane when he thought of introducing Margaret. The latter would be a much more imposing and colourful figure for a tragedy than Edward's bourgeois concubine. Similarly the inclusion of the Duchess of York, the mother of Edward, Clarence, and Richard, must have been a more tempting choice than the Duchess of Clarence, although the latter is mentioned in her husband's prayer for her safety and we might have expected to see her with the children when they appear shortly afterwards. Princess Elizabeth we may have a momentary expectation of meeting when Richard tells us in IV.iii. 'To her go I, a jolly thriving wooer.' She, too, is in *The True Tragedie*. But the dramatically effective wooing of Anne at the beginning of *Richard III* would probably have made a dialogue with the young Elizabeth too repetitious, and it was appropriate that Richard should have a final combat of wills and words with her mother the queen, who is so prominent in the early part of the play.

An expectation which is perhaps even more likely to be aroused than that of seeing Jane Shore is the actual sight of the murder of the princes. Here again *The True Tragedie* might have provided a model if any were needed. It is explicit on the title page about 'the smothering of the two yoong Princes in the Tower'. Tyrrel's account of the murder in Shakespeare's play is second-rate narrative at best and stands no comparison with the earthy dialogue of Clarence's murderers. One may surmise that one murder performed in view of the audience was felt to be enough, but the argument would not hold for a great many other plays, and anyway why show Clarence being killed rather than the princes? One may further surmise that the play was beginning to be rather long by the time Shakespeare got to Act IV, Scene ii, but then why the extremely long wooing scene soon afterwards? In this case Bullough may be right, that the staging of the murder in an earlier play was still too fresh in people's memory.

But perhaps the best answer is that Shakespeare sometimes ignored the most obvious dramatic attraction in order to exploit the less expected solution.

Honigmann has wondered about the absence of the trusted friend who betrays Buckingham to his captors:

> Whether or not Shakespeare slipped in supplying no more than hints about the treachery that led to Buckingham's capture is less easy to decide. Abjuring all enmity to the Queen, Buckingham hopes that if he forgets his oath he will be punished in his greatest need by a friend's treachery (II.i.32ff), and later recalls that his wish has come true (v.i.13). Buckingham's son states the facts in *Henry VIII* (II.i.107–11): his father, 'Flying for succour to his servant Banister' was 'by that wretch betrayed'. While writing Act II of *Richard III* Shakespeare perhaps planned a later scene depicting the treachery of Banister whom, according to Holinshed, Buckingham 'above all men loved, favoured, and trusted' – a grand climax after the play's other acts of treachery. If so, he changed his mind.[28]

I would add two things to support this conjecture. First, that in *Henry VIII* Buckingham puts some emphasis on his having been betrayed by a friend. And, secondly, that Banister has a small part to play in *The True Tragedie*. But Shakespeare may not have changed his mind at all. It is quite conceivable that he actually wrote a scene like the one Honigmann hypothesises and that it was later removed either by the author or by some other abridger. It is less probable, perhaps, that he wrote a scene, which may likewise be hypothesised, featuring Doctor Shaw and Friar Penker, who are summoned to Richard's presence at the end of III.v but never turn up. Shakespeare was content, one may assume, to merge them with the two clergymen (bishops in Hall and in the stage direction in III.vii) who at Buckingham's suggestion appear on either side of the would-be king during his meeting with the mayor and citizens.

Two other very minor cases of persons remaining absent or appearing contrary to expectations may be briefly mentioned. The fairly conspicuous part of Dorset, and his flight to Richmond, seem to point forward to his reappearance with Richmond's army from Brittany.[29] Instead we are told by a messenger when the rising is under way that he is in arms in Yorkshire. This would be a case of historical truth being in conflict with dramatic propriety, and it would be presumptuous to censure Shakespeare's decision in favour of the former. But that he did at need prefer fiction to fact is demonstrated clearly enough by the presence of Margaret.

The second case concerns Stanley, who surprisingly turns up in Richmond's tent on the eve of battle after Richmond has despatched Captain Blunt with a written message for him. Stanley's visit is extremely short and apparently serves mainly to repeat the excuse for his passivity which he already conveyed to Richmond by Sir Christopher Urswick on the former's landing in Wales (IV.v). He does, however, promise to help the Earl as best he may, and Shakespeare may have felt the incident to be necessary in order to motivate the reappearance of Stanley in the final scene. In both Hall and *The True Tragedie* there is a similar interview between Richmond and Stanley, though the meeting occurs somewhere between the armies.

Richard III is the most conclusive of Shakespeare's English history plays. It leaves no loose ends and prepares for no continued action. It naturally has backward perspectives to the plays which precede it, and it is no doubt a help to the understanding of the relations between the main characters to be familiar with the two *Contention* plays. The butchering of Rutland and the Duke of York at Wakefield, of Prince Edward at Tewkesbury by York's three sons, and of King Henry in the Tower, are especially recalled, as well as King Edward's marriage to Lady Elizabeth Grey and Clarence's betrayal of his father-in-law Warwick before the battle of Barnet where Warwick is killed. But *Richard III* is self-contained in that it briefly re-capitulates past events at all important points and has an entirely independent plot. It even approximately repeats passages from *3 Henry VI* so as to assimilate them, especially Richard's long soliloquy in III.ii of the earlier play, which is echoed in the opening soliloquy of *Richard III*. I emphatically disagree with Tillyard, who declares:

> In its function of summing up and completing what has gone before, *Richard III* inevitably suffers as a detached unit. Indeed it is a confused affair without the memory of Clarence's perjury to Warwick before Coventry, of Queen Margaret's crowning York with a paper crown before stabbing him at Wakefield, and of the triple murder of Prince Edward at Tewkesbury. The play can never come into its own till acted as a sequel to the other three plays.[30]

The best answer to this is provided by Honigmann:

> Shakespeare, so far as we can tell, did nothing to make his tetralogies available as such, either in print or in the theatre. Like the other dramatists of his time he had to plan even two-part plays largely, if not entirely, as two self-contained units: for *Richard III* . . . he devised a

firm internal structure, totally different from the loosely episodic
sequences of *Henry VI*. Themes and characters may survive from earlier
histories, but do so only when relevant to more immediate purposes.
Richard III, the first English play that has consistently held the stage,
stands triumphantly on its own.[31]

Among the characters who survive from earlier histories, one seems to
be specially introduced into *3 Henry VI* to prepare for his part in *Richard III*:
young Henry Richmond, whom King Henry sees as 'England's hope' and
'Likely in time to bless a regal throne' (IV.vi.67–76). He is Richard's
opposite and counterpart, but we catch only a glimpse of him in the earlier
play, and the lacking development of his character is in keeping with his
mainly symbolical role. Hastings is already King Edward's particular
friend and supporter in *3 Henry VI*. There is also a Sir William Stanley,
who helps to rescue King Edward from captivity and whom Edward
promises to requite for his 'forwardness' (IV.v.23). This must be the Lord
Stanley of *Richard III* who comes blundering in just as the news of
Clarence's death has been broken to Edward and demands 'A boon, my
sovereign, for my service done!' (II.i.97). Shakespeare obviously conflated
the two brothers William and Thomas and especially the parts they played
during the battle of Bosworth. In the third scene of the play, where this
composite person makes his first appearance, Lord Stanley's later title of
Earl of Derby is anticipated, but his part in that scene shows several signs of
being an afterthought, and he may simply have served as an excuse for
bringing in the name of Richmond at an early stage.[32] On the other hand,
some fairly central characters of *Richard III* are *not* in *3 Henry VI*, above all
Buckingham and the Duchess of York. Anne, Grey, and Dorset do not
appear in the earlier play either, though the marriage between Anne and
Prince Edward is arranged there. There is thus a certain amount of discontinuity between the two plays. There are many minor discrepancies, too,[33]
but no major ones, and *Richard III* commences smoothly from the situation
arrived at at the end of *3 Henry VI*. The really significant break in
continuity occurs about the middle of the earlier play, to be precise in
Richard's soliloquy in III.ii, when the loyal brother becomes a murderous
egomaniac.[34] His part in the remainder of *Henry VI* truly belongs to *Richard
III* and needs the latter play to be completed. But *Richard III* does not need
it. Nor, as pure drama and a very different kind of drama from its
predecessors, does it strictly need *any* support from the *Henry VI* plays.
    Within a wider epic framework where the fates of peoples and heroes are
recorded it is a different matter. There *Richard III* takes its place, not
necessarily as the last play of a tetralogy, but as the description of the last

phase in a power struggle beginning with England against France, continuing in civil war, and compacting itself into butchery of kith and kin before it finally narrows into a conflict within the evil mind:

> Then fly. What, from myself? Great reason why –
> Lest I revenge. Myself upon myself? (v.iii.186–7)

A central theme in this longdrawn struggle as dramatised by Shakespeare is the rise and fall of the house of York. And the increasing savagery of the conflict is in part a reflection of the way in which the Yorkist claim to the throne of England gradually changes from being based on legitimacy to expressing a naked power-lust.

Within this wider extra-theatrical framework we may wish to see Margaret, the bearer of memories, of ancient desires and hates, the keeper of accounts, the Norn, as the central character – paradoxically perhaps, since she is a Frenchwoman and the plays are about England. Those who had the good fortune to see Dame Peggy Ashcroft sustaining the part of Margaret from youth to age in the 1963 and 1964 Stratford-upon-Avon productions of 'The Wars of the Roses' are not likely to forget the dominance of that personality. Margaret paves the way for the Yorkist rebellion by depriving a weak king of his strongest support, then carries the burden of the struggle against the rival faction until its last forlorn and monstrous hope is on the brink of destruction. Only then does she fade into the shadows and give place to the symbolic deliverer. And it is in the wider framework of all the plays in which Margaret appears that Richmond's concluding speech in the last of those plays has its full force:

> England hath long been mad and scarred herself,
> The brother blindly shed the brother's blood,
> The father rashly slaughtered his own son,
> The son, compelled, been butcher to the sire:
> All this divided York and Lancaster,
> Divided in their dire division;
> O, now let Richmond and Elizabeth,
> The true succeeders of each royal house,
> By God's fair ordinance conjoin together!
> And let their heirs, God, if thy will be so,
> Enrich the time to come with smooth-faced peace,
> With smiling plenty, and fair prosperous days!

5   The Troublesome Theme of *King John*

Between the publication in 1591 of its probable main source, *The Troublesome Raigne Of John King of England*, and the mention by Francis Meres in 1598 of Shakespeare's tragedy of *King Iohn*, there is no external evidence to help us fix the date of composition of this play. For that matter it may have been the end-product of several stages of rewriting. In the absence of convincing proof for a very early dating (like that proposed by E. A. J. Honigmann in the new Arden edition) or a very late dating, I am inclined to agree with more cautious editors like Blakemore Evans, Herschel Baker, and Robert Smallwood and opt for a date between 1593 and 1595, preferably 'just before *Richard II*', as Smallwood thinks.[1] This would put *King John* between the first and the second tetralogies. The dating is of no great significance for my present purpose; but it does tell us something about Shakespeare's long-term planning, or lack of planning, of the history cycles if, after reaching the reign of Henry VII, he went right back to King John before attacking Richard II. There is something about the uncertain exposition of *King John*, too, which makes it resemble the problematic beginnings of the Lancastrian plays which it probably just preceded.

The opening speeches of *King John* go straight to the central issue of the drama: King John's possession of the crown of England and the threats to his hold of it by claimants who urge a better title. He is threatened first by his elder brother Geoffrey's son, Arthur, who is championed by the King of France and the Duke of Austria; and his efforts to obviate this threat fill up the greater part of the action, to the end of Act IV. Then he is challenged by the French Dauphin, who is married to his elder sister Eleanor's daughter, Blanche of Spain,[2] and the final act mainly concerns the invasion from France and the repulse of Lewis. This latter is effected more by policy than by arms, for the Pope has anticipated the Dauphin in disputing John's rule, and it is the papal legate, Cardinal Pandulph, who ultimately forces both sides to a composition. John's resistance and submission to the Pope intermittently provide important plot elements from the first scene of Act III on. John does not, however, live to see his last enemies defeated. Like that more indomitable soldier Tamburlaine he is struck down by sickness and deprived of life and crown by common mortality. But his son Henry inherits the kingdom and will hold his dominion unchallenged after Lewis resigns his claim to it. We are made to feel at the end that not only has John's possession of the crown and that of his heirs been successfully defended, but his right to it has been established. Strangely enough, for this impression is not brought about by his own character and achievements – in fact he himself has to die to make way for one unspotted by guilt – but by the perfidy of his external and internal adversaries represented by Lewis, Melun, and the monks at Swinstead, by the contrasting devotion and integrity of such of his followers as Hubert and the Bastard, and by the necessity we are made to feel of keeping the monarchy unassailed by doubts as to legitimacy. (This last point is one that recurs analogously in *1 Henry IV*.) In the broad outline of its plot the play poses a problem for which, after complication and conflict, it finds a dramatically, and to Elizabethans probably politically, satisfying solution.

This does not mean that it fulfils all expectations created in the opening scenes, or even that those scenes make it quite clear what to expect. Why, especially, is there so much talk of bastardy? Arthur's title to the succession seems at first to be in no doubt. As King Philip of France states the case to King John:

> That Geoffrey was thy elder brother born,
> And this his son; England was Geoffrey's right,
> And this is Geoffrey's;   (ii.i.104–6)

John does not actually contradict this statement. In the beginning of the play even Queen Eleanor admits to her son in confidence that she knows he is a usurper: just after the French ambassador has brought them King Philip's ultimatum on behalf of Arthur, John exclaims, 'Our strong possession and our right for us', and his mother replies:

> Your strong possession much more than your right,
> Or else it must go wrong with you and me:
> So much my conscience whispers in your ear,
> Which none but heaven, and you, and I, shall hear.
>
> (i.i.39–43)

And in Act iv, the Bastard, watching Hubert pick up and carry away the broken body of the young prince, significantly reflects:[3]

> How easy dost thou take all England up
> From forth this morsel of dead royalty!
> The life, the right and truth of all this realm
> Is fled to heaven;   (IV.iii.142–5)

Shakespeare only glancingly alludes to King Richard's will by which his surviving younger brother was to succeed him, so that John is not allowed even this support for his claim. Yet what does Eleanor mean by calling the supposedly legitimate claimant a bastard, when she starts shouting at Constance during the parley before Angiers?

> Out, insolent! thy bastard shall be king,
> That thou mayst be a queen, and check the world!
> (II.i.122–3)

Is this only filth stirred up in anger or is the accusation more substantial? It is followed by a rebuttal on Constance's part which may be a quibble – 'My bed was ever to thy son as true / As thine was to thy husband' – and by her counter-accusation relating to Geoffrey's parentage, which surely must be just as damaging to her son by that same Geoffrey as it is to Eleanor:

> My boy a bastard! By my soul, I think
> His father never was so true begot:
> It cannot be and if thou wert his mother.   (II.i.129–31)

Shortly afterwards there is another exchange of insults between the two women as Arthur begs for peace and Eleanor declares that 'His mother shames him so, poor boy, he weeps', provoking Constance to retort, again somewhat equivocally, 'Now shame upon you, whe'r she does or no!' As the scolding continues, Constance apparently gets the better of the argument and speaks repeatedly of Eleanor's sin and once of her 'sin-conceiving womb'. From the nature of the quarrel this cannot be sufficiently explained by a reference to original sin or to the Psalmist's 'in sin hath my mother conceived me', as editors have tried to do.[4] The charge is more specific and can only be taken to mean that either Geoffrey or his brother John was conceived in adultery. In the light of this assertion perhaps we may turn back and read an admission of conjugal infidelity in Eleanor's words to John, quoted above, about the weakness of his right. If they mean that Eleanor carries a guilty secret the reference here must be to John. On the other hand, what difference would it make if John was illegitimate by birth since he is not the rightful heir anyway, being the youngest son? The suggestion is puzzling, to say the least. And so is the suggestion made by Constance that Geoffrey was a bastard, for where would that put Geoffrey's son?

The question is strangely complicated by a seeming attempt to present Arthur as the son of Richard Cœur-de-lion. In his first speech in the play, King Philip,[5] addressing Arthur, speaks of Richard as 'that great forerunner of thy blood' (ii.i.2) and of Arthur as Richard's 'posterity' (l.6). And later in the same scene Constance tells Eleanor that Arthur is her (Eleanor's) 'eldest son's son' (l.177). Various explanations have been attempted, none very satisfactory.[6] There remains a contradiction between the explicit and historically correct presentation of Arthur as Geoffrey's son, which occurs at several points in the play, and the suggestion in the instances just quoted that he may be Richard's son. Was Shakespeare contemplating the possibility of making Arthur the Bastard's half-brother and Constance, like Lady Faulconbridge, a one-time captive to the charms of Cœur-de-lion?

It is worth noting that Shakespeare himself introduced the subject of adulterous relations as a new element in the quarrel between Eleanor and Constance. There is no hint of it in *The Troublesome Raigne*,[7] which on the contrary has firm statements about Arthur's legitimacy which Shakespeare does not repeat. Thus Constance in the earlier play declares that Arthur is 'heire to [John's] elder Brother, / Without ambiguous shadow of discent', and Arthur himself that his 'right discent can no way be impeacht'; and no one denies these assertions. Nor does Holinshed ever hint at bastardy in connection with Arthur. The main argument he gives to Eleanor for preferring John to Arthur is 'the difference of governement betweene a king that is a man, and a king that is but a child',[8] but this argument is used neither by the author of *The Troublesome Raigne* nor by Shakespeare, though they both repeat the real motive that Holinshed attributes to Eleanor, namely jealousy of Constance and fear of her power should she be allowed to rule through her son.

But Shakespeare did follow *The Troublesome Raigne* both in his sequence of scenes and the main contents of the scenes. And it was from this source play that he had the story of the bastard son of King Richard and Lady Faulconbridge, which is presented at some length in the beginning of both histories. In *The Troublesome Raigne* it functions as an anecdotal prelude, interesting and amusing in itself but without much relevance to the further development of the plot. It is enough to know that John has recruited a champion who is the son of the prestigious King Richard and therefore useful politically as well as for his physical prowess. It seems natural to suppose that Shakespeare wanted to give an added significance to the

Faulconbridge anecdote by making it an introduction to central problems affecting the rival claimants to the throne, in particular the question of John's title to it. In both the royal family and the Faulconbridge family there were two brothers whose rights were in dispute. Shakespeare may have seen a parallel between Philip the Bastard giving up his lands and John ceding his French dominions, but in other respects John would correspond to Robert Faulconbridge and Arthur (or his father Geoffrey) to Philip. Shakespeare emphasises the handsomeness of both Arthur and the Bastard and compares them both to their fathers in physical appearance. Thus Eleanor says of Philip:

> He hath a trick of Cœur-de-lion's face;
> The accent of his tongue affecteth him.
> Do you not read some tokens of my son
> In the large composition of this man?   (I.i.85–8)

And the King of France of Arthur:

> Look here upon thy brother Geoffrey's face;
> These eyes, these brows, were moulded out of his:
> This little abstract doth contain that large
> Which died in Geoffrey: and the hand of time
> Shall draw this brief into as huge a volume.   (II.i.99–103)

There is a revealing addition in *King John* to the *Troublesome Raigne* material: Shakespeare's King John judges Philip legitimate because, although born *out of* wedlock, he was nevertheless born '*after* wedlock':

> Sirrah, your brother is legitimate;
> Your father's wife did after wedlock bear him,
> And if she did play false, the fault was hers;
> Which fault lies on the hazards of all husbands
> That marry wives.   (I.i.116–20)

This liberal view, which probably derives more from the practical difficulty of determining fatherhood than from common or statute law,[9] could obviously have been introduced to make Philip's choosing bastardy rather than property all the more admirable. But it is equally possible that Shakespeare intended to give John's judgment a wider application as a point of reference for maintaining the legitimacy of Geoffrey or Arthur (in analogy with that of Philip) supposing either of the two former was not in fact the son of his reputed father. And not that only. The historical King Richard made a will in favour of John, dispossessing Geoffrey and Geoffrey's heirs. Shakespeare invented a similar will by which Philip was dispossessed in favour of Robert (i.i.109–11). He then let the king prove that will invalid:

> My mother's son did get your father's heir;
> Your father's heir must have your father's land.
> *Rob.* Shall then my father's will be of no force
>   To dispossess that child which is not his?
> *Bast.* Of no more force to dispossess me, sir,
>   Than was his will to get me, as I think.   (i.i.128–33)

The analogy between Philip's claim to the Faulconbridge estate and Arthur's to the realm of England would have become plain if the matter had been pursued. And the insinuations and accusations in Act II are clear enough signs that Shakespeare tried to work out a use of the theme of bastardy in the main plot. He may even have tried different solutions, one of them making Arthur, like Philip, the natural son of King Richard. But whatever may have been in his mind he did not pursue the subject of adultery and bastardy beyond the first scene of Act II,[10] or clarify his intentions in introducing it in relation to the royal rivals. He must eventually, I would think, have failed to satisfy himself as to the wisdom of pouring new wine into the old bottles of history, and he consequently left his scolding mothers to shoulder the responsibility of their mutual insults without either discrediting or verifying their accusations in the continued action. We are left with a fairly definite impression that Eleanor has been unfaithful in her marriage to King Henry, a rather less definite impression that this may have been when Geoffrey was conceived, and a vague suspicion that Constance, too, may have been unchaste.

For a while, in Acts II and III, the idea of unfaithfulness runs on as a kind of *leitmotiv*, used sometimes fairly conventionally about Fortune, sometimes about the French, or about both combined as in the following passage from Constance's speech to her son in II.ii.54–61:

> But fortune, O,
> She is corrupted, chang'd and won from thee;
> Sh'adulterates hourly with thine uncle John,
> And with her golden hand hath pluck'd on France
> To tread down fair respect of sovereignty,
> And made his majesty the bawd to theirs.
> France is a bawd to fortune and King John,
> That strumpet fortune, that usurping John!

In the second half of III.i there is a great deal of play on the word 'faith', both in a religious and a moral sense,[11] and the new agreement between France and England is seen as a marriage from which Cardinal Pandulph is trying to seduce one of the partners. But it is odd that Shakespeare hardly uses any imagery of marital unfaithfulness in the remainder of the play, even in relation to the English lords who defect to Lewis. And it is hard to see how he could have resisted the impulse to do so if he had chosen to develop the theme of bastardy. Certainly the concluding statement of the play would have found its natural place in a sequence of images of this kind:

> Nought shall make us rue
> If England to itself do rest but true!

As it is, the neuter pronoun 'itself', rather than 'herself', in the last line suggests that sexual implications, however figurative, were not in the forefront of his imagination as he completed his drama.

Altogether, the central problem of right or possession as it relates to the crown of England is only confused by the introduction and subsequent abandonment of the bastardy theme. The problem continues to dominate the plot, but the plot itself loses much of its interest towards the end.

Not only is the bastardy theme left undeveloped, but the conception of the Bastard seems to have undergone a change during the composition of the play, and one wonders if Shakespeare at first thought of giving him a larger role than he was eventually called upon to perform. Part clown, part chorus, he has all the most memorable lines to speak, and only Constance approaches his level of poetic utterance. The Bastard is no doubt both an entertaining madcap and a shrewd observer, but it is easy to exaggerate his importance in the actual business of the play.[12] The emphasis in *King John* is characteristically on argument, persuasion, and comment, while actions and events are often briefly reported, especially from III.ii, i.e. just before the middle of the printed text, on. This affects the Bastard's part not least. Most of the opening scene, 233 of its 276 lines, is devoted to him, and his soliloquy ends the scene. In the next scene, too, he is prominent, and he concludes it with his famous speech on commodity, but he is more a commentator on the action than a participant in it, though he does suggest the idea of the rival armies joining forces against Angiers. When he appears again in Act III he has little to say and that little mainly by way of comic interjections. He displays the Duke of Austria's head and makes known that he has rescued Eleanor, but we do not see him in action, and he goes off to England to 'shake the bags of hoarding abbots' and to disappear from view for the space of an act. From the middle of IV.ii on he is once more a central character and speaks the significant final lines of Acts IV and V. In the last act King John gives him 'the ordering of the present time' and we hear him threatening the French invaders, but there is only a report of his military success (v.iv.4–5) and he has no real share in the decisive events which conclude the play: the death of John, the advent of Henry, and Cardinal Pandulph's negotiation of peace, which all take him by surprise. One is actually unprepared to see him take the centre of the stage at the very end, or would be if one did not know that this is what he did in *The Troublesome Raigne* and did not realise that his chief role is a symbolical one, that of the spirit of England, the bearer of her martial traditions, the representative of all that is said by Chatillon in II.i (ll.67–75) about her proud adventurers. He may not be 'true begot' and the English as a whole may be a nation of bastards, it seems to be implied by Chatillon,[13] but he and they are certainly 'well begot'.

On the symbolic level the Bastard is a consistent enough figure. On the realistic level this is not equally true. He seems at first envisaged as an Edmund, out for his own advantage – and 'gods, stand up for bastards!' He does let his younger brother take his lands, but he has higher things in view for his own advancement. Having first obtained a knighthood and public recognition as the son of King Richard, he determines that a 'mounting spirit' like himself must observe the manners of the time and deal in compliments and flattery as others do in order to rise in the world:

> And not alone in habit and device,
> Exterior form, outward accoutrement,
> But from the inward motion to deliver
> Sweet, sweet, sweet poison for the age's tooth:
> Which, though I will not practise to deceive,
> Yet, to avoid deceit, I mean to learn;
> For it shall strew the footsteps of my rising.   (I.i.210–16)

Before Angiers he gives counsels of 'policy' to the belligerents (II.i.396) and, having observed their readiness to sacrifice ideals and principles to 'tickling commodity', resolves to take a lesson in self-interest from them:

> Since kings break faith upon commodity,
> Gain, be my lord, for I will worship thee!   (II.i.597–8)

This is obviously the right kind of person to send to England to ransack the church. Shakespeare could even have turned him into a schemer with the brazen ambition to become king and thus add one more to the number of

John's challengers. Indeed, since he is the son of Richard and determined to rise, audience expectation may to a certain extent be turned in that direction.[14] But we do not actually see him harassing the friars, as he does for comic and anti-Catholic purposes in *The Troublesome Raigne*. And he not only remains loyal to John when others rebel, but unquestioningly accepts John's son and heir as his sovereign, 'To whom', as he says,

> with all submission, on my knee
> I do bequeath my faithful services
> And true subjection everlastingly.   (v.vii.103–5)

There is a contradiction involved in these last words, as it happens, since only a few moments earlier the Bastard has promised to follow King John to heaven:

> I do but stay behind
> To do the office for thee of revenge,
> And then my soul shall wait on thee to heaven,
> As it on earth hath been thy servant still.   (v.vii.70–3)

But in any case his words both in the former and the latter of these quotations are those of a Kent, not an Edmund. Surely the Bastard has changed since the time when his inmost wishes were for his own advancement and gain.

The best analysis of the Bastard's character and function that I have seen is that of Julia C. Van de Water, writing in the Spring 1960 issue of *Shakespeare Quarterly*.[15] Van de Water takes issue with John Masefield, Middleton Murry, Dover Wilson, E. M. W. Tillyard and others who have elevated the Bastard into an ideal of royalty. He is not truly regal, she thinks, in any part of the play. But he does appear as two very different persons: 'in the first three acts he is little more than a thinly disguised vice, and in the last two the embodiment of active and outraged nationalism: the English patriot.' Van de Water goes as far as to assert that 'Not one element of the character of the first three acts survives in the Bastard of the concluding ones . . .. Obviously, we have two distinct characters under the name of the Bastard. There is, in reality, only cleavage at the end of the third Act where critics have persistently tried to find development.' This is putting it rather strongly, but my only actual disagreement with Van de Water concerns her view of the Bastard's efficiency in the latter part of the play. After his transformation, she says, 'He is a veritable whirlwind of activity and eloquence . . . .. So it is no surprise to learn that in the ensuing battle it is "Faulconbridge . . . alone [who] upholds the day".'[16] It seems to me that although his impishness may be left behind he rants and raves at the end of the play as he has done before, and we never really see him doing anything to the purpose. It is certainly none of his achievement that the French near-victory is frustrated. Gunnar Boklund is here nearer the truth: 'It is not Faulconbridge and his moral principles which ultimately save England. For all his patriotism he is not presented as a good general . . .. What saves England . . . is instead the intervention of Cardinal Pandulph.'[17]

The change in the character of the Bastard becomes suddenly apparent in the scene where Prince Arthur is found dead; and his new compassionate and responsible manhood is vividly expressed in his reflections on human frailty 'among the thorns and dangers of this world' and his sense that 'a thousand businesses are brief in hand'. But it will not do to put his conversion down to the chastening experience of finding a child who has died a violent death. Robert Smallwood thinks that 'the cynicism and detachment behind which he has sheltered are hammered out of him by the sight of Arthur's corpse' and that 'his personal moral goodness is now revealed'. 'There was a new sense of sternness about the Bastard as he confronted John's panic in the previous scene, but it is the sight of Arthur's corpse which hardens his resolution and reveals his quality.'[18] Smallwood suggests, then, that we are not absolutely unprepared for the change. But the 'new sense of sternness about the Bastard as he confronts John's panic' depends entirely on our interpretation of that short interview. Philip has never been afraid to tell the truth, or been awed by the presence of princes, nor is he now. It has to be noticed, too, that he is not ignorant of Arthur's death, or at least the rumours of his death, when he meets John. According to his own statement he has just heard the news from Lord Bigot and Lord Salisbury, and he tells John that the prince 'they say is kill'd to-night / On your suggestion'. (IV.ii.165–6). The king does not deny the report but sends the Bastard to bring the lords before him – he has a way, he says, 'to win their loves again' – and the Bastard willingly goes without enquiring farther. In *The Troublesome Raigne* it is different. Philip brings John bad news and sternly reproves his ravings, whereupon he is sent to mingle with the rebellious nobles to 'know their drifts'. But this happens after the death of Arthur and the discovery of his body, in which the Bastard does not take part. There is nothing in *The Troublesome Raigne* to indicate that Philip has knowledge of John's designs on Arthur's life, and he asserts in good faith when he meets the nobles at St Edmundsbury that

> For *Arthurs* death, King *John* was innocent,
> He desperat was the deathsman to himselfe,[19]

Shakespeare, on the other hand, seemingly makes the Bastard condone the murder of the prince in one scene and in the next scene call it 'a damned and a bloody work'. The change *is* abrupt, and there is an inconsistency of characterisation. One is reminded of Richard of Gloucester in *3 Henry VI*. Richard changes for the worse and Philip for the better, but they both change pretty suddenly.

Shakespeare may have had some difficulty in fitting the Bastard into the action around the finding of Arthur's body. John sends Hubert to bring 'the angry lords with all convenient haste' to his closet after he has first sent the Bastard on the same errand. On the heels of the Bastard he has already dispatched a servant, 'for he perhaps shall need / Some messenger betwixt me and the peers; / And be thou he.' The servant never gets there and the need for him does not arise. But when the Bastard finds the disaffected peers he tries to calm them and is answered by Salisbury: 'Our griefs, and not our manners, reason now.' Philip then replies, as if he is ignorant of Arthur's death:

> But there is little reason in your grief;
> Therefore 'twere reason you had manners now.
>
> (IV.iii.30–1)

For all the Bastard knows, if we remember the foregoing scene, Arthur has actually been killed on the king's command, and these lines would have been more appropriately spoken by Hubert, who thinks him still alive. The usually loquacious Philip remains silent for a long time on the discovery of the body and at the end of the scene forgets his allegiance to John to the extent of soliloquising on the fact that

> England now is left
> To tug and scamble, and to part by th'teeth
> The unow'd interest of proud swelling state.
>
> (IV.iii.145–7)

It is obviously the symbolic rather than the real Bastard who speaks and acts throughout this scene, and only on this view is it possible to explain the inconsistencies in his portraiture and in part to accept them. He has a dual personality, or rather exists on two levels and moves from one to the other towards the end of the play. In this way he can remain a central character although the relatively insignificant Pandulph has a much greater influence on the course of events than the Bastard.

Philip's brother and mother who play prominent parts in the opening scene, do not reappear later, and we hardly expect them to. It is a curious feature of *King John*, however, that many of the leading characters in the first half are women – Queen Eleanor, Lady Faulconbridge, Constance, and Blanche – and that they all vanish after the third act, almost as if the whole sex is annihilated. Of two of them, Eleanor and Constance, it is briefly reported that they are dead (iv.ii.119–23). We are prepared for Constance's death, but in the case of Eleanor we might have expected a greater participation in the plot than the author provided for her. She is represented at first not only as John's chief adviser (he always needs advice) but as one in authority and even as a military leader in her own right. It is she who makes the offer to Philip which determines his career, and it is to her that he first swears his faith:

> *Elea.* I like thee well: wilt thou forsake thy fortune,
> Bequeath thy land to him and follow me?
> I am a soldier and now bound for France.
> *Bast.* Brother, take you my land, I'll take my chance.
>
> . . . . .
>
> Madam, I'll follow you unto the death.   (i.i.148–54)

Chatillon describes her to King Philip as 'the mother-queen, / An Ate, stirring him [John] to blood and strife' (ii.i.62–3). But she is left behind in France after the peace treaty as regent of what is left of the English dominions, and the remaining action proceeds without her. She becomes one of those absent characters in Shakespeare's plays whose absence may be felt. The news of her death may even be a letdown for the audience. On the other hand there is no real need for her after her quarrel with Constance, in fact other people crowd in upon John and she would have got in their way. The only reason why she may be missed, apart from the general lack of women, is that Shakespeare gave her such major importance to begin with.

Some minor problems of consistency may be dealt with quite briefly. In the Folio text of *King John* the spokesman for the city of Angiers appears in the stage direction and speech headings of page 5 (sig.a3) as 'a Citizen' and 'Cit.' respectively. On pages 6–7 (a3v–a4) he appears in the speech headings first as 'Hubert', then as 'Hub.' There is no reason at all to suppose this person to be identical with the Hubert to whom Arthur is given in charge, though it is hard to say what accident of doubling, transcription, or printing led to the duplication of names.[20] If Shakespeare, departing from *The Troublesome Raigne*,[21] wished to make the two Huberts identical he would no doubt have made this clear in the dialogue. The genuine Hubert is Arthur's custodian. To this person Shakespeare makes John, after much roundabout talk marvellously dramatised, impart his unequivocal wish that Arthur should be put to death. In the source play the wish is not so explicit, and John promises Hubert further instructions. There are no further instructions in *King John*, but in both plays Hubert in the execution scene has orders, not to kill Arthur, but to put out his eyes with hot irons. Shakespeare's inconsistency about the commission seems to be due to a mixture of original invention where the source play was vague and dependence on the source play where it was specific, and this example seems as good as any to prove that *King John* followed *The Troublesome Raigne* and not the other way about.

The battle which is fought somewhere in Lincolnshire between the English and French forces on the eve of King John's death lasts until night-fall. The victory is undecided, but the French on the whole have the best of it, in spite of the death of Melun and the return of the English barons to their true allegiance; and this is so both in *King John* and *The Troublesome Raigne*. In Shakespeare's play it is during the following night that the Bastard loses half his army in the Lincoln Washes. There is no problem here. But in Shakespeare's version, and in that alone, King John has news of the wreck of a French supply fleet on the Goodwin Sands before he has actually retired from the battlefield and hours before the same news is brought to the Dauphin – repetitiously as far as the audience is concerned. When the news is reported to King John it is coupled with the information that 'The French fight coldly, and retire themselves' (v.iii.13), but when Lewis receives it he has just seen the English 'measure backward their own ground / In faint retire' (v.v.3–4). There may be an attempt throughout the sequence of battle scenes (v.iii–v) to show the advantage now swaying to one side now to the other. But it is odd that the same Messenger who brings the good news of French losses and a French retreat to King John simultaneously delivers the Bastard's advice that the king should retire from the field. And as a strange parallel to the double report concerning the French fleet, there is the Bastard's news of the English catastrophe in the Washes, imparted first to Hubert and repeated in the next scene in very similar words to the king.

Finally there is the problem of the long dialogue between Constance, King Philip, and Pandulph which appears in ii.iii wedged between the king's question in line 20, 'I prithee, lady, go away with me' and Constance's reply in line 68, 'To England, if you will'. It is no disrespect to Shakespeare's genius to see this passage as an interpolation added to an early draft of the play,[22] probably to dramatise the 'frenzy' which is mentioned later as the cause of Constance's death. The scene makes perfectly good sense without the passage, but Constance's complaints are no doubt an effective piece of theatre and some of her lines are truly moving. King Philip's final speech in the interpolated passage is tastelessly conceited, however, and may well have been meant for excision, since it begins with the king's exhortation to Constance, 'Bind up those tresses', and is followed by a repetition, 'Bind up your hairs'.

King John is a play which suffers from lack of focus. King John himself is obviously intended for the central character, and his tenure of kingship is the central problem.[23] But his importance is threatened by the Bastard, who keeps up a direct relationship with the audience and at the end assumes, or is invested with, an authority equal to that of any prince. The Bastard himself is not focused clearly, for he performs on two different levels and changes his moral features from those of an ambitious and high-spirited adventurer to those of a selfless patriot. And the action tends to break in the middle, when the scenes are transferred from France back to England. In the first half the Bastard is a mainly realistic character, women play conspicuous parts, Arthur is an active enemy, events are enacted, and conflicts are largely external. In the second half the Bastard is largely a symbolic figure, there are no women, Pandulph plays an important part, Arthur is a passive threat, events are reported, and conflicts are largely internal. What chiefly holds the play together and gives it unity is not so much the part of the Bastard or even the problem of de facto or de jure rule as the character of John. The portrait of John is consistent though he himself is not.[24] As Shakespeare saw him he is not without the makings of an admirable king, being quick and resolute in emergencies and able to inspire loyalty in his subjects. He even has a certain greatness in his opposition to Cardinal Pandulph and the Pope. But he has no staying power and his great weakness is his opportunism and readiness to yield to suggestions of immediate advantage. He has a conscience of sorts but no idealism. He represents England outwardly, but inwardly only himself, and his activity is therefore motivated by insecurity rather than by patriotism. He is dependent on the advice and support of others but, driven at last into being pushed and directed, and virtually abdicating his power, he is happy in having for his main adviser and champion one who will not be pushed and directed under any circumstances.

6 King Richard's Guilt and the Poetry of Kingship

If similarities in design and execution are an indication of closeness in time *King John* and *Richard II* must be near companions. Of the latter play Stanley Wells says that 'it is deliberately a play of character, thought, and emotion rather than action',[1] and the same may be said of *King John*. In both histories the central character is a weak king, or a king who proves weak in the testing after an initial show of strength. In both he resigns his authority to a contrasting character, a Faulconbridge or a Bolingbroke, who is a rising soldier and politician and serves 'commodity' or opportunity. In both plays the king causes the violent death of a rival to the throne and tries to disclaim the responsibility. In both there are women (Constance and the Duchess of Gloucester) vainly urging vengeance. And in both there is a trial by battle or by single combat. It will not be surprising to find that there are similarities in the ways in which some expectations are aroused and remain unfulfilled.

The likeness of *Richard II* to *Richard III* is of a more general kind. The elements of ritual and formal arrangement so often pointed out in *Richard II*[2] are also prominent in the earlier play, although they are there of a less ceremonial kind. There is also a similarity by contrast in the fates of the two kings bearing the same name, one a climber on Fortune's wheel for whom kingship holds no mystery but that of power, the other a monarch in descent almost from the start who clings to the sacredness of his kingly office. Both are consummate play-actors. But of the prophesying and cursing which point the course of events in *Richard III* there is relatively little in *Richard II*, and when the most ominous curse of the play is uttered by the dying John of Gaunt it remains ineffectual. In fact any comparison with *Richard III* and the other plays of the first tetralogy points up a shift of emphasis from careful plot structure to other aspects of dramatic composition, particularly the poetry.

Not that the main action lacks careful preparation. There are hints of Richard's political impotence and Bolingbroke's ambition from the opening scene on, and the idea of self-provoked deposition is introduced very clearly by York after Richard's decision to seize upon Gaunt's revenues and possessions: 'For how art thou a king / But by fair sequence and succession?' ii.ii contains the queen's moving premonition of sorrow, and in ii.iv the Welsh captain speaks of omens and signs which 'forerun the death or fall of kings'. The gardener in iii.iv, too, prepares us for the final death scene by his talk of lopping away superfluous branches. But with regard to incidental happenings *Richard II* offers frequent surprises. We are totally unprepared for the stopping of the trial by combat and the banishment of the combatants, and also for the arraignment of Aumerle in the beginning of the parliament scene. And there is only a brief forewarning of the death of Gaunt, of his son's precipitate return to England, of Richard's complete military collapse, and of Aumerle's involvement in the conspiracy of the Abbot of Westminster.

There is evidence of different phases of composition in signs of disturbance which can hardly be accounted for otherwise. Thus there are extensive passages in rhymed couplets (especially at the end or near the end of each of the first three scenes and at the end of iii.ii, v.i, v.iii) which on the whole are inferior in style to the blank verse in which most of the play presents itself. The rhymed parts may be of earlier provenance than the blank verse parts. But rhyming couplets are distributed throughout the play, with certain areas of concentration, and this would suggest sustained revision of a complete play in couplets rather than the addition of passages and scenes to an unfinished play or to excerpts from a finished play. I find it hard to understand why Dover Wilson, who sees such bad rhymed verse in the fifth act and thinks it pre-Shakespearean, is not also sceptical of some of the rhymed verse in the early acts. I also find it impossible to reconcile his statement that 'the tragedy of King Richard the Second has all the air of being composed in a single mood' with his belief in Shakespeare's dependence on a hypothetical source play which would account for 'the otherwise puzzling features of this text'.[3] We should perhaps keep an open mind about the possibility of composite authorship, but it cannot be ruled out that Shakespeare himself wrote a tragedy in rhyme at some early date and later revised it in its extant form. It is to be noted that the passages in which the murder of Gloucester is explicitly touched upon are for the most part in what is presumably the later verse medium.

There are substantial contradictions which follow the divisions between rhymed and blank verse. In i.iii Bolingbroke on hearing his sentence of banishment immediately comforts himself in the following couplets:

> Your will be done: this must my comfort be,
> That sun that warms you here, shall shine on me,

> And those his golden beams to you here lent
> Shall point on me and gild my banishment.   (ll.144–7)

Gaunt, however, is despondent:

> For ere the six years that he hath to spend
> Can change their moons, and bring their times about,
> My oil-dried lamp and time-bewasted light
> Shall be extinct with age and endless night,   (ll.219–22)

There follow thirty lines of which all but two are in rhyming couplets. Shortly afterwards, in a passage which returns to blank verse, it is Bolingbroke who is despondent and Gaunt the comforter:

> *Gaunt.* What is six winters? they are quickly gone –
> *Bol.*   To men in joy; but grief makes one hour ten.   (ll.260–1)

> *Gaunt.* All places that the eye of heaven visits
>   Are to a wise man ports and happy havens.   (ll.275–6)

No hint here of Gaunt's imminent death. Both Gaunt and Bolingbroke contradict what they have said only a few minutes earlier.

There are, even more surprisingly, two quite different versions of Aumerle's parting with Bolingbroke, one a brief but friendly 'Cousin, farewell', followed by a request that he should write (I.iii.249–50, in a rhymed passage), the other Aumerle's account to Richard (I.iv.3–19, in blank verse) of how he saw Bolingbroke off and counterfeited grief so as to avoid having to speak the word 'farewell'. There is further confusion as to who accompanies Bolingbroke on his departure: the Lord Marshal (I.iii.251–2, rhymed), Gaunt (I.iii.304–5, rhymed) or Aumerle (I.iv.1–19, blank verse).

In the rhymed passages of this part, then, we have a Bolingbroke who cheerfully accepts his banishment, is friends with Aumerle, and is seen off by the Lord Marshal and his father. These details are at variance with what we are told elsewhere and look like remnants of an original beginning or an early version or perhaps even an earlier play.

The contradictions as to the whereabouts of Bagot may be another sign of different phases of composition, unless they are simply due to carelessness. At the end of II.ii Bagot intends to join the king in Ireland (like the historical Bagot), but he is not in the king's company on his return, since Richard asks about him at III.ii.122, and he is wrongly reported to be at

Bristol at II.iii.164. The play tells us nothing about his capture by Boling-broke and there is no explanation of his reappearance in London, where he turns informer against Aumerle. At II.iii.164 he is possibly confused with the Earl of Wiltshire.[4] As for the latter, who is Richard's chief 'farmer' of the kingdom, it several times looks as if we may expect to see him on the stage, especially in the execution scene at Bristol, where Bagot and Greene are the only prisoners, but he remains absent throughout.

Such confusions and omissions – and there are others – reinforce the impression derived from a study of the larger movements of plot and theme that *Richard II* underwent some major changes of design in the course of its shaping. Stage adaptation and condensation would account for some, but certainly not all, of the irregularities.[5]

We may now turn to the major problem of composition. *King Richard the Second* opens with forceful accusations of embezzlement, treason, and murder. In the presence of the king and John of Gaunt, Gaunt's son Henry Bolingbroke throws these charges in the face of Thomas Mowbray, Duke of Norfolk. After a similar opening in a modern play we would probably expect an exciting story of detection and final apprehension. But the charges are vehemently rebutted by the defendant, and couched as they are in Elizabethan verse, blanketed to boot by a medieval setting, they probably in fact stir rather uncertain expectations. An audience in the 1590s may have known the to us anonymous play about the murder victim, *Thomas of Woodstock*,[6] and if so they would realise that the main accusation pointed slantingly at the king. If quick enough they would even catch the implication of a close kinship between killer and killed in Boling-broke's allusion to the blood of 'sacrificing Abel' crying 'for justice and rough chastisement'. They would be ready to notice symptoms of the king's uneasiness during the quarrel.[7] And even if they did not know *Woodstock* they would feel more familiar than we do with the political implications of the quarrel and would readily understand that King Richard had a personal, not just a magisterial, interest in a peaceful solution. In any case, as soon as we get to the second scene the accusation of murder is levelled directly at the king. Gaunt expressly declares that Richard was responsible for the Duke of Gloucester's death, and the widowed Duchess of Gloucester urges revenge. She evidently sees 'butcher Mowbray' as Richard's tool and prays for his defeat in the lists. Gaunt, it is true, refuses to touch God's substitute and implicitly admits the possibility that the assassination of his brother may have been justified:

> God's substitute,
> His deputy anointed in His sight,

> Hath caus'd his death; the which if wrongfully,
> Let heaven revenge.   (I.ii.37–40)

On his deathbed, however, he is provoked to denounce Richard in direct and violent terms:

> That blood already, like the pelican,
> Hast thou tapp'd out and drunkenly carous'd: (II.i.126–7)

And even the scrupulous York, speaking of Richard's father, Edward the Black Prince, is driven to insinuate Richard's guilt: Edward's hands, he declares, 'were guilty of no kindred blood'.

It may be worth observing that Bolingbroke's retrospective description of King Richard in *1 Henry IV* concentrates entirely on his frivolous and dissolute behaviour:

> The skipping King, he ambled up and down,
> With shallow jesters, and rash bavin wits,
> Soon kindled and soon burnt, carded his state,
> Mingled his royalty with cap'ring fools
> Had his great name profaned with their scorns,

and so on (*1H4*, III.ii). That, says Henry to his prodigal son, is what you are like now and what Richard was like 'When I from France set foot at Ravenspurgh' – almost as if that was all the reason for his insurrection. In *Richard II* we hear of the king farming out his land, being led by flatterers, and extorting money,[8] but his dissolute life is barely mentioned, and this lack of emphasis brings his actual crimes, murder and robbery, all the more into prominence.

The reasons for the murder are never discussed, but the underlying assumption of the play is obviously that Gloucester was an innocent victim of tyranny and malice.[9] This is definitely Bolingbroke's contention in maintaining that Mowbray

> did plot the Duke of Gloucester's death,
> Suggest his soon-believing adversaries,
> And consequently, like a traitor coward,
> Sluic'd out his innocent soul through streams of blood,
> (I.i.100–3)

The 'streams of blood' of course, are Shakespeare's contribution to the crime and help to make it more starkly real: the chronicles record that the duke was smothered or strangled. Gloucester's widow, naturally enough, describes him as a worthy son of his great father, Edward III, and the dying Gaunt, echoing *Woodstock* perhaps, calls him a 'plain well-meaning soul'. These descriptions are nowhere contradicted in the play (the chronicles, again, are another matter), unless one wishes to force an admission of Gloucester's disloyalty from Gaunt's words to the duchess quoted above or from York's exclamation in ii.ii.100–2:

> I would to God,
> So my untruth had not provok'd him to it,
> The king had cut my head off with my brother's.

It is strongly suggested, then, with only doubtful reservations, that Richard has committed an act of brutal tyranny against his own uncle. He had no justification for the murder. And the reason why he banishes Bolingbroke and Mowbray must be that he cannot tolerate having this murky affair pried into. This is what Hall and Holinshed jointly leave us to infer. Holinshed's report of Bolingbroke's accusation against Mowbray includes the murder of Gloucester; and the sentence of banishment as reported by Hall vaguely condemns 'Henry duke of Herfford [i.e. Bolingbroke] for diverse consideracions and because he hath displeased the kyng' and 'Thomas Mowbrey duke of Norffolke [. . .] because that he has sowen sedicion in this realme by his wordes wherof he can make no proofe'.[10] (Holinshed reports no reason at all for the sentence against Bolingbroke.) Shakespeare more eloquently makes Richard complain of the pride, ambition and envy of the combatants and the danger which their quarrel represents to the peace of England. This hardly makes sense as a reason for stopping the trial of their differences, and the most plausible inference we can draw from the play's treatment of the incident, if the banishment is not to seem insufficiently motivated, is again that the Gloucester affair must be hushed up. The only alternative is to see the banishment as an example of Richard's caprice and as a new act of tyranny. This could obviously have been Shakespeare's intention as well, but he would hardly expect us to forget the main reason why the lords had displeased the king. The sentence of banishment, incidentally, is agreed on in council, with Gaunt voting for it, as we can tell from ii.iii.233–46. But Gaunt has done nothing to dissuade his son from the combat. On the contrary, he has given him his blessing. And no one but the king can have proposed the sentence.

After Gaunt is dead and Bolingbroke and Mowbray out of the way, we learn, not quite unexpectedly but abruptly enough, of the death of the Duchess of Gloucester. So now Richard's most implacable accuser is dead too. There is no suggestion of foul play. Richard may be morally to blame, but the duchess simply expires, and in the remainder of the play there is not so much as a memory of her.

Next time we hear of Gloucester is one and a half acts later, when Bolingbroke reopens the murder case just before the deposition of Richard. This time Aumerle is the accused instead of Mowbray, a switch which is left unexplained and which needs an explanation considering the insistence on Mowbray in the beginning.[11] It is left unexplained, that is to say, unless we clearly see the accusations in both cases as really directed against the king. At any rate a decision is prevented once more. Mowbray, who was now to be a key witness for the prosecution, is reported dead, having purged whatever may have been his share of guilt in crusades to the Holy Land. Nor does the play include the trial of the lords appellants which Bolingbroke promises; and Aumerle is pardoned for another crime in the last act before the Gloucester mystery is brought up again. It never is.

There are quite a number of loose ends here. But the really remarkable circumstance is that after the first act Richard betrays not the slightest sign of a guilty conscience for any criminal or evil deed. And this in spite of John of Gaunt's deathbed curse:

> Live in thy shame, but die not shame with thee!
> These words hereafter thy tormentors be!   (ii.i.135–6)

In any other play, particularly *Richard III*, this curse or prophecy would be a prelude to great conflicts of defiance or remorse. Richard admits lightly enough in i.iv to having held 'too great a court' and shown 'liberal largess'. In the parliament scene he speaks vaguely of his sins and of sharing the guilt for his own deposition, and soliloquising in prison he blames himself for wasting time. But that is the full extent of his self-judgment. He reduces the 'grievous crimes' imputed to him by Northumberland to 'weav'd-up follies'. It is likely, as I suggested, that he betrays uneasiness in the first act on account of Gloucester's death, but he never throughout the whole play refers to Gloucester even obliquely. This could be explained in terms of Freudian psychology as a case of repression, were it not that the text of the play from Act ii on absolutely refuses to support a performance of Richard's part in which a sense of guilt is indicated by posture or gesture. I cannot find anything to substantiate Professor Leonard Barkan's remark at the conclusion of an otherwise interesting essay on 'The Theatrical Consistency of *Richard II*': 'Bolingbroke will be plagued to the end of his days by Richard's death, *precisely as Richard was by Gloucester's'* (my italics).[12] In fact we have the decidedly odd phenomenon of the suspected criminal going through the greater part of the play without awareness that a crime has been committed. And, what is more, he is never accused of the crime by his chief antagonist. Bolingbroke charges first Mowbray, then Aumerle, but not Richard. He cannot conceivably be ignorant of the fact that his father, uncle, and aunt hold the king responsible for the death of Gloucester. It is his father who brings him before the king in the first place. But however we choose to interpret his accusations against Mowbray and Aumerle, he never, apart from the one allusion to the blood of Abel, *voices* suspicion of the king, and never even by allusion after the first act. Nor does Northumberland or anyone else after York's exasperated outburst in ii.i. If the articles drawn up against Richard and presented to him in the parliament scene contain an indictment for murder (as they did in fact according to Hall and Holinshed) we do not learn of it because of Richard's blinding tears which prevent him from reading them.

These are plain facts drawn from the play itself, but the problem they pose has not been adequately recognised.[13] 'It is . . . Richard's limitation that he never grasps the significance of Gloucester's death to his own tragedy,' says Samuel Schoenbaum.[14] But if it is Richard's limitation it is *a fortiori* Shakespeare's. And it is equally that of his critics. Among the latter, A. P. Rossiter is probably the one who has most confidently expressed his sense of a major unconformity in the play, located, as he thinks, between Acts ii and iii and indicated by 'a discontinuity in character; some marked incoherences and dubieties in the story; a related uncertainty in the theme (tragic or political); and more than one kind of inconsistency in the texture of the verse'.[15] Rossiter blames it all on Shakespeare's assumption that his audience would be familiar with *Woodstock* and so fully aware of King Richard's guilt both in the murder of his uncle and in the plundering of his subjects. But even if we accept a degree of dependence on *Woodstock* – and I do not see why we should not – we would surely have to think Shakespeare quite uncharacteristically insensitive to the needs of his audience to withhold as much important information as this theory presupposes. There is no doubt a major unconformity in the play, but the causes probably lie elsewhere. In 1971 A. L. French published an article on '*Richard II* and the Woodstock Murder' in which he took issue with those who would minimise the importance of the murder and argued that to ignore it was 'to make nonsense of the play'. He was chiefly concerned to show that Richard's rage at having the affair brought up and particularly at 'being accused in public by Gaunt' started the train of events which led to

Bolingbroke's rebellion.[16] This is a valid enough argument and it is persuasively put forward, but no more than Professor Schoenbaum's admirable analysis of Act I or Rossiter's *Woodstock* theory does it explain why the murder charge is dropped. Derek Traversi, too, gives ample attention to the Gloucester plot in considering the opening of *Richard II*, and even calls the murder of Gloucester 'the mainspring of the following tragedy',[17] but, like French, he fails to show how inconspicuous the mainspring becomes as the play unfolds. Dover Wilson, in his Introduction to the New Cambridge *Richard II*, is aware of what he calls 'the vagueness, not to say inconsistency, which surrounds the question of Gloucester's murder' but thinks this is due to the prominence of the Gloucester business in a lost source play, which he hypothesises in analogy with *The Troublesome Raigne of King John*, and which Shakespeare, he says, may have 'compressed and distorted in the process of revision'.[18] As it is he thinks the murder has become 'a minor strand in the texture of the play', a view which obscures the element of inconsistency which he has previously called attention to. Later editors like Peter Ure, Stanley Wells, and Kenneth Muir represent the tendency of perhaps a majority of critics to underestimate the play's concern with the Gloucester affair and to see it right from the start as only 'a minor strand in the texture of the play'. Peter Ure maintains that Richard remains correctly impassive in the first scenes of the drama, 'playing the part of majesty with a fair efficiency'. His later fall 'is due to a specific deed', which is not the murder of Gloucester but 'the seizure of Gaunt's property'. And Ure finds a positive virtue in the design which enabled Shakespeare to deal first with one aspect and then another of Richard's character: 'Shakespeare bundled the narrative of causes into the first two and a half Acts so that he might more fully set forth the drama of the sufferer constrained to reduce himself from king to man.'[19] Geoffrey Bullough, who also sees two distinct Richards, traces them back to opposite traditions about the king to be found in the chronicles, the 'base fool' and the 'martyr', and thinks that Shakespeare made use of them both to give Bolingbroke 'fair reasons for rebellion yet not for usurpation'.[20]

No doubt Shakespeare often delighted in what William Empson has called 'dramatic ambiguity'.[21] Both King Henry IV and King John are ambiguously guilty and not guilty of murder, and we may be satisfied to feel the same about Richard. Whatever positive virtues we may find in the final arrangement of the play, however, it does look as if the author first planned to write an historical play which was also to be a revenge tragedy with a Richard haunted by guilt and overtaken by retribution – a play, perhaps, with certain points of resemblance to *Hamlet* – and then changed his design. There may be something, even a good deal, in Wells's suggestion that 'Shakespeare deliberately left the issue vague so that Richard would not be too much exposed to censure'.[22] but it is not the whole story. The issue is not so much vague as loose-ended. And there are definite indications of attempts to develop it. Shakespeare may have depended somewhat mechanically on Holinshed when he wrote the scenes involving Mowbray and Aumerle in the Gloucester plot, but he did elaborate on Holinshed in letting Mowbray specifically repudiate the charge of murder; and certainly his inclusion of the scene showing Gaunt and the Duchess of Gloucester discussing revenge against Richard was due to no mechanical copying of sources, even if *Woodstock* was in the background. The deliberate invention of this scene, as well as of Gaunt's dying curse, is strong evidence that at one time Richard's guilt for the murder of Gloucester was thought of by the author as an important plot element. Of the pre-Shakespearean source play posited by Dover Wilson we know nothing, but its existence would not basically affect Shakespeare's responsibility for the structuring of his own play. He was no longer a complete novice in the art of playwriting.

Why, then, was Richard's crime not kept in the foreground of the action? Could it be that Shakespeare got cold feet about pressing a similarity which might have aroused the displeasure of Queen Elizabeth? Lily B. Campbell points to the analogy between the assassination of Gloucester and the execution of Mary Stuart.[23] And Queen Elizabeth who, as we know, saw herself on a later occasion in the image of King Richard, would have been touchy on the subject of political murder. But if Shakespeare was thinking too hard of the queen he would scarcely have begun his *Richard II* at all. 'The reign of Richard had become a topic that wise men did well to avoid,' says M. M. Reese.[24] It seems more likely that he began by cashing in on the popularity of *Woodstock*, which of course centres on Richard's and his favourites' guilt in the death of the duke, and was guided away from his original direction by Holinshed, who in the last resort was more inclined to present Richard as a martyr than as a criminal.

One explanation which could do away with the discrepancy between expectation and fulfilment must be mentioned if only to be dismissed. It does look at times as if we have to do with a kind of morality play in which an impenitent sinner is finally punished by the agents of heavenly rather than earthly justice. This interpretation would find some support in John of Gaunt's refusal to take revenge out of the hand of God. It would also find support in the attitude of the Duke of York expressed in his assurance after the accession of Bolingbroke that 'heaven hath a hand in these events'. The idea of divine punishment no doubt thinly pervades the play and has a dramatic function, but, since Richard himself is entirely un-conscious of having offended the powers above, it can hardly be accepted as a central theme. His last words,

> Mount, mount, my soul! thy seat is up on high,
> Whilst my gross flesh sinks downward, here to die.
>
> (v.v.111–12)

must be supposed to be fully credible and directly contradict the idea of divine retribution. Heaven, not hell, is Richard's spiritual destination.

Bolingbroke, then, is no minister of heavenly justice. If the Gloucester theme was originally reintroduced just before the deposition of the king in order to provide divine sanction for his dethronement this becomes strangely irrelevant in the finished play. At most the idea of heavenly vengeance, so unambiguously introduced in the first act, is watered down to provide a vague metaphysical, not to say metadramatic, justification for Bolingbroke's action which it is left to the audience to feel, since it is not apparent to the *dramatis personae*. (To Bolingbroke and his followers the justification for the violation of Richard's divine right of kingship is practical, legal, and secular. It lies partly in the ostensibly voluntary submission of Richard and his nomination of Bolingbroke as his heir,[25] partly in the hoped-for confession of his 'grievous crimes'.) Shakespeare had to provide *some* metaphysical justification for Bolingbroke's rebellion and deposition of an anointed king. This was not to be a case of pure usurpation like that of Claudius or Macbeth in later plays, or of Richard III. A saintly king and a villainous Bolingbroke would be both unhistorical and uninteresting, apart from perhaps too much resembling characters which the author had already portrayed, Henry VI and Richard of Gloucester. On the other hand it had to be a case of some kind of unsurpa-tion. A villainous Richard and a saintly Bolingbroke would be even less use to him. This is quite likely one reason why he left the question of guilt undecided.

It is interesting to observe the various ways in which Shakespeare attempts to divide sympathy and understanding between the two main adversaries as equally as possible.

Richard's legitimacy is the main point in his favour, and this is not in question. But he relies too much on the sacredness of kingship, not admit-ting until suffering teaches humility that sacredness may be forfeited by the human incumbent of the kingly office. Some critics (Dover Wilson being one) are perhaps too ready to see the parallels drawn between Richard and Christ as a way of emphasising the martyrdom aspect of the king's downfall. It is more natural to see at least his own comparisons of himself to Christ, whether they are felt to be blasphemous or not (and there is a great deal of ambivalence here) as a sign of self-aggrandisement, which, with its complement in self-abasement, is a major fault of character.[26] The following passage from Holinshed may well have lodged in the dramatist's mind:

> Sir john Bushie in all his talke, when he proponed any matter vnto the king, did not attribute to him titles of honour, due and accustomed, but inuented vnused termes and such strange names, as were rather agreeable to the diuine maiestie of God, than to any earthlie potentate. The prince being desirous inough of all honour, and more ambitious than was requisite, seemed to like well of his speech, and gaue good eare to his talke. (III/490/2/57–65)

The other great weakness displayed in words and deeds is vacillation, most dramatically expressed in his stopping the combatants at Coventry almost in mid-career, and most spectacularly in his toying with the crown in the deposition scene. Neither self-aggrandisement nor vacillation is a criminal fault, however. Nor, apart from two scenes (I.iv and II.i) is there much in his utterances and general behaviour which can be called offensive. Practically all our impression of misrule is derived from the allegations of his critics and enemies. And they tend to blame his flatterers. It is all the more surprising that even these flatterers are not shown to be wicked. On the contrary, they demonstrate, on various occasions, both resolution, kindness, and fortitude. It is Greene who reminds the king (in I.iv) that 'expedient manage must be made' to deal with the Irish rebels, Bushy who comforts the queen with eloquent sympathy, Bagot who joins the king in Ireland when things begin to look black for his cause. Bushy and Greene meet death without flinching. Aumerle is the only royal favourite who does not behave unexceptionably. Describing his leavetaking with Boling-broke, he speaks of his own 'craft to counterfeit oppression of . . . grief', and thus prepares us to some extent for his conspiratorial role towards the end of the play. As for the queen, she has no properly dramatic part to play, and her sole function is obviously to elicit sympathy for her 'sweet Richard'.

Above all Richard makes his appeal by the great lines of poetry he is made to speak. It is doubtful whether Shakespeare meant to distinguish him in this way at first. The most memorable poetry in the beginning of the play is spoken by Gaunt and Bolingbroke. The quality of Boling-broke's verse, no doubt, is uneven. He reaches a low level in the rhymed couplets in which he speaks his farewell before the combat –

> O, let no noble eye profane a tear
> For me, if I be gor'd with Mowbray's spear!
> [etc.]   (I.iii.59ff)

But the lines beginning with the stichomythia between him and Gaunt in the ending of the same scene and including his penultimate speech in that scene bear the mark of genius:

> O, who can hold a fire in his hand
> By thinking on the frosty Caucasus?   (ll.294ff)

There is nothing to match this in Bolingbroke's subsequent utterances. Richard, on the other hand, from the moment he sets foot on the Welsh shore, moves us with the pathos and imagination of his words and with the poignancy of his reflections on majesty and mortality. It is as if Shakespeare, having struck some deep well of inspiration, could not bear to turn away before it was exhausted. One may imagine that he immersed himself more and more in the subject of kingship as he analysed Richard's predicament in verbal imagery and symbolic action, to the detriment, perhaps, of his plot, but to the immeasurable gain of the play's human appeal. Much of what Richard says has the character of soliloquy. Add to this the fact that he is the only person who technically soliloquises, and it is not to be wondered at that he governs our responses to the extent that we forget he has been a wastrel and murderer and remember him as a combination of ineffectual dreamer and royal martyr.

Bolingbroke's faults are at least as glaring as Richard's. Above all he is proud and ambitious. A modern audience may not realise to what extent this is emphasised in the play or how serious the vice of ambition was considered to be in the Elizabethan moral system.[27] William Baldwin dedicated *A Myrroure for Magistrates*, one of the possible sources for *Richard II*, 'To the nobilitye and all other in office', reminding them of Plato's warning, 'Well is that realme gouerned, in which the ambicious desyer not to beare office.' And when John Higgins brought out a supplementary volume in 1574 he wrote an Induction in which he reiterated a similar warning:

> The noble man to beare a noble mynde,
> And not him selfe ambiciously abuse:

Pride and ambition – they are very often linked and sometimes almost synonymous[28] – was the sin of Satan and the most pernicious vice of a courtier or statesman. In the presentation of Bolingbroke it is often suggested in images of height: 'high blood's royalty' (I.i.58,71), 'my height' (I.i.189), 'high Herford' (I.iv.2–3), etc. Richard is clearly aware of Bolingbroke's ambitious nature from the very beginning, witness his ironical remark 'How high a pitch his resolution soars!' (I.i.109), and there is an indication that his stopping the combat and banishing the combatants, which might otherwise be seen as a mere act of caprice,[29] is partly due to his fear of Bolingbroke's further climbing should he win. Here is the reason he offers:

> For that our kingdom's earth should not be soil'd
> With that dear blood which it hath fostered;
> And for our eyes do hate the dire aspect
> Of civil wounds plough'd up with neighbour's sword,
> And for we think the eagle-winged pride
> Of sky-aspiring and ambitious thoughts,
> With rival-hating envy, set on you
> To wake our peace . . .   (I.iii.125–32)

This is the only place apart from the more neutral context of v.v.18 where the word 'ambition' or its derivatives is used in the play, but the Marlovian 'aspiring' recurs in v.ii.9 (compare the phrase 'the aspiring blood of Lancaster' at the end of *3 Henry VI*), and the words 'pride', 'proud', and 'proudly' are applied to Bolingbroke a number of times in Acts III and v. Richard keeps up an appearance of impartiality in the quarrel between Bolingbroke and Mowbray and actually imposes a heavier sentence of exile on Mowbray than on his adversary, but there are constant indications that he favours the former and that Shakespeare wishes us to see Mowbray in a more favourable light than Bolingbroke.[30] The latter is presented in the very first lines of the play as 'bold' and 'boisterous' (he also sees himself in the deathbed scene of *2 Henry IV* as having snatched honour 'with boistr'ous hand'). When Richard warns us shortly afterwards that one of the appellants must necessarily be insincere ('yet one but flatters us') we are, or should be, made particularly sensitive to the tones of their speeches. And it is not long before we may detect a false note in Bolingbroke's affirmations of truth and loyalty which is absent in Mowbray's. The former is too eager to assure the king of 'the devotion of a subject's love', while the latter has to excuse his 'cold words' – the difference interestingly reminds one of that between Lear's eldest daughters and Cordelia.

The contrast between Mowbray and Bolingbroke is not made too obvious, but at the end of the first act we should at least suspect a

Machiavellian streak in Bolingbroke. The action as it develops shows him to be an opportunist who lets others – Northumberland, York, Exton – do the dirty work for him and rises in seeming innocence.

But this is not the complete picture, and Shakespeare does almost as much in the case of Bolingbroke as in that of Richard (it was perhaps more necessary in Richard's case since he begins by being in the wrong) to extenuate his faults and to attract our sympathy. In the first place Bolingbroke suffers gross injustice, not only in being exiled but even more in the confiscation of his title and revenues. This is made clear by as impartial a person as the Duke of York. And though Bolingbroke has no wife in the play to evoke vicarious pity, he does have another non-dramatic character, the gardener, to defend his military expedition into England in terms of natural necessity. He has the backing of Gaunt and wins that of York, who, after some characteristic hesitation, apparently lends his authority as Lord Governor to the execution of Bushy and Greene. He stoops to the common people and gains their devotion. And the discontented nobles, of course, flock to him. It would have been good for him if he had been praised behind his back, but at least Northumberland on the ride to Berkeley praises him to his face, whatever we wish to make of that (Northumberland does sound rather sycophantic). As in the case of Richard, whose favourites get some of the blame for his misrule, there is in Bolingbroke's case, too, a certain transfer of responsibility to others. Thus in II.i Northumberland can only be understood as inciting to rebellion against the king, long before Bolingbroke actually reaches for the crown.[31] Later the earl is so officious that Bolingbroke has to restrain him after Northumberland has thrice unsuccessfully urged King Richard to read the articles of impeachment. Richard himself takes some of the blame for his deposition.[32] And another officious person, Sir Piers Exton, carries out the act of regicide, which is performed by Bolingbroke's wish but not by his command. The new king shows magnanimity in pardoning first Aumerle,[33] then his bold opponent the Bishop of Carlisle. His dismissal of Exton and announcement of his intention to go on a pilgrimage to the Holy Land are the last two touches which help to make him an appealing character. Our final impression of Bolingbroke is probably of one whom astuteness, ambition, and circumstance have raised to greatness, but who will have to make strenuous efforts to defend his title to the crown both to his own conscience and to his subjects.

The attitude of the play as a whole remains ambiguous. There is not as in *Richard III* a clear case for dethroning a tyrant and murderer, and on the other hand the king is an accomplice to his own dethronement. His death, it could be said, is due to a misunderstanding. Who, then, is finally to blame? The author has it both ways and ultimately refuses to side with either of the two adversaries. Nevertheless, the play can be viewed on two levels, on neither of which it is entirely impartial. Bolingbroke has the last word, and politically *Richard II* is probably felt to be a pro-Bolingbroke play, just as the whole cycle of eight English histories has a Lancastrian bias culminating in the hostile portrait of the Yorkist Richard III. It should be noticed that Northumberland, the first time he addresses Bolingbroke after his coronation, wishes all happiness to his 'sacred state' (v.vi.6), using a word that has been almost appropriated by Richard and obviously assuming that Henry IV has inherited the divine authority which Richard was so confident of possessing.[34] And though Henry will never feel secure in possessing the grace he robbed from his predecessor, his reformed and God-fearing son will be seen to be divinely favoured at Agincourt and will close the second tetralogy – in a sense the conclusion of the whole historical cycle – with a vindication of his father's right. Certainly the supporters of Essex in 1601 must have regarded *Richard II* as a play which justified the coercion of an irresponsible monarch. It is interesting to note in this connection that Essex was a descendant of the Duke of Gloucester, whose place in the play is so problematic.

If we consider *Richard II* on the human level, however, without worrying about political right and wrong, our sympathy, it can hardly be doubted, is in the main for Richard, the murderer who becomes a murder victim, while the avenger is paradoxically left with the burden of guilt which the first murderer never assumed.

To sum up and conclude: the evidence suggests that Shakespeare began to write an historical revenge tragedy based on a murder and that he possibly wrote a rhymed version of this play before revising it. He may have been halted even while writing his first version by realising the impossibility of presenting Henry Bolingbroke as a divinely sanctioned executioner. Or the realisation may have come to him during revision, especially if it occurred to him at the same time that the Tudor myth, depending on Bolingbroke's usurpation, might be used as a *leitmotiv* in the history plays.[35] So Bolingbroke, when it comes to the point, does not invoke the king's guilt in the death of Gloucester as a reason for proceeding against him. Instead, a conflict is developed between ambition and opportunism on the one hand and legitimacy weakened by folly and irresolution on the other. Richard's misgovernment belatedly makes its appearance, without preparation, in the last scene of the first act. Then, after the death of Gaunt, it entirely displaces the murder theme. The misgovernment theme is in turn more and more effaced by the sacrilege theme and the conflict between divine right and mortal frailty, and the central issue becomes not the king's guilt or his irresponsibility, but the sacredness of his office. *Richard II* was not, after all, to be a story of crime and punishment, or even of sin and expiation, but of power and majesty. To fully understand why, we have to take into account the spontaneous and subconscious impulses which could have modified the author's design as consciously outlined, and it is easy to suppose him being carried away by the poetry of kingship as he continued his exploration of Richard's mind, even to the point of ignoring themes and issues which he had not intended to neglect.

In the economy of *Richard II* as it emerged the king enacts his own drama on a different level from that of his adversaries. They constantly want to incriminate him politically, but he remains unaffected. There is a curious lack of transition as far as verbal exchanges are concerned between Richard's granting of Bolingbroke's reasonable demands in iii.iii and his abdication as reported by York in iv.i. We are turned back for an explanation to Richard's own despondency, which is expressed most movingly in the moments before he descends to meet his peremptory petitioner at Flint Castle. Not events, then, so much as movements of the mind, become the mainspring of the completed action, as Peter Ure, following Coleridge, has pointed out.[36] In this process the action itself becomes attenuated and expectations are disappointed, in part no doubt deliberately, in part by the accident of composition. The revenge clamoured for at first is certainly accomplished at last, but it is no longer revenge and leads to an ironic reversal of guilt. So much abortive action may be considered a dramatic weakness. But this is made up for by psychological and thematic interest and by a poetry which, however lyrical, never ceases to be dramatic. Balm is not to be washed off with 'all the water in the rough rude sea' but it may be with a few tears. The sin of sacrilege cannot either be cleansed with water, but a voyage to the Holy Land will wash away the blood even of regicide.

7 Down-trod Mortimer and Plump Jack

The beginning of *Henry IV* links up fairly closely with the ending of *Richard II*. It is true that we hardly expect to find King Henry 'shaken' and 'wan with care' only a twelvemonth after his coronation. It is also true that he now speaks of a regular crusade to the Holy Land like those in which his old opponent Mowbray participated rather than the voyage, or pilgrimage, which he planned at the end of *Richard II*. In fact he no longer speaks of washing the blood off from his guilty hand. But at least he has an interval of peace at home,[1] and the Jerusalem theme is renewed. With *Richard II* in fresh memory an audience might be expected to know what lies behind King Henry's decision to commence 'new broils . . . in stronds afar remote', and in any case we are three times reminded of the king's guilty conscience as we proceed through the two parts of *Henry IV*.[2] The intended crusade is not mentioned again in the first part after the end of the opening scene but it is reverted to in the second play several times and finally resolves itself in Henry's death in the Jerusalem chamber. It almost looks as if the whole action of the two plays could have been designed to show Henry overcoming the obstacles and dangers which beset him on his way to Jerusalem,[3] finally reaching his goal in a surprise dénouement which the author had his eye on from the start as a theatrical effect worth exploiting. Fulfilment in so far as this particular piece of plotting is concerned is long delayed but finally effected. This is more than can be said of some of the other plot elements.

After the awkward cancellation of the intended crusade – it is proclaimed after it has already been prevented – we find Henry, like Richard, faced with intractable nobles who refuse to obey orders. King Henry's peace has been broken on the Welsh and Scottish borders, and the prophecy uttered by the Bishop of Carlisle in *Richard II*, of bloody wars to follow upon Henry's usurpation, may seem about to be fulfilled.[4] So may Richard's prophecy concerning the treacherousness of Northumberland, who now joins his son and brother in rebellion against the man he helped to the throne. Henry, like Richard, is defamed behind his back as a murderer. The initial conflict in the later play, however, is centred on Henry's legitimacy rather than on criminal guilt as in Richard's case. And to aggravate this problem the claim of Edmund Mortimer, which was not allowed to complicate the issue between Richard and Bolingbroke, is now brought forward. Mortimer had already appeared on the stage in *1 Henry VI* as an old and dying man to pass on his claim to the Duke of York, but since he is not mentioned in *Richard II* there now has to be an explanation of his pretension to the crown. (We are not here concerned with Shakespeare's inaccuracy, following his sources, in confusing two different Mortimers.) This explanation is given by Worcester and Northumberland in I.iii.143–55. They do not repeat the details of Mortimer's and Bolingbroke's descent from Edward III, which are explained at some length in *1 Henry VI*, but briefly declare that King Richard when he 'set forth / Upon his Irish expedition' proclaimed Edmund Mortimer 'the next of blood' and 'heir to the crown'. Northumberland was present and 'heard the proclamation'. Functionally the role of Mortimer resembles that of the Duke of Gloucester in *Richard II*, though one is alive and the other dead. Mortimer is absent from most of *Henry IV* and might have been dispensed with altogether for all the expectations he fulfils in the unfolding of the plot, but he is the subject of much of the altercation and conspiracy in the beginning, and like the Duke of Gloucester he provides a motive for revenge against the king. In the first and third scenes the name of Mortimer is sounded no fewer than sixteen times, plus once when he is called the Earl of March; largely, of course, because Hotspur insists on repeating it in his indignant outbursts against King Henry's refusal to ransom his brother-in-law. Even before he hears of Mortimer's claim to the throne Hotspur swears he 'will lift the down-trod Mortimer / As high in the air as this unthankful King' (I.iii.133–4). Mortimer appears in person in the Bangor scene, where, in A. R. Humphreys's words, 'from Holinshed's brief reference to his capture and his marriage to Glendower's daughter Shakespeare makes the sensible negotiator, the devoted son-in-law and husband'.[5] It is Mortimer who tells us of the rebels' appointment to meet at Shrewsbury and his own intention of keeping the appointment:

> Tomorrow, cousin Percy, you and I
> And my good Lord of Worcester will set forth
> To meet your father and the Scottish power,
> As is appointed us, at Shrewsbury. (III.i.79–82)

It is Mortimer, too, who has the last few words of the Bangor scene: when Glendower calls him 'to horse immediately' he answers cheerfully 'With all my heart', and we must suppose him ready to gallop off with the others. But whether he falls asleep in the stable or loses his way, he at any rate strangely disappears. Even more strangely, he is not missed by his companions at Shrewsbury, who *are* worried, however, by the default of Northumberland and Glendower; and it is not till the short conversation between the Archbishop of York and Sir Michael in IV.iv that his absence from the field is so much as remarked on.[6] Shakespeare again casts him for a part in the Welsh campaign which the king announces at the end of *1 Henry IV*:

> Myself and you, son Harry, will towards Wales,
> To fight with Glendower and the Earl of March.
>
> (v.v.39–40)

Yet Mortimer is entirely forgotten in the second part, when the Welsh campaign is already over at the beginning of the action, and remains unseen and unmentioned throughout *Henry V*, although the traitorous Earl of Cambridge hints at a motive for his own revolt which can be none other than the advancement of Mortimer (this is confirmed in *1 Henry VI*). Mortimer apparently became a superfluous character when *Henry IV* took a turn from its original direction.

For that, like *Richard II*, it evidently did. Mortimer's title to the crown is the cause which first rallies the rebels, and that is how the dying Mortimer is at pains to explain the rebellion to his young kinsman in *1 Henry VI*:

> The reason mov'd these warlike lords to this,
> Was, for that – young King Richard thus remov'd,
> Leaving no heir begotten of his body –
> I was the next by birth and parentage; (*IH6*, II.v.70–3)

In *2 Henry VI* Jack Cade calls himself a Mortimer. And, to return to *Henry IV*, we have an audio-visual demonstration of Mortimer's claim to the better part of England in the presumably large map of the kingdom and the principality produced by Glendower and the discussion of the partition of the country which follows. As late as the eve of battle Hotspur states the rebels' complaints against King Henry and the purpose of the rebellion in terms for which Holinshed provided no suggestion as far as Mortimer's title was concerned. He is speaking of Bolingbroke:

> Then to the point.
> In short time after he depos'd the King,
> Soon after that depriv'd him of his life,
> And in the neck of that task'd the whole state;

> To make that worse, suffer'd his kinsman March
> (Who is, if every owner were well plac'd,
> Indeed his King) to be engag'd in Wales,
> There without ransom to lie forfeited;
>
> . . . . .
>
> And in conclusion drove us to seek out
> This head of safety, and withal to pry
> Into his title, the which we find
> Too indirect for long continuance.   (IV.iii.89–105)

Then there is an abrupt and inexplicable deflation of Hotspur's defiance. When Blunt asks, 'Shall I return this answer to the King,' he meekly replies, 'Not so, Sir Walter. We'll withdraw awhile,' and promises to send an answer in the morning. This answer, conveyed by Worcester, substantially repeats Hotspur's complaints of Henry's usurpation and disgrace of his former supporters but omits any mention of the death of Richard and of a rival claimant. In other words Shakespeare turns Holinshed's two briefly-reported parleys into a repetition of the same thing with one major difference: the question of legitimacy raised by Hotspur and omitted by Worcester. To accentuate this impression of a double treatment, the king's promise of a complete and speedy redress of grievances and of a 'pardon absolute' is first communicated to Hotspur by Blunt, then repeated by the king himself to Worcester. It is finally suppressed in Worcester's report to Hotspur, on the mistaken assumption that the latter has not heard of it. And there are other irregularities. The rebels at Shrewsbury are surprised by Vernon's news that Glendower 'cannot draw his power this fourteen days', although Mortimer already told them at Bangor that 'My father Glendower is not ready yet, / Nor shall we need his help these fourteen days' (III.i.83–4). (At.IV.iv.18 we belatedly learn that Glendower's absence is due to his being 'o'er-rul'd by prophecies'.) In the evening at Shrewsbury Worcester urges his impetuous nephew to delay the attack and wait for reinforcements, while in the morning it is Worcester who is spoiling for the fight. There is no indication that Vernon is present during Worcester's interview with the king, but afterwards it is assumed that he was there. Up to a definite point, then, Mortimer's claim continues to be urged and Hotspur is his inflexible champion, then, in the middle of an outcrop of irregularities, the claim is dropped and the rebellion is subsequently fuelled by arguments of ingratitude and tyranny. Just as, in *Richard II*, the accusation of murder directed at the king is replaced by general charges of misgovernment, in *1 Henry IV* the charge of illegitimacy (compounded with murder) is dropped in favour of general complaints of oppression.

And the reason? Once more it is tempting to ask whether Shakespeare may have hesitated to press an analogy which might have displeased the queen. As in the case of King Richard and the Duke of Gloucester, Lily Campbell finds Queen Elizabeth and Mary Stuart behind Henry and Mortimer, too.[7] Obviously the dramatic portrayal of an insurrection against the reigning monarch supported by arguments of legitimacy would hardly recommend itself to Elizabeth, and Shakespeare may have developed the initial conflict of his play to the point where it would have become too topically sensitive and then defused the most explosive issues. But it seems just as likely that the steady refusal of his sources to support a more significant role for Mortimer forced him to modify his plans. A more structurally determined explanation of the eclipse of Mortimer and his claim may also be offered. I said in my last chapter that I agreed up to a point with the view of the Gloucester mystery that 'Shakespeare deliber-ately left the issue vague so that Richard would not be too much exposed to censure'. Similarly it may be said that the position of the Lancastrians must not be too much exposed to challenge. As the plot of *Henry IV* is unfolded, Prince Hal begins to assume importance as a worthy heir, and his legitimacy needs to be built up. It must not be jeopardised by too much questioning of his father's right.[8]

Hal comes into full prominence in the *Henry IV* plays less often than we may be inclined to suppose. For what such indications are worth, he is not included in the full title of the first part as recorded in the Stationers' Register and printed in the quartos, which singles out King Henry, Hotspur, Falstaff, and the battle of Shrewsbury for advertisement, while the Folio concentrates on the king and Hotspur. Nor is he in the registra-tion entry for the second part, though the printed quarto and Folio titles mention his coronation. But if we examine the structure of the first part we will find a pretty regular alternation of Hotspur and Hal scenes as if the two are constantly balanced against each other; Falstaff's five times reiterated 'when thou art king' in I.ii, echoed by Hal's 'when I am King of England' at II.iv.13, as well as the mock enthronement in II.iv, create a major expectation of Hal's succession; and the reformation of the prince is undoubtedly an important component of the plot of both plays.[9]

Perhaps the relatively frequent occurrence of the verb 'redeem' in some form or other in *1 Henry IV* (it is used twice each by the prince, the king, and Hotspur) may be taken as a sign that the idea of redemption was play-ing all the time at the back of Shakespeare's mind. We are certainly given ample notice of Hal's reformation, beginning with the first mention of Hal in *Richard II*, v.iii, where Bolingbroke discerns 'some sparks of better hope' in his son. His first soliloquy in *1 Henry IV*, 'I know you all, and will awhile uphold / The unyok'd humour of your idleness', etc. (I.ii.190ff), has even been thought over-explicit.[10] The mock banishment of Falstaff in II.iv has more than a touch of seriousness, and the serious interview with the king in III.ii shows the prince promising with great sincerity to redeem his bad reputation 'on Percy's head'. In v.ii his enemy Vernon prophesies an astonishing change in him. In *2 Henry IV* there are renewed promises of reformation. Thus in his conversation with Poins in II.ii the prince exclaims:

> By this hand, thou thinkest me as far in the devil's book as thou and Falstaff, for obduracy and persistency. Let the end try the man.
>
> (ll.43–5)

And in II.iv he feels himself 'much to blame / So idly to profane the precious time'. Whether or not he is genuinely depraved and in need of redemption will no doubt continue to be hotly debated as long as critics go on repeating the battles of their predecessors.[11] I shall have more to say on this subject when I come to deal with *Henry V*. But those who think the prince remains a mere spectator to the crimes and debauchery of his cronies and put all the emphasis on Warwick's favourable interpretation of his behaviour in Part II, IV.iv, should notice, as they often fail to do, that it is Hal who asks Falstaff in the beginning of the first part, 'Where shall we take a purse tomorrow, Jack?' (I.ii.96). In fact the prince plans a highway robbery while the king is planning a crusade. It is Hal who tells Falstaff to dismiss the king's messenger with a bawdy jest about his own mother[12] and who strikes the Lord Chief Justice 'about Bardolph' the thief, though we do not actually witness the latter incident. In the second part he also feels compunction on several occasions for playing the fool with the time (II.ii.134), and we must suppose he is speaking of fooling and not education. Professor Sengupta insists on Hal's imaginative and emotional inferiority to Falstaff but believes he is 'never defiled by Falstaff's company',[13] yet one can more easily overlook the inferiority than the defilement. All in all it is probably fair to say that Shakespeare remained undecided and even inconsistent about the prince's moral character. And this impression is reinforced by his failure or refusal to give Prince Harry a part in the concluding military operations in *2 Henry IV*. At one moment, near the end of Act II, it looks as if Hal is all set to rush off to the battlefield. This is when he blames himself 'So idly to profane the precious time':

> When tempest of commotion, like the south
> Born with black vapour, doth begin to melt
> And drop upon our bare unarmed heads.
> Give me my sword and cloak. Falstaff, good night.
>
> (*2H4*,II.iv.358–63)

One wonders whether these lines could have strayed from Part I, for when next we hear of Hal in Part II, which is not till after the whole rebellion is over, he is reported to be either hunting at Windsor or dining with 'his continual followers' in London. There is no explanation of why he does not do his bit for his country unless we are to assume continued profligacy. But this may be one of the signs of the patchwork nature of *2 Henry IV*.

Prince Hal at first represents just another liability to the insecurely seated monarch. Then he not only redeems his own lost opinion but in doing so helps to vindicate his father's legitimacy. As we have the *Henry IV* plays this is done twice over, first in Part I, then in Part II, and opinions differ widely as to whether the repetition was envisaged in Shakespeare's original plan or the effect of a more or less accidental adjustment, and whether *Henry IV* is one play in two parts, or a dramatic diptych, or two separate plays. Dover Wilson, closely followed by E. M. W. Tillyard, is probably the leading exponent of the view that the two parts structurally make one whole and that they were intended for consecutive performance (on alternate afternoons according to Wilson). His suggestion that Shakespeare's 'symbolic arrangement' restricts Part I 'to the theme of the truant prince's return to Chivalry, and leaves the atonement with Justice, or the Rule of Law, as a leading motive for its sequel',[14] has won considerable support. Wilson sees the two parts as stages in a sequential development. Another possibility is to see them as parallel and complementary phases of a process which is to be understood emblematically rather than chronologically. This is the view of Irving Ribner, who in turn refers to G. K. Hunter.[15] A. R. Humphreys gets it both ways by explaining that 'while the historical events are in chronological sequence, the moral events (Hal's redemption in chivalry and justice) are in parallel'.[16] Bullough, on the other hand, faces the problem of repetition squarely and argues that 'a pattern of repetition in political matters [i.e. a series of rebellions in the unquiet time of King Henry IV] was essential to Shakespeare's historical and moral purpose. But repetition was also deliberately chosen by the dramatist in planning the serious and comic material affecting the Prince.' He explains: 'Shakespeare was not as yet interested in stages of growth in character, and the Chronicles suggested that the Prince's behaviour was inconsistent and declined after Shrewsbury.'[17]

Some of these views are perhaps influenced by a general reluctance to recognise signs of broken planning and improvisation in Shakespeare, a reluctance which is understandable but not necessarily laudable. The now common argument that Shakespeare planned a history in two parts devoted to the themes of chivalry and justice respectively, is hardly as well-founded as its frequent repetition might suggest. Hal's adoption of the civic virtues in the second part comes only as a surprise ending, though the audience has been prepared for the surprise. And anyway, why should he be made to disavow his chivalric virtues in order to demonstrate his submission to the law? A better explanation of the overlapping plots is provided by Harold Jenkins in his essay on *The Structural Problems in Shakespeare's Henry the Fourth*, which was published in 1956. Professor Jenkins's basic contention is that 'through the first half of Part I the Hotspur plot and the Falstaff plot show every sign of moving towards their crisis together', that then the Falstaff plot is slowed down to be completed in a separate play, and that consequently there has to be another reformation of the prince as if the first had not taken place. Jenkins does not try to get rid of this inconsistency by either minimising it or making it symbolical but suggests an analogy with heroes of folklore, who can always be 'at the same point twice', as he says. He refrains 'from assuming that a second part was necessarily planned before Part I was acted', but here, I feel, he might have been more confident. There are, as I shall show in a moment, indications that Shakespeare had already produced too much Falstaff material before he got to the battle of Shrewsbury to make it possible to finish his plot in a single play. Having all this material, he relegated some of it to a sequel, which would also have to contain the death of the king, the accession of Hal, and the rejection of Falstaff.[18] One consequence, as we shall see, is that the sequel – 'that ramshackle rag-bag of a piece', as one critic has called it[19] – is without a proper beginning. The overcrowding of the projected play also led, it would seem, to a certain amount of condensation and omission, and there are traces of both in Part I.

The clearest signs of condensation are probably in the extant opening scene. To begin with, after Henry has announced his determination 'forthwith' to levy 'a power of English' to march 'as far as to the sepulchre of Christ', there is a bit of clumsy patching in lines 28–30, where he explains that 'this our purpose now is twelve months old' and does not need to be proclaimed. This is followed by Westmoreland's supererogatory report of the previous night's council meeting, at which the king must be assumed to have been present and where the plans for a crusade were already interrupted, as we now learn, by news of Mortimer's defeat in Wales and of a big battle in progress at Holmedon. Next, without a transition, the king has suddenly had news of the outcome of the battle and has even had time to send for Hotspur, who is to answer for his refusal to yield up prisoners. It is hard to defend this huddling of events as a legitimate method of exposition. A better explanation could be that the original draft began with a council scene in which the crusade was announced much as it is now, and that this was interrupted by a series of messages from the two battle-fronts which were later digested into Westmoreland's expository report in order to save acting time. In the original version the king might also have had an opportunity to take in Sir Walter Blunt's news and to send for Hotspur.

The omitted matter may have included a scene in which the Lord Chief Justice sends for Falstaff, and another, or the same, in which Prince Hal delivers the famous blow on the Justice's ear. In *2 Henry IV* (I.ii) we learn that the Lord Chief Justice sent his summons to Falstaff before the latter's expedition to Shrewsbury, which of course belongs to Part I, and that Falstaff refused to come. We also learn, or can infer, that Bardolph for an unspecified reason was had up before the Justice, that Hal on that occasion forgot himself so far as to strike the Justice in his 'very seat of judgment' and that he was consequently rebuked and committed to prison. This must also have happened before Shrewsbury, else it would coincide with the prince's absence in Wales. The omission from the extant Part I of these suggested scenes showing the summoning of Falstaff and the scuffle in court undoubtedly robs the final rejection of the unruly knight as well as Hal's reconciliation with the Lord Chief Justice of some of their over-tones.[20]

In any case, what chiefly protracted the action and made it impossible to contain it within the normal length of a play must have been the comic subplot. There is no such subplot in *Richard II*, unless one wishes to see York as a Polonius and the revelation of Aumerle's conspiracy as comic relief. In *Richard II* Shakespeare was lured by poetry and may have chosen to leave out some of the action rather than lengthen the play. In *Henry IV* he was seduced by humour. As soon as Falstaff shaped himself in his imagination he was himself obviously a captive to his invention. Having made the most of the Gadshill episode, in which he dramatised a highway robbery, he must next send his hero to Shrewsbury. And since Hal by the king's orders was to march through Gloucestershire, so must Falstaff, there to press soldiers for his charge of foot. So we have his meeting with Justice Shallow and the conjunction of two of Shakespeare's most marvellous comic characters. The meeting must undoubtedly have been designed as part of a single Henry IV play and could only belong to the Shrewsbury plot. Shallow is not necessarily a Gloucestershire man in the recruiting scene as we now have it, but this may be the result of adaptation,[21] and he is definitely a Gloucestershire justice both at the end of *2 Henry IV* and in *The Merry Wives of Windsor*, where he reappears. As such he could have nothing to do with preparations for the Gaultree Forest campaign. One may at a pinch suppose Falstaff going *from* York to London by way of Gloucestershire in order to call on an old acquaintance, but he would hardly make a long detour to recruit in western England on his way to a battle about to be fought in the north. Moreover, the Falstaff who turns up with Corporal Bardolph at Shallow's house to press a few ragged wretches into the king's service is not the prestigious post-Shrewsbury commander of Part II whom 'a dozen captains stay at door for'. I see no special signs of 'the deference with which Justice Shallow receives him and his man Bardolph' which Dover Wilson discovers.[22] Nor can I agree with Derek Traversi that the Shallow episodes characteristically belong to Part II in their emphasis on age and decline.[23] Falstaff is old already in *1 Henry IV*, and his age is amply insisted on in the mock examination in II.iv, in fact it is given quite precisely: 'inclining to threescore' (l.419). This Falstaff definitely belongs in Part I. Shadow, Wart, and Feeble are so obviously examples of the scarecrows collected by Falstaff for his Shrewsbury command and described in his soliloquy in Part I, IV.ii, that it is natural to see them as belonging to the company which he refuses for very shame to march through Coventry and who are criticised by the prince and Westmoreland on the same occasion as 'pitiful rascals', 'exceeding poor and bare, too beggarly'. There would be little point in repeating the pitiful rascals theme in two separately planned plays.[24] It should be noticed, too, that Falstaff arrives in Gaultree Forest without any soldiers, having, at least by his own account, ridden post from London. So the recruiting scene in *2 Henry IV* rightly belonged with the Coventry scene in *1 Henry IV*.

The remainder of the first Shallow scene as well as the second, third, and last may be naturally explained as expansions and extensions for use in Part II. There is a fault in the recruiting scene at the point where Falstaff has 'pricked' his four champions and says he 'cannot tarry dinner'. He then goes to dinner while Bardolph takes bribes to free two of the men. Subsequently the choosing starts all over again, when Falstaff asks 'which men shall I have?' and Shallow suggests the very four who have already been pricked. In the beginning of the scene (III.ii.24–5) Shallow tells Silence that Falstaff was only a boy when he himself was a student at Clement's Inn, but just before the dinner break he speaks as though they were of an age and companions in revelry (ll.189–213).[25] In the second and third Shallow scenes a new person appears, who is important enough to make us wonder why he is not present in the recruiting scene. This is Justice Shallow's factotum Davy, who, as Falstaff observes, is both his servingman and his husband. His name is once repeated five times in a line. He was obviously not thought of till new Shallow scenes were invented for Part II.

That the partial overlapping of Parts I and II is not a question of parallelism, as some critics maintain, but of division, is further borne out by clear signs of textual disturbance in places where there is also episodic repetition. In *1 Henry IV*, III.iii the prince orders Bardolph, who is Falstaff's servant, not his, to carry letters to Prince John and the Earl of Westmoreland, both of whom were on their way to Shrewsbury in the previous scene (III.ii.170–1). The lines are very irregular if they are meant to be verse, and John is mentioned twice:

> Go bear this letter to Lord John of Lancaster,
> To my brother John, this to my Lord of Westmoreland.
> (III.iii.194–5)

The prince then orders Peto to horse, 'for thou and I / Have thirty miles to ride yet ere dinner-time'. Hal has appeared with Peto instead of Poins as his special companion once before,[26] but Peto is Falstaff's lieutenant in IV.ii.9 and his association with the prince is confusing. The thirty miles can only be understood as the first stage on the road to Shrewsbury. In spite of this the prince tells Falstaff to meet him next day in London, in the Temple hall 'at two o'clock in the afternoon'. There he shall know his charge, although the prince has just revealed that he has procured him a charge of foot. Now if we turn to *2 Henry IV*, I.ii.239–41, we there find Falstaff, about to set out for York and in need of cash, ordering his page, in words almost identical with those of Hal in the first part, to carry letters to the same recipients plus the prince:[27]

> Go bear this letter to my Lord of Lancaster; this to the
> Prince; this to the Earl of Westmoreland;

Once more Lancaster and Westmoreland must be already on their way to the scene of battle (see I.i.132–5). The letter to the prince is delivered in II.ii, but apparently by Bardolph instead of the page, though the page is present. As for Peto, he makes an anomalous appearance in *2 Henry IV* (II.iv.351ff) as a bringer of news from Westminster which fits in with his unlikely appearance as the prince's companion in *1 Henry IV*. It is hardly probable that these similarities between Parts I and II, riddled and surrounded by confusions as they are, represent deliberate parallelism in the two plays. They are more probably the results of carelessness in excerpting material from a one-play version for use in a new context, and of patching up the resultant gaps.

The uncertainty about the time of King Henry's and Prince Hal's return from Wales may be an indication that Shakespeare had a lot of material to arrange in designing his second part. In I.ii Falstaff has heard that 'his Majesty is returned with some discomfort from Wales' (ll.102–3), and at the end of the same scene he dispatches his letter to the prince on the obvious assumption that he is back in London. Bardolph delivers the note in II.ii with the words, 'He heard of your Grace's coming to town – there's a letter for you' (ll.94–5). But in II.i Gower informs the Chief Justice that the king and the prince 'are near at hand', i.e. still on their way, and Falstaff asks in apparent ignorance, 'Comes the King back from Wales, my noble lord?' (ll.133–4, 172). Finally, at the end of II.ii, the prince, having received and read Falstaff's communication, instructs the page and Bardolph to make a secret of what Falstaff already knows: 'no word to your master that I am yet come to town (ll.153–4). One may hazard the guess that Shakespeare wrote the two almost contiguous confrontation scenes between Falstaff and the Lord Chief Justice as alternative versions and intended to keep only one of them, but it would probably be impossible to say which he meant to use. He may have decided to keep them both without seeing the minor contradictions this would involve. The contradiction in the Bardolph scene could be linked with the irregularities, including Bardolph's appearance as the messenger, attending the whole business of the letters.

Apparently some material which may have been planned for the original *Henry IV* also found its way into *The Merry Wives of Windsor*. As Falstaff comes away from Shallow's house in *2 Henry IV*, with or without Shallow's dinner in his belly, he is in a derisive mood about the old justice's boasting of the wildness of his youth and works himself into a state of combined vindictiveness and rapacity:

> Well, I'll be acquainted with him if I return, and't shall go hard but I'll make him a philosopher's two stones to me. If the young dace be a bait for the old pike, I see no reason in the law of nature but I may snap at him: let time shape, and there an end. (III.ii.322–7)

After the rebels have been tricked and routed in Gaultree Forest he obtains leave to return through Gloucestershire in order to visit Master Robert Shallow, Esquire. He now sounds pretty confident:

> I have him already tempering between my finger and my thumb, and shortly will I seal with him. (IV.iii.128–9)

We are now quite prepared for a frontal attack on Shallow's purse, and perhaps even a quarrel, on Falstaff's return to the justice's estate. In the event there is, surprisingly, nothing of the sort, though we learn later that Falstaff has got his thousand pounds. Nor is there any unfriendliness in the second and third Shallow scenes, except that Falstaff is satirical of his host behind his back and promises to 'devise matter' out of him for the amusement of the prince. But in the beginning of *The Merry Wives* Shallow incongruously turns up at Windsor and demands reparation of Falstaff for breaking open his lodge, killing his deer, and beating his men. Falstaff unabashedly admits to all this and defies Shallow to do his worst: he will only be laughed at. The quarrel is then patched up, we must assume, by Master Page, who invites everyone to dinner. It has no further importance in *The Merry Wives*, and Shallow has no significant function in the remainder of the play. Once more expectations remain unfulfilled. To explain why they are aroused in the opening scene of *The Merry Wives* is largely guesswork, but it is not unreasonable to suspect that this scene contains matter left over from *Henry IV* which Shakespeare was too thrifty to waste.

To fill in the action of Part II of *Henry IV*, Shakespeare chiefly added new Falstaff material, so that the second part became much more a Falstaff than a King Henry play. The blustering knight's encounters with the Lord Chief Justice help to provide a central theme of law, incidentally helping, too, to integrate Justice Shallow into this new setting. But Falstaff's new grand manner and continued impecuniosity and his attempts to remedy his need of money by borrowing from all and sundry – highway robbery now being out of the question – is a more important plot element. We meet him in the second scene of the play attended by a page, having consulted a doctor, ordered satin for a fashionable short cloak and 'slops', and sent Bardolph to buy a horse. He tries to touch the Lord Chief Justice for a thousand pounds, then sends letters presumably with a similar purpose to Prince Henry, Prince John, the Earl of Westmoreland, and Mistress Ursula, wheedles Mistress Quickly into not only remitting his old debts but providing a new loan, and at the end of the play has obviously been successful in getting his thousand pounds from Justice Swallow. It is all the more remarkable that we do not actually see him squeezing Shallow. In addition, his association with Mistress Quickly and Doll Tearsheet expose him as a lecher as well as a coward, braggart, and drunkard. Along with Doll Tearsheet, Ancient Pistol is introduced as a new humorous character. He was successful enough to be included with the king, the prince, and Falstaff on the title page of the printed quarto.

One consequence of continuing the Falstaff antics was involving the prince in further familiarity with his disreputable companions. In Part I he was reconciled to his father and redeemed his compromised royalty by his courage and gallantry at Shrewsbury, climbing suddenly to a peak of glory by overcoming his rival Harry Percy. Now he relapses into his old ways. Not entirely, since he is more an observer of Falstaff's debauchery than a participant in it, but sufficiently to give an impression of renewed wildness. It is in Part II that we hear of Hal's hitting the Lord Chief Justice in court (I.ii.55–6); and, significantly, Clarence thinks the Justice 'must now speak Sir John Falstaff fair' after King Henry's death (v.ii.33). According to Bullough, Shakespeare cannot be held alone responsible for the obvious breach of consistency: 'the Chronicles suggested that the Prince's behaviour was inconsistent and declined after Shrewsbury.' But one would expect an awareness of this inconsistency in the play if the dramatist actually meant to show a relapse from reform to licence, and there is no such awareness. This does not matter if we choose to see *2 Henry IV* as an independent play. There is a sound enough plot in the transformation of a prince from a haunter of taverns to an ideal heir of the realm even if it occurs for the second time. But it would have been impossible then and it is scarcely possible now to consider *2 Henry IV* apart from *1 Henry IV*.[28] Nor is there consistency, even within Part II, in the king's attitude to Hal. As the action begins, they have been fighting in Wales together, but there are no details of this campaign and we learn nothing about the relationship between father and son during the expedition. We can only assume that the confidence and admiration established at Shrewsbury continue. When we actually see the king, which is not till the first scene of Act III, he is greatly worried about the state of the kingdom and the threat from Northumberland but oddly makes no mention of his son who has proved himself such a doughty champion. Next time King Henry appears, in IV.iv, when he is already on his deathbed, he begins by praising Harry to his brother Thomas of Clarence:

> For he is gracious, if he be observ'd,
> He hath a tear of pity, and a hand
> Open as day for melting charity:
> Yet not withstanding, being incens'd, he's flint,   (ll.30–3)

Then abruptly he switches to the deepest despondency in his view of the prince and of the future of England when Harry will be king:

> The blood weeps from my heart when I do shape
> In forms imaginary th'unguided days
> And rotten times that you shall look upon   (ll.58–60)

It is in this mood that Harry finds him when he returns with the crown.

It is the mood which is needed for the dramatic conflict and resolution at the end of the play.[29] But it does not at all agree with the optimistic description of the prince to Clarence, and in fact that passage shows signs of being interpolated, perhaps after being transferred from a different context, in that it is both preceded and followed by similar questions as to the whereabouts of Harry and why Clarence is not with him. It also introduces a subject which remains entirely irrelevant both in *Henry IV* and *Henry V*: that of Clarence acting as a mediator between his brothers, who might otherwise fall out. Nothing in this play or the next bears out the king's seeming prophecy of dissension among the brothers, and Clarence nowhere performs the function which is here assigned to him. He does not appear in *Henry IV* before the deathbed scene and has no speaking part in *Henry V*.[30] Perhaps Shakespeare at one time planned to make him more important. As it is, the Clarence scene may indicate a stage of vacillation in the final shaping of the play, particularly as regards King Henry's attitude to Hal. It may have represented the relationship between the two after Shrewsbury in a one-play *Henry IV*. But it is hard to think it was meant to be finally included in the two-part treatment of the father-and-son theme.

The other new material that was introduced into *2 Henry IV* concerned the rising in the north. This is barren and unpleasant stuff involving deceit and butchery in place of the heroism of Part I. It also employs only secondary characters, apart from Falstaff. But some military activity there obviously had to be if the play was to remain a history and since we are still in 'the unquiet time of King Henry the Fourth'. It is not inconceivable that Shakespeare initially thought of doing something with the expedition against Glendower and Mortimer which is proclaimed at the end of *1 Henry IV*, and then found too little to build an interesting action on. We are left with news of the king and the prince – one ill, the other 'exceeding weary' – returning from what we gather to have been an unsuccessful incursion into Wales, and with the comforting information imparted to the king some time later that Glendower is dead. It more clearly looks as if he intended to use Northumberland in some striking and significant action – one of the components of the 'integrated double action' which Harold Jenkins finds in Part I but not in Part II.[31] Northumberland is a prominent and active character in *Richard II*, where he partly displaces Holinshed's Archbishop of Canterbury, and Richard utters a prophecy against him and Bolingbroke which is remembered by the latter in *2 Henry IV*. But his part in subsequent events is mainly negative. He is too ill (or 'crafty-sick' according to Rumour) to come to the aid of his son at Shrewsbury and prefers discretion to valour when the Archbishop of York takes the field with Mowbray and Hastings. Nevertheless, *2 Henry IV*, after Rumour's induction, opens with a long scene featuring Northumberland as the recipient of conflicting battle news, and at the end of the scene apparently deciding to throw in his lot with the archbishop. If this scene was meant to introduce Northumberland as an important actor in a new play it would serve a natural dramatic purpose. As it is, it simply contains matter which spills over from the first part. Northumberland remains remarkable mainly for his absences. He comes on stage once more, when he is dissuaded by his daughter-in-law, Hotspur's widow – of all people – from risking his life. Then he is not seen again. But from the concluding speech of *1 Henry IV* on there is frequent talk on the king's side of Northumberland being 'busily in arms' along with 'the prelate Scroop'. Thus the Lord Chief Justice tells Falstaff, 'I hear you are going with Lord John of Lancaster, against the Archbishop and the Earl of Northumberland', and Gower has information that

> fifteen hundred foot, five hundred horse
> Are march'd up to my Lord of Lancaster,
> Against Northumberland and the Archbishop.
>
>   (ii.i.169–71)

The king's conversation with Warwick in iii.i is chiefly about Northumberland, whom he sees as the greatest threat to his state.[32] He has heard that 'the Bishop and Northumberland / Are fifty thousand strong' (ll.95–6). Whether all this was meant to indicate that the king's side are misinformed about the state of affairs on the other side, or that a more active role was being prepared for the shifty earl, is hard to say. The fact remains that the last we hear of him after his remarkable discretion at York is the brief report, brought to the dying king in iv.iv, that

> The Earl of Northumberland and the Lord Bardolph,
> With a great power of English and of Scots,
> Are by the shrieve of Yorkshire overthrown.   (ll.98–100)[33]

After so much expectation so little fulfilment. It is possible, it is true, to find a significance in Northumberland's very ineffectiveness which gives it a dramatic colour. Derek Traversi, interpreting his role largely in a symbolical sense, sees it as a comment 'upon the universal implications of sedition'.[34] Shakespeare, too, may have found comfort in seeing it in this way after finishing his play, and who knows what subconscious artistic impulses helped him to body forth his character? But his surface intentions were evidently for a more stirring presentation of Henry's one-time friend and now chief adversary. As it is, Northumberland plays a part in the beginning of *2 Henry IV* which is structurally not unlike the parts played by the Duke of Gloucester in the beginning of *Richard II* and by the absent Mortimer in the beginning of *1 Henry IV*. And I think we may add Justice Shallow in *The Merry Wives*.

Perhaps it was impossible to do more with Northumberland than keep him hovering in the background as a threat to the king's peace and a reminder of the 'by-paths and indirect crook'd ways' by which Bolingbroke met his crown. But in any case he would have been pushed aside by the tide of inspiration which carried the comic scenes to the centre of this history play. In fact in both the *Henry IV* plays the emergence of inspiration during the process of composition seems to have been particularly disruptive. Many of the structural weaknesses seem to be due to a yeasting of material which necessitated a division into two plays where one would have given a firmer plot (though not necessarily a better plot, all things considered). King Henry's crusading plans remain unfulfilled until the end of Part II, when he dies symbolically in the Jerusalem chamber, and in a sense until the climactic events of *Henry V*, as we shall see. Hal's definitive reformation and his rejection of his loose companions − as well as his succession − are likewise deferred to the end of the second part, making his fall from grace and loss of the king's confidence an unexpected interlude. The prince seems surprisingly inactive in the second part after his energetic activities in the first, especially since he has no share in the military operations that we witness. Only the disappointed expectations attending Mortimer cannot be easily explained by the expansion of the play's material. His prominence, in person or by proxy, during the expository phases of *1 Henry IV*, and the important role he is made ready for, create a sense of disproportion when our expectations fail to materialise, and make us suspect not just rearrangement but substantial changes in Shakespeare's plotting.

One person more than lives up to the expectations he arouses: Sir John Falstaff. His appearance at Gaultree is an anticlimax, especially if we have Shrewsbury in mind, and we never actually see him closing with Shallow. Nor do we ever witness his reformation. But he so abundantly imposes his presence that the scene of his rejection makes a natural climactic ending not only to the second part of *Henry IV* but to the two parts combined. He so abundantly infects us with his fatuous optimism that most of us are shocked at the roughness of the rejection although we should have been sufficiently forewarned. It is often pointed out that there is an increasing severity in the prince's treatment of Falstaff in the second part as compared to the first. But Hal is nowhere more brutal than in the mock banishment in Part I:

Why dost thou converse with that trunk of humours, that bolting-hutch of beastliness, that swollen parcel of dropsies, that huge bombard of sack, that stuffed cloak-bag of guts, that roasted Manningtree ox with the pudding in his belly, that reverend vice, that grey iniquity, that father ruffian, that vanity in years?   (II.iv.442–9)

Mockery here becomes deadly serious and brings out an almost over-whelming pathos in Falstaff's reply. We understand him perfectly when he urges, 'banish plump Jack, and banish all the world'. But the prince is tight-lipped: 'I do, I will.' If we have forgotten this by the time the coronation procession of Henry V passes through the streets of West-minster the fault is partly ours, but not altogether. So much matter has intervened which cannot have been contemplated when the first rejection was penned, but which has kept us excited, moved, and amused.

8 The Disunity of *King Henry V*

King Henry V, it seems to be generally agreed, 'was almost certainly written in the spring or summer of 1599'. The main evidence is the allusion to the Earl of Essex's expedition into Ireland contained in the chorus before the fifth act. Essex 'left London on 27 March 1599 and returned on 28 September in the same year having failed in his task'.[1] The allusion to Essex, however, only proves that the lines containing it, and possibly the whole chorus, were written in the spring or summer of 1599. It tells us nothing about the dating of the rest of the play, some of which could theoretically have been composed much earlier. There is good reason to believe that the 'wooden O' referred to in the prologue is the new Globe theatre and not the Curtain.[2] The Globe may not have been completed till August or September 1599 but it must have been going up in the early summer, and if Shakespeare was giving final shape to a play at that time it would be natural for him to anticipate its effect in the new theatre. So the prologue, too, may be a late addition, supposing *Henry V* was first begun soon after the completion of *2 Henry IV*, i.e. possibly as early as 1597.

That *Henry V* was not all written at one time has long been recognised, though as far as revised and additional matter is concerned suspicion has almost exclusively focused on the comic subplot, especially the Eastcheap scenes, which contradict the chorus's initial announcement of a general removal to Southampton.[3] It is time now to see that the 'faults' of the play reveal a much more extensive stratification. There are structural anomalies both in the main plot, the comic underplot, and the choruses.

The French campaign which furnishes the major part of the action is foretold at the end of *2 Henry IV*, but it is not quite clear whether it has been finally decided on as the trumpet sounds for the beginning of *Henry V*. The most prominent character in the two scenes which make up the first act is the Archbishop of Canterbury, who does not reappear in the remainder of the play. In the first scene he confides to the Bishop of Ely that he has offered the king a large bribe to side with the clergy against the 'exhibitors' of the bill for the expropriation of church property.

The ostensible purpose was to aid the king 'in regard of causes now in hand. . . . As touching France'. Obviously Harry is already engaged in preparation for a war. Obviously, too, he has already sent into France to press his territorial claims, as we definitely learn at 1.ii.246 from the mouth of the French ambassador. He is now expecting the French king's answer, which Canterbury thinks he 'could with a ready guess declare / Before the Frenchman speak a word of it' (1.i.96–7). But Canterbury also informs the Bishop of Ely that he was about to expound to King Henry

> The severals and unhidden passages
> Of his true titles to some certain dukedoms,
> And generally to the crown and seat of France,
> Deriv'd from Edward, his great-grandfather   (1.i.86–9)

when they were interrupted by the arrival of the French ambassador, who 'upon that instant / Crav'd audience'.

In the next scene we are surprised, or should be, to find that the French ambassador is nevertheless kept waiting while the archbishop delivers a long peroration on the Salic law, explaining in detail why it does not apply to the realm of France and showing that the French kings always ignored it anyway. And he does more than that. He persuades a hesitant Henry to decide for war even before he has heard King Charles's answer to his demands. Then he again offers the bribe as if it has not been offered already, in words which almost repeat those which he employed when speaking to the Bishop of Ely. There is some debate as to whether Scotland or France should be attacked first. There is Canterbury's fable of the bees. The king finally declares that he is 'well resolv'd'. Only then is the French mission called in and proves to be, not King Charles's ambassador, but 'messengers sent from the Dauphin'. 'For we hear,' says Harry, 'Your greeting is from him, not from the king' (1.ii.235–6). In his interview with these messengers he finds no use whatever for the legal briefing he has just received. He does in passing refer to 'my throne of France' and in five lines appeals to the will of God and speaks of putting forth his 'rightful hand in a well-hallow'd cause' (ll.289–93). But apart from this there is nothing in his answer to the Dauphin's messengers to indicate that he is thinking of his legal title. On the contrary, the Dauphin's insult provides him with a totally different motive for war both from that suggested by his father at the end of *2 Henry IV* – 'to busy giddy minds with foreign quarrels' – and from that supported by the bishops. It is now a question of revenge:

And tell the pleasant prince this mock of his
Hath turn'd his balls to gun-stones; and his soul
Shall stand sore charged for the wasteful vengeance
That shall fly with them: for many a thousand widows
Shall this his mock mock out of their dear husbands;
Mock mothers from their sons, mock castles down;
And some are yet ungotten and unborn
That shall have cause to curse the Dauphin's scorn.

(ll.281–8)

This does not mean that the argument from right of descent has been forgotten for good. When Exeter goes as ambassador to the King of France in II.iv it is precisely this right that he urges, and he even brings a written pedigree so that King Charles may be convinced of Henry's being 'evenly deriv'd' from Isabella's son Edward III.

What *is* forgotten as the play proceeds is the Dauphin's insult. There is one reminder of it, in the special message which Exeter has for the Dauphin in II.iv, but that is all. What is more, there is no hint of the particular antagonism which we might legitimately expect to find between King Henry and the Dauphin, and they are never brought face to face. We are told of Harry's encounter with Alençon[4] but of none with the French prince. In fact the latter plays an increasingly inconspicuous part. We may suppose him to be the *de facto* ruler of France as we listen to his messengers insulting the King of England, and again when Harfleur capitulates because the Dauphin cannot relieve the town. Indeed Holinshed points out that the Dauphin occasionally had 'the governance of the realme' because of his father's 'disease of frensie'.[5] But Shakespeare makes no mention of King Charles's disease, and contrary to Holinshed's account puts the king rather than the Dauphin firmly in charge of the French preparations for defence. He even (here following the chronicles) makes Charles order the Dauphin to stay in Rouen as the French get ready for their main battle against the English (III.v.64–6). In spite of this the Dauphin in the Folio version of Shakespeare's play takes part in the fighting; but it is the Lord High Constable, not he, who is in command, and the Dauphin's most sustained contribution to the dialogue is his fatuous praise of his horse. After the battle he vanishes without a trace as far as the play is concerned, and he does not take part in the meeting of royalty and nobility in the last act. So much for Harry's 'chid[ing] this Dauphin at his father's door' (I.ii.308).

There may not be one explanation to cover all these anomalies. But a great deal can be explained if we suppose that Shakespeare made fairly extensive alterations after writing the first draft of his play. In that draft it is reasonable to suppose that he stayed closer to *The Famous Victories of Henry the fifth* than he did in his final manuscript. *The Famous Victories* was registered for printing as early as 1594 and Shakespeare would have seen it on the stage. For that matter he may have read the authentic playbook before the debased and obviously fragmentary text was published in 1598. Even that corrupt version is enough to show that he followed its main plot outline.

In *The Famous Victories* Harry sends the Duke of York on an embassy to France immediately on his succession. The embassy is expressly for the King of France and to claim the crown of France. It is 'Jockey', or Oldcastle, who informs us of this:

> Did you not see with what grace
> He sent his embassage into *France*? to tel the French king
> That *Harry* of England hath sent for the Crowne,
> And *Harry* of England wil have it.[6]

When Harry asks the Archbishop of Canterbury his opinion of this 'embassage into France' the latter in a relatively short speech explains the king's right to the French crown, guesses King Charles's answer, urges King Henry to 'take [his] sword in hand, / And conquer the right', and assures him that his 'Country men are willing with purse and men' to aid him. York returns, followed by the Archbishop of Bourges, who comes from the French king to reject Harry's claim to the crown and to offer him instead a sum of money with the Lady Katharine in marriage. The French ambassador is *also* charged with a commission from the Dauphin (and in this connection refers to himself as 'a messenger'): the presentation of the tennis balls. Harry at once promises war and destruction. There follow an episode in which the Lord Chief Justice is assured of the new king's favour and one in which three clowns are pressed for soldiers, whereupon we move to the court of France, where the king presides over his council. The Archbishop of Bourges returns to report his unsuccess and to say that Harry 'is alreadie landed' in France. He *then*, on the Dauphin's enquiry, describes Harry's reaction to the mockery of the tennis balls. King Charles forbids his son to take part in the fighting, and Harry looks for him in vain at Agincourt. There is this exchange between Harry and the French herald:

> HEN. 5 But I pray thee what place hath my lord Prince *Dolphin*
> Here in battell.
> HERALD And it please your grace,

My Lord and King his father,
Will not let him come into the field.
   HEN. 5 Why then he doth me great injurie,
I thought that he & I shuld have plaid at tennis togither,[7]

and so on, for another eight lines of threats to the Dauphin.

This plot differs from the underlying accounts of Henry V's reign given by Hall and Holinshed in a number of ways which show that Shakespeare borrowed his sequence of events from *The Famous Victories*. Neither Hall nor Holinshed says anything about an English mission to France *before* the parliament in which the Archbishop of Canterbury plays such a decisive part. Consequently neither reports an answer from the French before the Duke of Exeter has been dispatched to make King Henry's claim known to the King of France. In both accounts Exeter is received by King Charles before Henry has embarked on his invasion. Both Hall and Holinshed describe one formal embassy from France to England, after war has been decided on but before hostilities have commenced. This embassy is led by the Archbishop of Bourges, who tries in vain to appease King Henry by offering him an annual grant of money and the Lady Katharine in marriage. Bourges is sent by the Dauphin, but his mission has nothing to do with tennis balls. Shakespeare refers to it only in the chorus before Harfleur.

In practically all these matters Shakespeare uniquely agrees with *The Famous Victories*. Assuming, then, that he initially followed the earlier play in outlining his action, he must have changed his plans, first to accommodate the Archbishop of Canterbury's long perorations and exhortations, and secondly to bring the Dauphin more into the foreground. The detailed disquisition on the Salic law and the genealogies of the French kings contained in I.ii was lifted straight from Holinshed, who clearly made the archbishop put the idea of war into Henry's head; just as that dignitary virtually does in the second scene of Shakespeare's play, thus contradicting the first scene, where preparations for war are already in progress. Perhaps the author meant to cancel the first scene, or at least its conclusion, since it also anticipates the bribe which Canterbury offers to Harry in Scene ii. Why he should prefer the longwinded casuistry of the archbishop to the dramatic compactness of the conversation between Canterbury and Ely seems puzzling to us today. But the opening scene of the Folio, that of the two bishops, is altogether omitted in the quarto text, and whatever else the begetters of that text may have forgotten one would expect them to remember how the play began on the stage.[8] On the other hand, the exposition of the Salic law and the business which follows are relatively intact in the quarto, so it was indubitably used in performance. We can only conclude that there was a livelier historical interest in the English sovereign's title to the French crown then than there is now and that it was activated by uncertainty as to the prospects and intentions of France's Henri IV. Queen Elizabeth was continually feeding the French king with driblets of men and money and had not quite given up her hopes of restoring at least Calais to English rule. Interest in the French monarchy could certainly be counted on in the court circles for whom the second scene of Shakespeare's play may have been principally devised.[9]

As for the Dauphin, Shakespeare may have felt that the play lacked colour as originally designed, and if we may judge by the rather wooden scene of Exeter's embassy to King Charles this may well have been the case. The highlighting of the episode of the tennis balls, which in itself must have seemed especially attractive, and the general forefronting of the quarrel between Harry and the Dauphin, would make it all more temperamental. Not that the Dauphin could be turned into another Hotspur, but he might still be made to serve as a foil to Harry. English audiences were used to seeing the Dauphin as the arch-enemy, and if Shakespeare had in mind any sequential performance of *Henry V* and *1 Henry VI*, as the final chorus of the former play could be taken to indicate, it would be useful to make the Dauphin fairly conspicuous in both. Then, too, there was Hall's suggestion that the famous tennis balls might have precipitated the war. While Holinshed separates this incident from the dynastic conflict by placing it in the first year of Henry's reign, Hall places it immediately after the return of Exeter from his embassy to King Charles and says that 'Whether he wer moued with this unwise presente, or espiying that the Frenchemen dalied and vaynely delayed his purpose and demaund,' King Henry at this time 'determined fully to make warre in Fraunce' (Fol.xliv). Whatever King Henry's motives, Shakespeare scrapped the French king's ambassador whom he found in *The Famous Victories* to make way for the messengers from the Dauphin. In so doing he limited Harry's initial territorial claim (as referred to by the messengers) to 'some certain dukedoms', a moderation for which he had no authority in his sources but which enabled him to escalate the conflict when Harry's anger was roused.[10] Equally without warrant or precedent he introduced the Dauphin into the Agincourt scenes, to be put to shame in the ignominious defeat of the French. But these changes were not effected without leaving traces of the original plotting. Thus there are reminders of the French king's embassy not only in the Archbishop of Canterbury's anticipation of its import (even he could hardly have guessed the Dauphin's message) but still more clearly in the French Lord

High Constable's later description of how the ambassadors (now in the plural) were received by Henry:

> With what great state he heard their embassy,
> How well supplied with noble counsellors,
> How modest in exception, and withal
> How terrible in constant resolution.   (II.iv.32–5)

This is no description of the fury provoked by the Dauphin's insult, and there is not a word here of tennis balls. It is the original reception of King Charles's, not the Dauphin's, ambassadors that Shakespeare follows up with Exeter's mission to the French king, when Henry's legal right is maintained and his genealogy presented.[11] There is purely verbal evidence of revision as well. In Shakespeare's final version as we have it in the Folio, King Henry listens with remarkable patience to the archbishop and his other counsellors and then declares:

> Now are we well resolv'd; and by God's help,
> And yours, the noble sinews of our power,
> France being ours, we'll bend it to our awe
> Or break it all to pieces   (I.ii.222–5)

On the entry of the Dauphin's messengers immediately after the remainder of this speech he begins again: 'Now are we well prepar'd to know the pleasure / Of our fair cousin Dauphin.' The near-repetition of the opening formula is an example of the loops in the dialogue mentioned in my opening chapter (p. 10), often found in places where the text seems to have been disturbed, usually by interpolation. In this case it seems possible that the first speech, 'Now are we well resolv'd . . .' down to line 233, was to have preceded the entry of the French king's ambassador and really became superfluous when the Dauphin's mission was substituted for Charles's. In the scene of Exeter's embassy to France there is a similar repetition. Having heard King Henry's message to himself, King Charles tells Exeter, 'To-morrow shall you bear our full intent / Back to our brother England.' There follows Henry's special message to the Dauphin, at the conclusion of which King Charles again declares, 'To-morrow shall you know our mind at full', this time eliciting an expression of impatience from Exeter. The evidence strongly suggests that the greeting to the Dauphin, which is in reply to his gift of tennis balls, was interpolated into an already completed scene in which Exeter's errand was for King Charles only.

Like *The Famous Victories*, Shakespeare probably kept the Dauphin away from Agincourt in his first version of the play and may even have copied his predecessor in letting Henry enquire after his insulting challenger on the battlefield. Both the surviving texts of Shakespeare's *Henry V* have retained King Charles's peremptory order to his son to stay in Rouen (III.v.64–6). In the quarto the Dauphin apparently obeys, at least he does not appear in the Agincourt scenes. Instead it is the Duke of Bourbon who rhapsodises about his horse and who after his first exit is maligned by the Constable for his cowardice. In the Folio text the Dauphin is present at Agincourt. The Duke of Bourbon has only two short speeches besides a silent appearance as a prisoner, but his two bursts of speech in IV.v make him conspicuous enough – daring the other lords to follow him in a last desperate sally – to make us wonder why we have not seen him before. It is tempting to suppose that the quarto has somehow preserved the original casting and that Bourbon was partly replaced by the Dauphin when Shakespeare decided to give the latter a larger share in the action. It may not be entirely irrelevant to observe that the man who was crowned King of France in 1594 was a Bourbon. Shakespeare could hardly avoid having Henri IV sometimes in his thoughts as he wrote a play about a soldier-king and battles in France; and the quarrel between the Constable and Orleans about the Dauphin's (or Bourbon's) valour in III.vii possibly reflects the divided opinions of both Englishmen and Frenchmen concerning Henri IV. (Orleans' oath, 'By the white hand of my lady, he's a gallant prince', and the Constable's bawdy retort, 'Doing is activity, and he will still be doing', may even be an allusion to the amorous propensities of a king who was known as 'le Vert-galant'.) Altogether, the quarto's retention of Bourbon, which may safely be taken to represent stage practice, probably indicates that there was some indecision, either on Shakespeare's part or on that of the players, attending the expansion of the Dauphin's role in the play.

To turn to the underplot, if indeed it amounts to that in *Henry V* as we know it, there can be no doubt that the death of Falstaff, however movingly described, has no real business in the beginning of the play. It is an isolated extension of *2 Henry IV* and was to all appearances included only because the author had rashly promised in an epilogue to continue his story 'with Sir John in it' and then found no real need for him. Why the Eastcheap scenes should come after the chorus has announced our presence in Southampton and so necessitate two temporary transfers back to London is another problem which has not been finally solved. As for the rogues who now appear in those scenes, Bardolph and Pistol are recognisable as the swashbucklers we have already met in *2 Henry IV*, but Nym featured only in *The Merry Wives* before he came into *Henry V*, and we have hardly been prepared for his broken betrothal to Mistress Quickly or for the marriage of the hostess and Pistol.[12] Bardolph and Nym are quickly despatched once we have seen them briefly in inaction at Harfleur, and though we are given a reason for Bardolph's hanging, there is no advance notice of Nym's. Pistol, as befits his new role of innkeeper, is to be sutler to the camp (II.i.111–12), but we nevertheless find him with the foot soldiers at Harfleur and Agincourt. His behaviour on both occasions is sufficiently in character, but his capture of Monsieur le Fer parallels Falstaff's seizure of Coleville in Gaultree Forest. And it is Falstaff, not Pistol, who has enjoyed the favours of Doll Tearsheet to our certain knowledge and so would be the more likely to lament her demise, as Pistol does in v.i.[13]

A number of critics, from Duthie and Dover Wilson on, find evidence in the le Fer incident and the lament for Doll that some of the part now belonging to Pistol was designed for Falstaff.[14] Thus J. H. Walter simply declares that 'Falstaff, true to his form in *1* and *2 Henry IV*, captured M. le Fer and in v.i was humiliated by Fluellen'. He also points out the reference to the speaker's age in the Doll speech in v.i. 'So far,' he says, 'there has been no reference to Pistol's age, and he has given no indication that would justify the statement, "Old I do wax". The one person in whose mouth this speech would be appropriate is Sir John Falstaff.'[15]

Falstaff, or his prototype Oldcastle, does not go to France in *The Famous Victories*, but he may well have done in Shakespeare's original play. The author's promise in the epilogue to *2 Henry IV* surely creates expectation of something more than an off-stage death. When he wrote that epilogue Shakespeare was banking on the popularity of the bibulous knight and hoping to use him again in spite of his banishment. (It seems possible, too, that when he changed the name from Oldcastle to Falstaff it occurred to him to take the character right through *Henry IV* and *Henry V* to cycle back as a kind of indestructible comic-strip hero into *Henry VI*. In this way he would identify him with the cowardly Sir John Falstaff who is there deprived of his Garter and once more banished by the king on pain of death.)

If Falstaff went to France, so would his followers. As it is there seems to be no particular reason why Bardolph, Pistol, Nym and the boy should go to the wars.[16] In *The Famous Victories* there is at least a captain to press their counterparts into the service. But Shakespeare's Sir John already has his retainers. And it would be reasonable to suppose that it was originally Falstaff, not Fluellen, who belaboured them at the breach at Harfleur, however vainly. Fluellen, as Walter remarks, 'is unannounced, and the abject terror in Pistol's appeal (ll.22–5) loses much of its humour unless the audience knows who Fluellen is'.[17] In fact the audience could be excused for thinking that Pistol's 'Be merciful, great duke' is addressed to an actual duke. Besides, Fluellen is wanted in the following scene and his exit and re-entry, both unmarked, are awkward; his remaining on stage during the boy's soliloquy would be even more so;[18] nor does he recognise Pistol when he sees him again at the bridge (III.vi). In the quarto it is Nym who answers Fluellen, 'Abate thy rage sweete knight,' a form of address which obviously fits Falstaff, as might also the 'good bawcock' and 'sweet chuck' by which Pistol tries to mollify his tormentor in the Folio. If the original version of the play had 'sweet knight' and this was changed to 'great duke' Shakespeare may have thought of replacing Falstaff by the Duke of Gloucester, who has 'the order of the siege', but not made his intention sufficiently clear, or else decided that Fluellen would do as well. In any case it seems likely enough that the author first intended to employ Falstaff as a captain in the French campaign and Pistol as sutler, perhaps reserving the death of Falstaff for somewhere near the ending of the play – after all, he did half promise to show him dying of a sweat.

Whether or not this was really his plan and irrespective of how far he proceeded in executing it, Falstaff was eventually left out. Dover Wilson thinks this was because of the untimely 'desertion or expulsion of Will Kempe' from the company of actors,[19] but his theory has found little support, and there is little inherent probability in Shakespeare's making such drastic changes for the sake of one actor. Another theory, for which J. H. Walter is a spokesman, has it that the change was made in deference to the Brooke family: 'it is probable that the Brooke family, realizing that they could not stop people from calling Falstaff Oldcastle, determined to prevent Falstaff appearing on the stage in a third play, and in this they were successful.'[20] There is no solid evidence that the Brooke family did intervene in this way, however, and it seems fair to suppose that having gained their point in effecting a change of name they had to swallow the rest. Nor can the theory that the removal, or omission, of Falstaff was made for artistic reasons be as easily dismissed as it is by Walter. Falstaff, it could be asserted, had already assumed too much importance in the history cycle, creating a redundancy in *1 Henry IV* and practically engrossing *2 Henry IV* to himself. It would be very hard to keep him within bounds in another play, and Henry V must be given ample room to display his new virtues. It would not be too strange if Shakespeare after three plays (assuming that *The Merry Wives of Windsor* was written before *Henry V*) felt he had had enough of the fat knight. As for the comic element of the last play of the tetralogy, Pistol had probably proved himself a popular hit, since he is mentioned on the title pages of both *2 Henry IV* and *Henry V* in their quarto editions. He would not be directly associated with the king, and he could more easily than Falstaff be kept in his place. In *Henry V*, says Irving Ribner, Shakespeare could use the character of Pistol 'entirely for its value as comedy, without the relation to the king and the direct involvement in the central political issues of his tetralogy which had been from the first an integral part of Falstaff'.[21] There is in fact a proliferation of comic material in *Henry V*, as if the absence of Falstaff had set the author free to devise an all the greater variety of characters and incidents for our amusement. At one level there is the satirical treatment of the French lords, at a quite different level the scenes featuring Princess Katharine – Shakespeare had also promised at the end of *2 Henry IV* to make us 'merry with fair Katharine of France'. At a third level there are the four captains, at a fourth the quarrel between the king and a private,[22] and at a fifth and the lowest (though the first four are not in descending order) Pistol and his thieving companions.

And now the choruses. These are certainly not in complete agreement with the main body of the play. In the first place there is no regular correspondence between the ordering of the choruses and the Folio act divisions, but this bit of editing may have been bungled by Jaggard or his compositors. In the second place, and this is more serious, the choruses form rather imperfect links between the scenes they follow and anticipate. The first chorus (not counting the prologue) takes us to Southampton and tenses us for the outcome of a conspiracy against the king's life, then changes its mind and introduces a low-comedy scene set in London. The second chorus takes us to sea after we have heard in the preceding scene that the king is 'footed' in France already. The third chorus rather superfluously (speaking in terms of drama, not poetry) describes the king's visits to his troops by night, which we are about to witness; while the fourth, on the contrary, summarises in narrative the events of a long period of time which is skipped in the dramatic action and then returns us to a quarrel which began before that interval. It has been suggested that the choruses serve more as linking commentaries to guide our responses than as expository devices,[23] but even from this point of view they are sometimes misleading. Thus the first and second choruses convey the impression that not only 'all the youth' but all the manhood of England flock to France, leaving their country 'Guarded with grandsires, babies, and old women'; yet Westmoreland, surveying Harry's little 'band of brothers' at Agincourt, wishes for 'But one ten thousand of those men in England / That do no work to-day'. The third chorus gives a very different picture of the king from that of the disguised moralist who quarrels with one of his own privates.[24] And the epilogue contradicts the confident expectations of future strength and peace created in the conclusion of the play proper: for not only does Harry in despite of the epilogue and historical truth promise Katharine a prodigious soldier for a son, one 'that shall go to Constantinople and take the Turk by the beard', but the King and Queen of France foresee a future when war will 'never . . . advance / His bleeding sword 'twixt England and fair France' and when 'ill office, or fell jealousy' will never 'Thrust in between the paction of these kingdoms'.[25]

There is no reason to think that the choruses were part of the original version. Their omission from the extant quarto text may simply mean that they were felt to be unnecessary in a theatrical abridgment, but their bad jointing into the sequence of scenes is a better indication of added material. To take the geographical location of the first Eastcheap scene, it was more likely the added chorus that introduced a contradiction here and so had to be corrected, than the scene itself that caused the contradiction by being inserted after the chorus was written, as Pollard and Wilson suggested.[26] There is a similar scene in a similar place in *The Famous Victories*, and it is hard to see where else it could go. The prologue and choruses with their strong appeal to the imagination of the spectators, their rousing patriotism, and their unproblematic presentation of the hero-king could well have been inspired, as I hinted at first, by the prospect of performance in a new theatre, which no doubt was the pride of the shareholders and the company. The sonnet which forms the choric epilogue would have been added on the same occasion to link the latest and last of the history plays to its predecessors and to remind the audience of the whole historical cycle. And perhaps it was more natural in 1599, after the peace treaty between France and Spain, to speak of the loss of France, as the sonnet does, than it was in the years when Queen Elizabeth was continually sending contingents of soldiers across the Channel and was still hoping to regain Calais.

The text of *Henry V* which was printed in 1623 was evidently to some extent a conflated version, containing passages from different stages of composition and revision, some of which had been meant for excision.[27] I have mentioned a relatively insignificant example: the king's concluding speech after hearing his counsellors in I.ii, which is rendered superfluous by the unexpected nature of the embassy scene which follows. Another example is the double description of the English army in IV.ii, first by the Constable, then by Grandpré. The former's speech is preceded by a message that 'The English are embattail'd, you French peers', and by the Constable's immediate order, 'To horse, you gallant princes! straight to horse!' He concludes his speech of twenty-three lines as follows:

> Then let the trumpets sound
> The tucket sonance and the note to mount:

For our approach shall so much dare the field
That England shall couch down in fear, and yield.

(iv.ii.34–7)

There is little need for Grandpré to enter after this with his 'Why do you stay so long, my lords of France?' followed by a speech of seventeen lines on the miserable condition of the English and their horses. In fact Shakespeare may have felt he was too much dishonouring Henry's band of heroes in Grandpré's description and decided to scrap it. But Heminges and Condell thought otherwise, or didn't notice. The whole scene is missing in the quarto.

There is one complex of scenes and passages of central importance which might have been tidied up by the author had he lived to oversee the printing of his work, but in which it is now hard to determine whether any substitutions and omissions were intended. I refer to the two long night and morning scenes in the English camp which straddle the French scene we have just considered. The clearest indication of irregular composition is to be found in the repeated assignations for the lords to meet at the king's tent and Henry's failure to turn up. At iv.i.24–7 Harry tells the Dukes of Bedford and Gloucester:

> Brothers both,
> Commend me to the princes in our camp;
> Do my good-morrow to them; and anon
> Desire them all to my pavilion.

He also tells Erpingham, who offers to attend him, 'Go with my brothers to the lords of England: / I and my bosom must debate awhile.' He then goes off into the night to debate, not with his bosom, but with Pistol and the three privates and, between these encounters, to listen to the debate of Fluellen and Gower. He subsequently soliloquises at some length on greatness, ceremony, and the responsibilities of kingship, and when Erpingham comes to look for him because the nobles are, understandably, 'jealous of [his] absence' he again instructs the faithful captain:

> Good old knight,
> Collect them altogether at my tent:
> I'll be before thee.   (ll.292–4)

Whereupon he falls to his prayer, 'O God of battles! steel my soldiers' hearts', until, next, Gloucester comes to remind him that the day and his friends are staying for him. There is a break for the scene in the French camp, and when we return to Henry's headquarters we find Gloucester asking 'Where is the king?' and Bedford replying, 'The king himself is rode to view their battle.' (IV.iii.1–2). Only after Salisbury, possibly tired of waiting, has bid a last farewell before battle to the other lords does Henry at last keep his rendezvous, in time to hear Westmoreland (or Warwick in the quarto) wish for more soldiers, and to deliver his resounding lines on the glory to be won 'upon Saint Crispin's day'. A somewhat deflated Salisbury[28] returns as a messenger to say that 'The French are bravely in their battles set' (IV.iii.69), Montjoy reappears with a message from the Constable, who was ready to charge when last we saw him, and then, finally, the Folio stage direction briefly signals '*Alarum. Excursions.*' as the battle commences.

If we were to pursue a direct link through these tangled passages it would have to go, as Duthie and Wilson have noted,[29] from the king's first instruction to his brothers for a meeting at his tent, and his wish to debate with his bosom, straight to his 'God of battles' prayer followed by Gloucester calling for him and the actual meeting of the nobles. Into this simple sequence are inserted a large number of episodes which are less logically linked and which to some extent are repetitive, the most important being Harry's discussion with Bates, Court, and Williams at three o'clock in the morning.[30] Some of these episodes, like Harry's long soliloquy on ceremony and Salisbury's farewell, could no doubt be forgone without dramatic loss. But Shakespeare apparently felt a need at this point to clarify Harry's attitudes and motivations and to examine the whole question of right and wrong in war. And whether or not we think him successful in doing so there seems to be a general feeling that the nocturnal campfire scene is a masterstroke of atmosphere-creation and dramatic commentary.

We have now ourselves reached a point where we must take a closer look at Shakespeare's portrayal of the titular hero of his play. The portrait has probably been disturbed somewhat by the process of revision of which we have found so many traces. But was it ever entirely clear? And above all was it ever completely guileless?

The common view of the character variously known as Hal, Harry, and Henry is probably that epitomised in the lines spoken by the Archbishop of Canterbury in the opening of *Henry V*:

> The breath no sooner left his father's body,
> But that his wildness, mortified in him,
> Seem'd to die too; yea, at that very moment,

> Consideration like an angel came,
> And whipp'd th'offending Adam out of him,
> Leaving his body as a Paradise,
> T'envelop and contain celestial spirits.   (I.i.25–31)

This picture only needs to be supplemented by that of the impetuous and unvanquishable soldier and the heroic embodiment of English patriotism. It is not seriously disturbed by the contradictory view of the prince's reform (as gradual and deliberate, not sudden and miraculous) suggested by the Bishop of Ely:

> And so the prince obscur'd his contemplation
> Under the veil of wildness; which, no doubt,
> Grew like the summer grass, fastest by night,
> Unseen, yet crescive in his faculty.   (I.i.63–6)

There have always been voices raised against the idealisation of Harry, however. Some have thought Shakespeare asked us to admire a man with too many objectionable traits, others that the author was out of love with the paragon he suddenly had on his hands and failed to breathe real life into him.[31] Among the latter, E. M. W. Tillyard has probably gone to the farthest extreme in asserting that Shakespeare had committed himself to a task which it was beyond the powers even of his versatile genius to perform: that of reconciling the detached ironist (as Tillyard sees him) of the *Henry IV* plays with the 'simple forthright energetic man' of the concluding play of the trilogy. King Henry, in Tillyard's words, 'is utterly inconsistent with his old self and with any of the pieces of self that make up his patchwork character in the present play [*Henry V*]'.[32] John Palmer, too, thinks that Shakespeare was committed to presenting his hero 'in a setting of formal grandeur alien to the resources of a poet who writes from nature'. But he contends that the author solved his problem by letting the picture of the ideal monarch emerge from 'comments delivered by friends and followers', while 'the words and actions of the King himself' show him to be a human being behaving as successful people do behave in political life. 'There is neither censure nor commendation.'[33]

What Tillyard perhaps failed to recognise was Shakespeare's struggle to qualify his portrait of the national hero. The idea that Shakespeare was being ironical about Harry is an old one, but in recent years it has been urged with particular insistence, e.g. by Roy W. Battenhouse, who also cites a number of earlier proponents of the idea. Battenhouse himself is especially concerned with the lack of Christian spirit in Henry's semblance of piety:

> There can be 'glistering semblances of piety,' yes. But the heart of the action will suggest no substantial Christianity. Thus reconstructed the history will be double-edged. It will allow some spectators, blinded by a surface patriotism, to admire as their own ideal its particular heroism. But it will permit others to discern, as various modern critics have, an ultimate emptiness in the pageantry, a suspicious fulsomeness in the rhetoric, and a kind of heroism in Henry more suggestive of 'a very amiable monster' (Hazlitt's phrase), or of 'some handsome spirited horse' (Yeats's phrase), than of a truly human being.[34]

The image of Henry V as Shakespeare's model king has been further deflated by C. H. Hobday, William Babula, and Andrew Gurr.[35] 'Whatever Shakespeare may say about Henry,' says Hobday, 'in his heart he regarded him as a murderer. Faced with the demand to depict such a man as a hero, he took refuge in the irony which permeates the whole play, and constantly juxtaposed the fine talk of honour and religion with the realities of human greed and cruelty.'[36] Babula especially focuses on Henry's evasion of responsibility, and Gurr's main theme is the self-interest shown by the various members of the English commonwealth, individually and collectively, and by the king in particular.

A number of critics have emphasised the irony of Henry's claiming the French crown by virtue of a right which he denies to others and which would actually disinherit him from the English crown if strictly observed. The Earl of Cambridge, whom he condemns to die, has conspired against him on behalf of Mortimer on exactly the same grounds as those which Henry urges on his own behalf vis-a-vis the French, and, though Cambridge's motive is muted in the play, the better-informed members of Shakespeare's audience would probably see the connection. Irony, it has been argued, is present from the beginning.[37] I completely agree that this is so. But the irony, of course, is not immediately apparent.

In all three plays in which he appears, Harry is deliberately drawn so as to represent in certain essential respects a contrast to his father. In particular we are assured in many ways that he is not proud and ambitious. Whereas the words 'pride', 'proud', and 'proudly' have a high frequency in *Richard II*, where they are chiefly (though not exclusively) used in connection with Bolingbroke, they occur with diminishing frequency in the two parts of *Henry IV* and there mostly refer to Hotspur (twice to Bolingbroke). In *Henry IV* and *Henry V* they are connected with Henry of Monmouth only as his pride is denied. A typical instance may be found in the famous scene in *2 Henry IV* in which the prince defends himself to the king after taking away the crown. He is willing that God should for ever keep the crown from his head if, as he says, it did 'swell my thoughts to any strain of pride'. (*2H4*, IV.v.170). As for the word 'ambition', it occurs only once in the *Henry IV* plays, and it is Hal who uses it about Hotspur (v.iv.87).[38] It also occurs once in *Henry V*, when the king blames his father's ambition for making him the rough fellow he is (v.ii.236). He speaks jokingly, of course, but the word was loaded. Anyway, if Bolingbroke's chief sin was pride it is purged not only by his dying in Jerusalem but in the humility of his son, demonstrated most spectacularly before and after the battle of Agincourt.

For the victory at Agincourt is obviously a confirmation of the divine favour enjoyed by Henry V. He has been careful to secure the church's blessing for his expedition, and from the very start he has almost ostentatiously subordinated his own purposes to the will of God. Even in his answer to the Dauphin's messengers Shakespeare interposes the lines

> But this lies all within the will of God,
> To whom I do appeal; and in whose name
> Tell you the Dauphin I am coming on,
> To venge me as I may and to put forth
> My rightful hand in a well-hallow'd cause.   (I.ii.289–93)

After the great battle, too, Harry is ready to give credit for victory to his divine champion:

> Come, go we in procession to the village:
> And be it death proclaimed through our host
> To boast of this or take that praise from God
> Which is his only.   (IV.viii.115–18)

The victory itself, under such circumstances, can only be seen as a sign that the monarchy has been reconsecrated and that Harry has regained what was lost in the death of Richard. His legitimacy is based both on true inheritance and divine right.

Shakespeare may have felt it to be necessary to make Harry as pious as possible and omits few occasions to have him express his religious sentiments.[39] His reform is not only moral and behavioral but of the nature of a revivalist conversion, and this is apparent even at the end of *2 Henry IV*. In the light of his new personality his advice to Falstaff, 'Fall to thy prayers', is seen to be meant quite literally. And the general effect in so far as regards his military campaign is to turn it into a crusade. In fact it becomes King Henry IV's crusade inherited by his son. The identification is already implicit in Henry IV's last long speech:[40]

> I . . . had a purpose now
> To lead out many to the Holy Land,
> Lest rest and lying still might make them look
> Too near unto my state. Therefore, Harry,
> Be it thy course to busy giddy minds
> With foreign quarrels, that action hence borne out
> May waste the memory of the former days.
>
> (*2H4*, IV.v.209–15)

The motivation for foreign quarrels given here is purely political and hardly very elevated, but we are reminded a few lines further on of the king's guilty conscience, and Harry's prayer before Agincourt leaves no doubt that he is carrying on his father's attempts to expiate for the murder of King Richard. The French easily enough fit into the role of turks and infidels in this crusade. They are proud, boastful, vain, and treacherous, and while the English constantly call upon God for help, the French only exclaim and swear by God and the devil: 'O diable!', 'O Seigneur! le jour est perdu!', 'Mort Dieu!' etc. The Constable, joking or quarrelling with the Duke of Orleans, once compares the Dauphin (or Bourbon) to the devil (III.vii.119–20), and Harry, in the beginning of the night scene at Agincourt, speaks of the French as 'things evil' and associates them as a body with 'the devil himself'.

We may yet feel that Harry's piety and humility change him too unbelievably from his unregenerate Adam. At times they seem positively nauseating, as when he first begs God's forgiveness for having bragged to the French herald and then rebukes his brother Gloucester for his natural fear that the enemy may attack while the English power is weakened by illness: 'We are in God's hand, brother, not in theirs' (III.vi.174). After a while one begins to detect a false note in the description of this sanctimonious puritan. And the suspicion grows as one turns back to the beginning of the play to read again. As they come on stage the two prelates of the opening scene are discussing a bill which has been reintroduced in parliament to dispossess the church of all its temporal lands. The value of these lands would maintain not only a large number of earls, knights, and esquires 'to the king's honour' but also

> to relief of lazars and weak age,
> Of indigent faint souls past corporal toil,
> A hundred almshouses right well supplied;   (i.i.15–17)

They greatly fear a confiscation which could have consequences of such magnitude but hope to get the king on their side, 'For', as the archbishop says,

> I have made an offer to his majesty
> Upon our spiritual convocation,
> And in regard of causes now in hand,
> Which I have open'd to his grace at large,
> As touching France, to give a greater sum
> Than ever at one time the clergy yet
> Did to his predecessors part withal.   (i.i.75–81)

Probably the dominance of the two bishops in the opening scenes and the discussion of the confiscation bill raise false expectations that the fate of the bill will become an issue in the play. In other words we have another parallel to the undeveloped openings in the earlier plays of the tetralogy. In this case, however, the issue is soon forgotten, and what we have is a good example of a topic introduced for the sake of character portrayal, realistic background, and, not least, satire. These are the men who lend their religious support to the invasion of France, backing it with a bribe which the archbishop offers again to the king's face.[41] Obviously the worldly interests of the churchmen and their gilded persuasions underlie some of King Henry's faith in a monopoly of providence. This means that there is an authorial irony behind his frequent pious ejaculations. If we realise this it is easier to understand why Shakespeare gave him such a pharisaical prayer to speak before the battle:[42]

> Five hundred poor I have in yearly pay,
> Who twice a day their wither'd hands hold up
> Toward heaven, to pardon blood; and I have built
> Two chantries,   (iv.i.304–7)

and so on. Not a very dignified prayer for a king in a moment of national crisis. There is no need to speculate whether Shakespeare was having a fling at popish reliance on good works. His audience would certainly know that Henry was a Catholic king and that the prelates of the first act represent the Church of Rome. But this is not of primary importance. The important thing is to realise that Henry's piety is superficial. It is really a political, not a personal, phenomenon, just as his father's plans for a crusade became more and more a political affair. And this may be what the irony in the presentation of Henry V is partly meant to convey. Not that the treatment of the devout king is entirely ironical. Probably Shakespeare wants us to think him subjectively sincere. But the author quite obviously did not put his heart into Hal's conversion. It is not a true conversion but a deliberate adoption of a new role. Shakespeare felt constrained to show the reformation at work and to make it evident even to the groundlings. But he found the soldier-hero who was first revealed at Shrewsbury much more congenial to his poetic inspiration. And the soldier follows hard on the heels of the meek monarch of the beginning of the play:

> But tell the Dauphin I will keep my state,
> Be like a king and show my sail of greatness
> When I do rouse me in my throne of France:
> For that I have laid by my majesty
> And plodded like a man for working-days
> But I will rise there with so full a glory
> That I will dazzle all the eyes of France,
> Yea, strike the Dauphin blind to look on us.
> And tell the pleasant prince this mock of his
> Hath turn'd his balls to gun-stones;   (I.ii.273–82)

This, and not the nocturnal moralist, is the man who fires his soldiers' courage at Agincourt:

> But if it be a sin to covet honour,
> I am the most offending soul alive.
> No, faith, my coz, wish not a man from England:
> God's peace! I would not lose so great an honour
> As one man more, methinks, would share from me
> For the best hope I have.   (IV.iii.28–33)

It is these rousing accents, which even admit taking the name of God in vain, which no doubt endeared the play to patriotic Elizabethans and which usually sound best on the stage to this day. These, and the bluff humour of the wooing scene, where there is no piety except that briefly expressed by the Queen of France at the end, and where, in contrast to all other occasions, King Henry invokes the Lord only in a lighthearted oath. The love of honour and glory and the rough heartiness, these are qualities which seem to belong to Harry, and they are quite inconsistent with the religious humility he is so often made to parade. There is a jarring switch from boasting to meekness in lines like the following, as if Harry suddenly remembers his new role in the midst of being himself:

> And some are yet ungotten and unborn
> That shall have cause to curse the Dauphin's scorn.
> But this lies all within the will of God,   (i.ii.287–9)

Oddly enough, however, there seems to be irony at work in the presentation of the soldier-hero as well. Harry is not only exceptionally brave and chivalrous, one who gives strict orders to spare the country he has invaded (iii.vi.110–17), he is also exceptionally cruel and callous. At Harfleur he disclaims all responsibility for the atrocities which may be committed by his own soldiers if they are once let loose:

> And the flesh'd soldier, rough and hard of heart,
> In liberty of bloody hand shall range
> With conscience wide as hell, mowing like grass
> Your fresh-fair virgins and your flowering infants.
> What is it then to me, if impious war,
> Array'd in flames like to the prince of fiends,
> Do, with his smirch'd complexion, all fell feats
> Enlink'd to waste and desolation?   (iii.iii.11–18)

His order to cut the throats of the French prisoners has been much debated. There seems to be some confusion in the play as to the motive for it – it occurs three times in different connections. Shakespeare may have wanted to make it follow upon the fleeing Frenchmen's sacking of the English tents, but even so it is bound to leave a painful impression, especially with a modern audience. Harry the soldier is by no means always the ideal of chivalry, and his romantic rhetoric has a good deal of unpleasantness to disguise. It is too powerful, perhaps, for the hollowness to be audible, but it is still histrionic.

If there were contradictions in the presentation of Harry in the two preceding histories, they are nothing to the schizophrenia we find in *Henry V*. In that play, though Harry is not the man of bits and pieces that Tillyard makes him out to be, he is at least two persons and those two opposites: the meek and pious Christian hero and the bragging conqueror. They occasionally embrace, as in Henry's answer to Montjoy in iii.vi, where he boasts that his sick men are hardly better than so many Frenchmen and quickly adds:

> Yet, forgive me, God,
> That I do brag thus! this your air of France
> Hath blown that vice in me; I must repent.   (ll.155–7)

At such moments one may have a feeling that Harry is one person with conflicting impulses fighting for mastery. But this kind of inner conflict, interesting as it might have been, is not really dramatised, and more often than not the two components of Harry's character are kept apart. The prologue invites us to see him as 'warlike Harry', and both at Harfleur and in the wooing scene he identifies himself as a soldier, 'A name that in my thoughts becomes me best' (III.iii.6), but the archbishop introduces him rather as a scholar, the night scene makes him a moral philosopher, and the last chorus sees him entering London more as a saint than a soldier, 'Being free from vainness and self-glorious pride'. In both his main manifestations he is equally unsmiling, and though his solemnity may be in part due to his no longer having Falstaff or Poins to spar with, it may also to some extent be a sign of the author's withdrawal of sympathy. Of Harry's two new identities it seems clear that Shakespeare preferred the soldier. But he even more relished the old madcap, and he gave him a last fling in the wooing scene.

It is tempting now to ask whether Shakespeare was ironical about Henry of Monmouth all along. Were Hal's promises of reform in the *Henry IV* plays only the putting-off of an unpleasant duty to the day when it would be inevitable? Certainly we cannot help feeling that the prince enjoys his dissipation while it lasts, especially since the audience is made to enjoy the spectacle of it. This is John Palmer's opinion:

> Henry undoubtedly enjoys the low life of Eastcheap. The plea that he consorts with low companions merely in order that he may surprise the world later on with a timely reformation is merely his way of finding a good and sufficient reason for doing something he wants to do. That he should pitch on this particular kind of reason is equally characteristic. It is a good, worldly reason, but it is not an attractive or a generous reason.[43]

Palmer in general takes an extremely harsh view of Hal and perhaps makes his self-justification too conscious a piece of hypocrisy. But on the background of the prince's behaviour one cannot help suspecting the sincerity of his protestations. In *The Famous Victories* there is merely debauchery and no caveat, till Henry's heart is miraculously touched at his father's deathbed. And in Shakespeare's plays more is suggested concerning the debauchery of his youth than we actually see and hear. Tillyard tries very hard to defend his behaviour: 'Unable under his father's eye to face being the impeccable prince, he compensates by practising the regal touch among his inferiors and proving himself the king of courtesy.'[44] But this is wide of the mark. The unregenerate Hal is not merely the heir apparent schooling himself for the task of government by steeping himself in the life of his future subjects – though he undoubtedly is this too. As Shakespeare depicts him from the end of *Richard II* on he is much more the young profligate with little genuine thought of present or future responsibility.[45] His father cannot be completely misinformed:

> Inquire at London, 'mongst the taverns there,
> For there, they say, he daily doth frequent
> With unrestrained loose companions,   (*R2*, v.iii.5–7)

And Harry Percy has to be believed:

> His answer was, he would unto the stews,
> And from the common'st creature pluck a glove,
> And wear it as a favour;   (ll.16–18)

Shakespeare was constrained by truth and tradition to turn this forlorn hope into a virtuous and victorious monarch, but it would not be surprising if he felt at times that he was doing violence to his image of the royal madcap. Hal is much more convincingly himself when he allows Falstaff to take the credit for slaying Hotspur than when he gives God the credit for the victory at Agincourt.

With Falstaff out of the way, Harry is firmly in the centre of the action, and our appreciation of *Henry V* must largely depend on what we expect of this central character. *Henry V* can be made to seem a simple, stirring drama of patriotism and heroism, and perhaps most people experience it in that way. In fact it is one of the history plays which embody the most contradictory attitudes and where it is hardest to determine the author's position in relation to such central themes as war and religion.[46] The frequent failure to recognise this complexity may be partly due to stock responses in times of war and national peril, from which we have never been far removed (witness Sir Laurence Olivier's screen interpretation of 1944, in its turn enthused over by Dover Wilson in 1945).[47] But it is perhaps just as much due to the image of Prince Hal we carry over from the

Henry IV plays and from the changes in his character which both those plays lead up to. We expect the king to be a model king after his reformation, and we consequently tend to see him as a model king, not noticing, or not seriously paying attention to, the ironical qualifications which Shakespeare has added to his portrait. This may be why the play sometimes offends with its simple pseudo-Marlovian rhodomontade and apparent chauvinism. Whereas if we see how unstable is the attitude of the creator to his hero, and to what extent that hero is a man of contradictions, we may lose some of the thrills down the spine, but we will probably have a finer understanding of Shakespeare's struggle to convert refractory material into art.

Coming at the end of the second tetralogy, *Henry V* marks the resolution of the conflict begun when Bolingbroke was banished and disinherited. And Harry Monmouth is as much the hero of Elizabethan royalism as Henry Tudor. To Shakespeare as an author and to his audiences *Henry V* came after the *Henry VI* plays and *Richard III*. It does not immediately look forward to the dynastic conflicts between the houses of York and Lancaster or to new wars in France. In fact, as I have pointed out, the play proper concludes with visions of everlasting peace, and it is only by disregarding Shakespeare's interpretation of the achievements of Henry V that one can see the sequence of eight plays in their historical order as a dramatisation of the Tudor myth. But this is not saying that his interpretation of Henry V cannot, or must not, be sidestepped in taking an overall view of the two tetralogies. Shakespeare himself would probably in retrospect have seen the complete series as one cycle, with *Henry V* at a half-way point, or, better, with *Henry V* and *Richard III* at opposite ends of an imaginary diameter. The final chorus or epilogue of *Henry V* perhaps indicates as much in pointing on, or back (depending on order of history or order of composition), to the reign of Henry VI and the loss of his father's conquests, 'Which oft our stage hath shown'. And there may even be something in the inclusion of such persons as Bedford and Salisbury and the mention in Henry's great Agincourt speech of Talbot and Warwick to indicate an attempt at linking up with *Henry VI*.[48] But in emphasising didactic elements it is easy to exaggerate the unity of conception which admittedly is present in the two tetralogies, and to underestimate the climactic effect of *Henry V*. Apart from the death of Falstaff, *Henry V* is quite independent even of *Henry IV*, but it still has all the qualities of a resounding finale, to its own action and that of the preceding plays. At least all the surface qualities: the success, the romance, the rhetoric..

9 All Is True, or the Honest Chronicler – *King Henry VIII*

Probably a majority of critics have seen *Henry VIII* as a play separated not only in time but in kind from the early histories. It is certainly different, but not because of the amount of pageantry it contains, as is often asserted, nor because of its use of mythic elements, Christian or pagan, nor because of its alleged looseness of plot.[1] *Henry VIII* is unlike Shakespeare's English history plays of the 1590s because of its new approach to the treatment of character.

The pageantry is there, and the prologue apparently draws attention to it:

> Those that come to see
> Only a show or two, and so agree
> The play may pass, if they be still and willing,
> I'll undertake may see away their shilling,
> Richly in two short hours.

The citizens, we are told in the beginning of Act IV, 'have shown at full their royal minds' by celebrating the coronation of Anne 'with shows, / Pageants and sights of honour'. There is contemporary testimony, too, as to the magnificence with which the play was presented, thanks paradoxically to the fire which destroyed the Globe on that fateful midsummer afternoon in 1613. Sir Henry Wotton, describing the fire in a letter to Sir Edmund Bacon, has this to say of the spectacle he saw before it broke out:

> The Kings Players had a new Play called *All is True*, representing some principal pieces of the Reign of Henry 8. which was set forth with many extraordinary circumstances of Pomp and Majesty, even to the matting of the stage; the Knights of the Order, with their Georges and Garter, the Guards with their embroidered Coats, and the like: sufficient in truth within a while to make greatness very familiar, if not ridiculous.

We must distinguish between dramatic and theatrical features, however. Sir Henry's sarcasm in that last sentence is levelled at the production of the play and does not implicate its essential nature. The ceremonial processions and arrangements that we witness have no structural importance and little thematic significance. They provide no action or information which does not sufficiently emerge from the dialogue, and are in fact spectacular additions to the basic dramatic scenes. Those who went to gape at shows could no doubt see away their shillings and feel richly rewarded without paying too much attention to more sophisticated matters. In an age when court masques had become popular it must have been tempting to transfer some of their attractions to the public theatre, and it was a simple matter to copy a few itemised descriptions of stately processions from Holinshed and use them for stage directions. There are perhaps more great ceremonies in *Henry VIII* than in the early plays, what with the trial of one queen, the coronation of another, and the christening of a princess, plus a formal meeting of the privy council. But there are funerals, coronations, and parliaments in the early plays as well, and Shakespeare, had he been so inclined, could as easily have inserted directions for additional pageantry in them as he did in *Henry VIII*. Indeed, for all we know, a number of dumb shows may have been included in the staging of the early history plays which do not appear in the printed texts, and we have no certain knowledge that Shakespeare himself included the directions for these spectacles in *Henry VIII*. The play is not dependent on them, and the characters are even occasionally impatient of ceremony. King Henry dispenses with the reading of the cardinals' commission from Rome at the beginning of Katherine's trial, and the queen refuses to submit to the impersonal forms of the tribunal. In the light of Katherine's personal dignity we might even be tempted to read a certain irony into Anne's submission to ceremony. It is hard to understand how Irving Ribner can characterise *Henry VIII* as 'a patriotic pageant'.[2] If we pay any attention to Queen Katherine's complaints of being friendless among enemies, or indeed to the actual state of a country where such men as Buckingham, Norfolk, Suffolk, Surrey, and Sands represent the ruling class, we can hardly find much occasion for patriotic complacency.[3] The patriotism is seriously qualified within the play and the pageantry is extraneous to its main concerns.

Nor are the mythic elements at all conspicuous. They are in fact concentrated in Cranmer's final prophecy of a golden age under Elizabeth and James I, which is briefly anticipated earlier in the play in Suffolk's praise of Anne Bullen (III.ii.50–2). Howard Felperin finds a double pattern of myth, 'Tudor and Christian', in *Henry VIII*. The Tudor, or historical, myth is 'that of a Tudor golden age emerging under the watchful eye of God from a long ordeal of tyranny and dissension'.[4] But that ordeal is not dramatised or even referred to in *Henry VIII*, which has very few links backward to the Plantagenet tetralogies. The ordeals it dramatises are those of individuals, except for Wolsey's rapacious taxation scheme, which is quickly quashed by Henry's intervention. Theological dissensions are kept strictly in the background, and when an individual, Cranmer, is accused of heresy, Henry again personally intervenes to vindicate him. Prophecies of an age of peace and prosperity, it should be remembered, occur at the end of *Richard III* and *Henry V* as well, albeit not as oracularly uttered as in *Henry VIII*. There is little sense of 'an overriding philosophy of history, that God directs all' in Shakespeare's last play, in spite of sympathetic interpretations which find it there.[5] As for 'the providentially governed pattern of worldly fall and Christian conversion', this is not turned into a myth in the sense that it directs the movements of the play. It is true that Wolsey and to some extent Buckingham suffer a 'fortunate fall',[6] but Katherine is in no need of conversion, and Henry needs only to have his eyes opened. Nor does the conversion of the most villainous character of the play, Wolsey, have any consequences for the subsequent action or for any of the other characters except perhaps Cromwell, since Wolsey's pernicious manipulations are continued by Gardiner. As Frederick O. Waage has remarked, 'In *Henry VIII* those personal qualities in the principals which would allow them to insure the tranquil continuity of their state emerge only when death is denying them the power to insure that continuity.' Waage thinks the play is characterised by 'Shakespeare's *inability* to mythologize history', an inability which was caused, as Waage sees it, by the disappointment of millennial expectations on the death of Prince Henry in 1612.[7] Ronald Berman has suggested the presence of a pagan fertility myth enacted by Henry and Anne, with 'Anne and her daughter [. . .] envisaged as Ceres and Proserpina'.[8] He might have extended his interpretation to include Katherine and Wolsey, for there is a *death* of nature as well as a rebirth if one is looking for mythic archetypes. But this is a typically modern explication which adds no significance to Shakespeare's treatment of historical persons and events. And in any case it would still have to be mainly based on the last act, with very little support from the central parts of this domestic and political drama.

The looseness of plot has been frequently alleged, and the New Penguin editor, A. R. Humphreys, takes an extreme position: 'the play lacks integrated character . . . it is made up of notable episodes laid in sequence rather than generated dynamically one from another.'[9] This question of structure used to be commonly seen as an aspect of the problem of authorship, and the more sentimental scenes, like those depicting the good ends of bad or worldly men, were attributed to Fletcher. But as in the case of *1 Henry VI*, an influential body of opinion seems now to have swung in favour of Shakespeare's sole authorship, though it is generally conceded that Fletcher may have contributed a few lines and passages.[10] I am content to leave the arbitrament to others and to take my stand, for the present purpose, with the upholders of Shakespeare's authorial integrity. Which means that if we find divided intentions it does not necessarily indicate divided responsibility. And should it ever be established that *Henry VIII* is the result of composite authorship it will at least not affect our analysis of the play itself.

With this in mind let us consider the complaints that have been made and can be made of the loose plot structure. Irving Ribner reviews the 'poorly-connected series of episodes' which, in his opinion, constitute the play:

> It begins with the fall of Buckingham, who is promptly forgotten. Then follow the king's sudden infatuation with Anne Boleyn at a ball given by Wolsey, the trial of Queen Catherine, the sudden fall of Wolsey and the parallel rise of Cranmer. The coronation of Anne Boleyn is presented in great detail. There follows the plot of Gardiner against Cranmer and the Archbishop's absolution by the king, and the play ends with the report of Elizabeth's birth and an elaborate display of her christening, at which Archbishop Cranmer officiates as godfather and ends the play with an elaborate prediction of the great age of peace and prosperity which she is one day to bring to England.[11]

R. A. Law gives his support to Ribner, makes a similar enumeration of scenes, and asks rhetorically, 'Are not such incidents . . . presented to us primarily because Holinshed also records these events during his long account of King Henry's reign?'[12] It is particularly the last act, and within it the last scene, that of Cranmer's prophecy, which have been found inconsequential, or even incompatible with the rest of the play. In 1850 James Spedding declared that the play 'falls away utterly, and leaves us in the last act among persons we scarcely know, and events for which we do not care'. Law contends that 'This last act destroys all vestige of unity in the drama as a whole', while Waage calls the last scene 'an artificial appendage tacked on at the end to redeem the somber vision of the play as a whole'.[13] Another main stricture is 'that the characters are inconsistent, that Buckingham, Wolsey, and Katherine become weak at their falls'.[14] This may also be seen as an aspect of plot structure, but we will leave it aside for the moment.

It may be easily agreed that the structure is episodic and that the play focuses in turn on such divergent concerns as the destruction of Buckingham, the royal divorce, the unmasking of Wolsey, the vindication of Cranmer, and the birth of Elizabeth. In all these actions different characters successively take the centre of the stage and it is hard to decide where to place the centre of interest. If Henry's divorce and remarriage are the main issue one has to wonder what Buckingham is doing in the first two acts, and there is a major unconformity in his disappearance. If, on the other hand, the machinations and disgrace of Wolsey are mainly in question this would make sense of Buckingham but not of Cranmer. In other words the beginning and ending seem not to belong to the same play. It is certainly true that the last act brings a whole new set of people into prominence.

King Henry, of course, is there all along, but what does he *do* in the play? We do not see him courting Anne except by the briefest of glimpses, or indeed rejecting Katherine except by his silence when she pleads. Nor do we see him facing up to Wolsey openly. In fact we never actually see him overcoming anyone by force or persuasion. He is acted upon but he acts through others, both in toppling Buckingham, securing his divorce, and exposing the cardinal. Only when he steps in to save Cranmer in the fifth act does he become an agent in terms of plot and staging. We do get some information as to his activities by means of narrative and by implication. But even so the impression of his role tends at times to be blurred. And the same is true of Wolsey. Thus in the trial of Katherine there comes a point at the end of Act II when the king exclaims against Wolsey and Campeius for trifling with him: 'I abhor / This dilatory sloth and tricks of Rome.' Up to that point the cardinals have obviously been more zealous than the king in pursuing the divorce and it is not made at all clear why the roles seem to be suddenly reversed. To add to the uncertainty they are not actually reversed in the sequel to the abortive trial until after the prelates' private interview with the queen, when we learn (in III.ii) that Wolsey has asked the pope to halt the divorce proceedings on account of the king's being 'tangled in affection' to Anne Bullen. Another blurring of roles takes place when the lords gather for their final onslaught on the cardinal and find that all they need to do is push home King Henry's attack. They are at once the king's instruments and his substitutes, and their ambiguous status is emphasised by their not having a written commission from the king. Not unnaturally Wolsey accuses them of envy and malice. The hunt is now theirs.

This blurring is an aspect of what is probably the major plot weakness of the play: the lack of adequately dramatic aims and motivation for the behaviour of the principals. It is shown in the ambiguity of the king's reasons for wanting a divorce, but it is mainly noticeable in the behaviour of Wolsey, the chief fomenter of trouble. At the beginning of the play Wolsey is already as powerful as he can ever hope to become in England. His plans to climb to the papacy do not really affect the plot, nor are they revealed till the moment of his disgrace (III.ii.210–13). His action against Buckingham lacks maturation and his action against Katherine is not in reality directed against her but against her nephew the emperor (II.i.162). Neither Buckingham's fall nor Katherine's serves to advance him. So apart from satisfying his spite it is hard to see what he is after.

The plot, then, is undoubtedly loose in many ways. But strangely enough, and whatever adverse critics may think, it has no remarkable faults or inconsistencies.[15] When expectations are specifically raised and then disappointed they concern relatively unimportant matters, or there are fairly plausible explanations for their not being fulfilled. Thus Buckingham in I.i promises to denounce the cardinal to the king and expose his treason, but since Buckingham is arrested and himself accused of treason before he can reach the king's ear we must assume that he never has a chance to counter-attack. In IV.i the Third Gentleman expresses confidence that Cranmer 'will find a friend will not shrink from him' in Thomas Cromwell if matters come to a head between the archbishop and the Bishop of Winchester, and if we remember these words we are likely to be surprised at the feeble support that Cromwell ventures for his friend at the critical moment in the privy council, actually voting with the others for his arrest. But it has to be left to King Henry, of course, to come to Cranmer's aid. I have mentioned King Henry's impatience with the 'dilatory sloth' of the cardinals, whom we find immediately after his petulant outburst busily serving his cause with the queen. Other unfulfilled expectations I doubt if there are. It is worth observing that there is no open conflict between Katherine and Anne and we are nowhere led to expect one. Katherine does not even mention Anne at any time. Shakespeare could obviously have written a play in which such a conflict was featured, but he chose to keep the two women apart and the divorce distinct and separate from the marriage except for a very brief verbal hint (II.ii.17–18), and a vague suggestion through the ordering of scenes, that the king has a double motive for divorce. Katherine and Anne relate to the king and Wolsey, not to each other. Anne on the whole is kept in the background (unless we wish to stress her prominence in the coronation show), but by reasons of state she is closely woven into the causal fabric of the play and by her personal history she is firmly linked in the sequence of events.

Modern audiences no doubt have stock responses to Anne Bullen, and our sentimental romantic interest in her character could hardly have been foreseen by Shakespeare. He wrote a play principally about the fall of Katherine and Wolsey, into which the king's romance with Anne was woven more or less incidentally. Anne has speaking parts in two scenes, both of which represent Shakespeare's additions to the scanty material about her in Holinshed, and she appears as a mute in the coronation procession. But apart from these manifestations she is only the subject of talk and rumour, particularly in the long central scene in which King Henry's secret marriage to her is revealed. This is when Wolsey exclaims:

> There was the weight that pull'd me down, O Cromwell,
> The king has gone beyond me: all my glories
> In that one woman I have lost forever.

Henry VIII is a play of a peculiar nature, and it is possible that the dramatist to some extent thought of Anne as a symbolic figure whose importance would be adequately demonstrated in the magnificence of the coronation scene and indirectly in that of the christening of her daughter Elizabeth (where she is absent). She still seems to have an importance in excess of her part in the play, however, and this impression is largely based on the one relatively long scene entirely of Shakespeare's invention where she is really allowed to speak her mind. In the course of a conversation with a fruity Old Lady she asserts that she would not be a queen 'for all the riches under heaven'. Everything points to her sincerity, but we are never given an opportunity to see it practised or to share in her thoughts and emotions again.

The only difficulty caused by the divided treatment of the two queens is that the lords are made both to grieve at Katherine's misfortune and to rejoice at the happy prospects of her supplanter. There is a contradiction here if one brings their utterances together, but it is a functional contradiction in that it serves to keep our sympathies uncomplicated.

In architectural elevation there may not be anything very imposing in *Henry VIII*. It is no towering edifice, based and buttressed, one substructure resting upon another. But everything is meshed, consequential, and more subtly interrelated than one may suspect at first. The lords' attack on Wolsey merges inextricably, as we have seen, with that of the king. The trial of Buckingham is not merely a display of power on the part of Wolsey but provides a perspective for the king's fears as to what may happen should he die without legitimate issue,[16] and also a point of reference for his warning to Cranmer near the end of the play that justice may be overborne by corruption.[17] The vision of Katherine's heavenly coronation follows upon Anne's earthly coronation. And so one might go on.

The last example is one of those mentioned by Foakes in illustration of the pattern of contrasts and oppositions which governs the play.[18] G. Wilson Knight, to whom Foakes is largely indebted, sees this pattern as a juxtaposition of sombre and light-hearted scenes with thematic overtones of far-reaching import:

> We have accordingly a series of warmly conceived humanistic scenes countering our three falling movements. Those were moralistic, on the pattern of medieval stories of the falls of princes; these are eminently Elizabethan. Effects are deliberately got by juxtaposition, as when Buckingham's execution follows Wolsey's feast and the death of Katharine the coronation of Anne. We attend diversely two views of human existence; the tragic and religious as opposed by the warm, sex-impelled, blood; the eternities of death as against the glow and thrill of incarnate life, of creation. These two themes meet in the person of the King.[19]

Foakes particularly emphasises the trials of Buckingham, Katherine, and Cranmer as keystones in the structure of the play, and includes that of Wolsey to make four:

> The character of these trials which form the groundwork of the plot is at once public, as they affect the state, and personal, as they affect the protagonists. The conflict they present between the public interest and private joy and suffering is indeed at the heart of the play, and all the contrasts already discussed between neighbouring scenes relate to it.[20]

Both the pageantry and 'the numerous scenes of walking lords or gentle-men, who discuss what has happened or is to happen . . . play a vital part in establishing this general conflict', according to Foakes.

All this is no doubt close to the truth. There is a pattern, almost a rhythm, of reversals and contrasts, to some extent dependent on an alternation of sad and humorous scenes. There is an insistence on ceremony and some use of the language of ritual. And there is a general conflict between public and private interests. But Knight is carried away by his own poetic imagination and patriotic eloquence far beyond the facts and qualities of the play itself when he finds everything not only in *Henry VIII* but in all of Shakespeare's work coming to a great climax in Cranmer's prophecy.[21] And Foakes, more sober, yet allows himself to be moved to praise of the wrong things when at the end of his structural analysis, turning from form to theme, he declares:

This careful organization goes to shape a play radically different from Shakespeare's earlier histories in dealing with peace, and in having for its general theme the promise of a golden future, after trials and sufferings terminating in the attainment of self-knowledge, forgiveness, and reconciliation.[22]

One would like to think the prologue and epilogue as well as the rest of the play were written by Shakespeare. But even if they were by Fletcher or someone else, that someone could hardly have misunderstood the tenor and subject of the play so completely as to speak of woe and pity in the prologue and emphasise the role of Katherine in the epilogue if the general theme was 'the promise of a golden future'. What Knight and Foakes see as the promise of a golden future are rather, as Lee Bliss has it in one of the most lucid and perceptive essays on *Henry VIII* I have come across, an attempt on Shakespeare's part to present an ideal contrast to the England of Henry VIII as Shakespeare actually described it.[23] The praise of Elizabeth and James I 'fulfills the didactic function of panegyric in the Renaissance: idealized portraits which heighten the subject's exemplary traits in order to incite emulation'.[24]

Knight and Foakes claim too much for this play and too little: too much for the patriotic ritual, too little for the psychology. This is probably because they misinterpret the significance of the pattern. Its interest is not in epic breadth but in moral insight. Where they come closest to recognising this fact is in what they have to say about the spiritual and political development of the king. Some critics seem to think that King Henry starts in almost abject dependence on Wolsey and grows in sense and authority till he is in complete command both of himself and his kingdom. This would make *Henry VIII* a play about the education of a monarch and King Hal another Prince Hal. Wilson Knight, however, whose portrait of Henry is a small masterpiece whatever one may think of his opinions, realises that even at first Henry 'is not all under the influence of Wolsey',[25] and Foakes sees him 'as a strong, regal figure, the embodiment of authority', though 'initially this authority is subdued under the sway of Wolsey'.[26]

Henry develops not from weakness to strength but from being deceived and deluded to becoming clearsighted, and this development is one of the main strands of the action. A good deal of suspense is made to hang on the question: how long will the king continue to be taken in by the cardinal and how will he react when he is undeceived? There is a parallel development on the external, political level from his having a papist counsellor, queen, and heir[27] to his having a quasi-protestant counsellor, queen, and heir.

This movement in the play points naturally enough onward to Cranmer's vision of the reigns of Elizabeth and James. But to emphasise it too strongly would mean to see Katherine as an undesirable encumbrance at best and an evil influence at worst, one whom the king happily gets rid of along with Wolsey, whereas in fact she is depicted as a very saintly Catholic.

There is vision and perspective nevertheless, provided we are not put off by the strangeness of the good king and the good queen appearing on opposite sides of a conflict. The double standard that this division implies is actually the key to the central mystery of *Henry VIII*. For Shakespeare in his last play staked his all on the knowledge that he had fitfully acquired and taught throughout his career as a dramatist, that which had gone into the making of a Bolingbroke, a Shylock, a Macbeth, a Cleopatra, a Lear, a Leontes, even a Caliban: the knowledge that goodness and badness in most human beings are relative to the point of view and that it is humanity which rises and falls and rises again with its individual members.[28] So Henry is a good man when judged by his own standards and a good king when judged by his subjects but an ungrateful and cruel husband when judged by his wife and queen.[29] He is independent enough in exercising authority but not, at first, in knowing how and when to delegate it. In this respect he is the opposite of the Henry VI of the *Contention* plays, who is clearsighted enough but incapable of exerting his authority. His flirtation with Anne while still married to Katherine is not allowed to damage his character in the opinion of his subjects, but it adds a touch of ambivalence to his moral standing in the totality of the play.

Wolsey, the consummate hypocrite, the Tartuffe of Renaissance politics, has few redeeming qualities. But it is this most unlikely person who is selected for the explicit demonstration of Shakespeare's moral theme. In the conversation between Katherine, herself about to die, and her gentleman usher, Griffith, in iv.ii, Wolsey's epitaph is spoken in two contrary and juxtaposed character sketches first by Katherine, summing up all the bad qualities we have seen in evidence, then by Griffith, not denying his faults but reminding Katherine and us that

> From his cradle
> He was a scholar, and a ripe and good one,
> Exceeding wise, fair-spoken and persuading:
> Lofty and sour to them that lov'd him not,
> But to those men that sought him, sweet as summer.
> And though he were unsatisfied in getting
> (Which was a sin) yet in bestowing, madam,
> He was most princely: (iv.ii.50–7)

Griffith calls to witness the colleges founded by Wolsey at Ipswich and Oxford and concludes by speaking of the cardinal's good end:

> His overthrow heap'd happiness upon him,
> For then, and not till then, he felt himself,
> And found the blessedness of being little;
> And to add greater honours to his age
> Than man could give him, he died fearing God.   (ll.64–8)

This speech has the effect of making Katherine wish for an equally unbiased obituary for herself by 'such an honest chronicler as Griffith'. The conversation is also designed to show that for all her loyalty and patience, Katherine is not free from baser feelings of bitterness and hatred. Even in death, we see shortly afterwards, she has human failings. Her pride, which has been so admirable, flares up in a last moment of anger with the messenger who hurries in unceremoniously to announce the presence of Capuchius.

Shakespeare's historical characters were not given to sudden conversions in the early plays. In the case of Wolsey there was Holinshed's authority for his conversion, and Shakespeare in his late maturity was obviously disposed to give prominence to openings for grace. But in the early histories, too, men and women at the point of death were often made to speak with an insight and sometimes with a charity they did not possess before. Thus both Hastings and Buckingham in *Richard III* blame only themselves for their misfortune and recognise the justice of God in the punishment which overtakes them, and the Yorkist butchers Edward and Clarence are both allowed to die in a spirit of religious humility. There is nothing quite so extraordinary, then, in the pious deaths of Buckingham and Wolsey as some critics maintain, nor are any of the characters inconsistently drawn merely because they are seen from different angles.

There *is* a case for inconsistency, as I have demonstrated in detail in my introductory chapter, in the portrayal of Buckingham during his last journey from Westminster to the Tower (II.i.55–136). He first declares to Sir Thomas Lovell that he forgives everybody, but immediately afterwards, speaking to Sir Nicholas Vaux, utters a curse against his 'base accusers, / That never knew what truth meant'. Since it is hard to see what Shakespeare could have intended by making the duke so contradict himself, I am inclined to think, not that Shakespeare nodded but that one of the speeches was an afterthought and that the other should have been deleted if the author had been firm enough or his editors observant enough. It seems likely, too, that the first speech, that addressed to Lovell, was the original one, being closest to Holinshed, and that it should have been replaced by the second speech, the one addressed to Vaux. This would mean that Buckingham is less humble and forgiving in his last moments than some would like to think. What cannot be denied if nothing is omitted in the scene as we have it, is that Buckingham's last sentiments are bitterly misanthropical.[30] Perhaps Shakespeare, as he finished his play, came to feel that the pious deaths of his two main opponents, Wolsey and Katherine, were enough, and that three would be too many. He precisely did not want too much abstract patterning. So insight and fortitude Buckingham may have gained, but not reconcilement with his enemies. It is possible to say that he makes a good end, but in observing the good ends made by various characters in *Henry VIII* we must not blind ourselves to the weaknesses they all also display, Buckingham in particular.

Shakespeare's mature experience of life itself must have had a lot to do with the balanced and mellow vision of humanity which we find in his later plays. But his early immersion in the chronicles of England gathered by Holinshed and Hall and his return to them during the composition of *Henry VIII* must have played an important part in shaping the psychological relativism which went along with his charitable treatment of both repentant and unrepentant sinners (Gardiner is let off very lightly in *Henry VIII*), especially when he portrayed men and women who once had real life. Holinshed and Hall themselves drew on different sources for their information and judgments and frequently present divergent or contradictory views of individual characters. Or they disagree between them about people and events.[31] Shakespeare may at times have been led into contradictory presentations more or less unwittingly by simply following his sources, and certainly his pictures of men like Richard II and Bolingbroke to some extent reflect the shifting attitudes of the chronicles. But he could hardly avoid being consciously struck by many of the contradictions and reflecting on their causes. He would have learnt to look all round a person before trusting any one account. As early as the two Richard plays he had begun to probe inside his characters and to debate the question of identity. *Hamlet* represents his supreme moment of relativism in this internal exploration of the psyche. It is a further step, philosophically, and perhaps psychologically, to the existential view that we are what we seem to be, and that we may seem different beings to ourselves and others at different times and in different circumstances. This is a typically modern view, but it is anticipated by Shakespeare, and it is this kind of realisation which is dramatised in *Henry VIII*, where contradiction and ambiguity in the character portrayal are turned into a creative principle, one is tempted to say a principle of structure, so that the characters appear now in one line of vision, now in another. That is why it seems likely enough that the subtitle, or alternative title, of the play was indeed *All is True*, the name by which Sir Henry Wotton referred to it in his letter to his nephew. I take this to mean not primarily that everything is 'historically authentic'[32] but that seemingly contradictory points of view are equally true. In fact the relativism extends beyond the interpretation of character to the understanding of manners, actions, and events. As Lee Bliss puts it:

> Even before the appearance of the king, the first scene sets up a world in which establishing the 'truth' in any given situation is exceedingly complicated: prior certainty repeatedly dissolves in the face of later revelations. As the play progresses, its probable subtitle 'All is True' and the references to 'truth' in the Prologue become increasingly perplexing and ironic. If the facts of history remain constant, those treaties, taxes, deaths and births, rises and falls, become subject to many, even contradictory, interpretations. Any artistic work of course 'interprets' through necessary selectivity and compression, but Shakespeare has dramatized the essential limitations in our knowledge of 'truth' or human motivation through a proliferation of explanations within the play itself.[33]

Henry VIII is remarkable not chiefly for the depth of its probing and its subtlety of penetration, those qualities which we find so strikingly manifested in the great tragedies, but for its wisdom of understanding. Shakespeare may have sensed some of this wisdom in Holinshed, but he brought it out and fleshed it. And to demonstrate his ultimate answer to the riddle of identity he had to use characters who were also true in the sense of being historical. He, too, is the honest chronicler.

We should not be misled, then, by the looseness of the action. *Henry VIII* is a play of character rather than of plot and intrigue. And the action is chiefly organised to give prominence to changing points of view with regard to characters, so much so that we are constantly assailed by conflicting impressions of them. It is by and by made perfectly clear that Buckingham is innocent of treason and the victim of injustice, but we cannot entirely doubt his surveyor's testimony against him. Wolsey is several times revealed as a machiavellian conspirator, but we cannot entirely doubt his professions of disinterested service. Henry's political sincerity seems unquestionable, but we cannot deny his concupiscence. Anne is both flirtatious and modest. Only Katherine and Cranmer are practically irreproachable, but Cranmer conducts the final divorce proceedings against the queen, and Katherine has the disadvantage of being a Spanish papist and perhaps an illegitimate wife. Not that papism is made a fault of character, and the religious issue is not brought into the open until the last act. But we must count a little on the bias of Shakespeare's audiences.

That bias is itself counteracted as it enters into the ambient vision of the play. Katherine appears in some of the best scenes: in three of them fighting Wolsey and in a fourth preparing for death. The play could well have been conceived as her tragedy, and one may fancy the prologue and epilogue reflecting a lingering-on of that conception. As it is, she becomes part of the human comedy, and her Catholicism one of the elements to be illuminated from opposite sides. There are obviously good and bad Catholics. Just as there are good and bad Englishmen. Just as England itself is viewed by the author's mature understanding – confirming what he knew since he wrote his first history play but never expressed so clearly as when he gave his sympathy to a foreign queen[34] – as imperfect in fact but perfect in potential.

10 Shakespeare at Work

We know nothing about Shakespeare's earliest attempts at playwriting, but it is intrinsically improbable that he made no attempts before he tackled *Henry VI*, or whatever play of the canon may be assumed to be the first in time. It seems likely enough, too, that some of the plays we still have were built on earlier versions which were discarded when they had served their turn. This may be particularly true of the histories. In the case of three of them there are extant source plays, presumably by other hands than Shakespeare's. In the case of at least two others – *1 Henry VI* and *Richard II* – there are what look like fossil remains in the form of primitive rhymed verse and imperfectly assimilated action which point to immature productions of Shakespeare's own underlying the more confident re-handling. He may have borrowed feathers from Greene and his fellow wits but would be unlikely to lift passages verbatim from their plays. He more probably salvaged lines from his juvenilia and threw away the worser part of them.

The first play of the *Henry VI* trilogy as we have it now really consists of a double plot, the intrigues at the English court and the war in France, the latter centering on the English champion Talbot and the French Amazon Joan of Arc. I have indicated my reasons for believing that there was a separate Talbot piece before any of the surviving *Henry VI* plays. And judging from the Talbot plot of *1 Henry VI* this hypothetical early play was a work so neatly planned as to look almost schematic in its symmetrical opposition of armies and leaders and its alternations of military gains and reverses, beginning with a setback for the English forces and ending with a victorious peace for them. Surprises there are in plenty, but expectation and fulfilment are contrived so as to leave no unconformities of major importance. Then some time after completing this play, and having for all we know written others in the meantime, the rising dramatist planned a history of a more ambitious kind based on the reign of King Henry VI, involving a large cast of characters, and centering on the ascent and tragic fall of the Duke of York. It was obviously to be called 'The Contention betwixt the two famous Houses of York and Lancaster'. I have argued that during the process of composition this play broke into two parts because of the superabundance of material to be found in the chronicles. The careful plotter is still evident in *The First Part of the Contention* and the beginning of *The True Tragedy of Richard Duke of York* (i.e. the present *2* and *3 Henry VI*), but in the remainder of the latter play the plotting gets very shaky as dramatic material is added by stages to fill in the action of a semi-independent historical tragedy. And there is a startling fault in the middle of it as Richard of Gloucester reveals new machiavellian qualities and the author begins to prepare for another sequel in which a villainous Richard will be the chief protagonist. *The True Tragedy* is thus wedged between two other plays both conceived in a more unified vision, and suffers structurally. The most that can be said for its unity of conception is that it is organised thematically around the struggle for political power and that it achieves a kind of symmetry between a Yorkist martyrdom in the first act and a Lancastrian one in the last.

The *Whole Contention* covered the life of Henry VI from his marriage to his death in the Tower. The Talbot play covered the beginning of his reign. What more natural than that the Talbot material should be turned into the first part of a trilogy on the whole reign of the unfortunate king? The transformation could be easily enough effected by adding or developing a parallel plot alongside the sequence of battles, which would provide a link with the *Contention* while at the same time showing the origins of the struggle between the two famous houses of York and Lancaster. And this second plot could be roughly integrated with the original Talbot story by suggesting that dissension among the English nobles was the main cause of the critical situation in France. Finally, the coming of Margaret and her romance with Suffolk could be prepared for by a glimpse of the preliminaries to her career as Queen of England. In some such way *1 Henry VI* may have come about.

Apparently *Richard III* was already in the author's mind while he was still working on *3 Henry VI*, and he probably wrote it soon afterwards. Once again, as in *The Whole Contention*, he seems to have had difficulties in limiting his treatment to a two or three hours' traffic, but this time there was no division into two plays, and though *Richard III* is unusually long the plot remains firm. It was now not mainly a question of organising the abundance of material provided by the chronicle sources. The author's imagination was powerfully at work, building up expectations and systematically bringing them to fulfilment. Even so he may have had to jettison certain characters and scenes to prevent his drama from growing out of all proportion. Parts for Jane Shore and Humfrey Banister (who betrays Buckingham) may well have been contemplated if not written, and Tyrrel's account of the murder of the princes seems a poor substitution for the actual spectacle of the murder.

While attention to plot structure seems to have been a primary concern in Shakespeare's earliest career, this is not so evident in the history plays that followed after *Richard III.* Either the action and the treatment of central isues were not planned in advance with the same care as before in these later plays, or else the initial plans were not adhered to as consistently as in the earlier plays. Beginning with *King John* (supposing it came before *Richard II*), there is a marked tendency to change the direction or focus of the plays in midstream, so to speak. In each case the opening scenes introduce business which promises to become important but which is not pursued to a conclusion or which is pushed into the background. In *King John* there are the theme of bastardy and the roles of the Bastard and Queen Eleanor, in *Richard II* there is the idea of revenge for the murder of the Duke of Gloucester, in *1 Henry IV* the claim of Edmund Mortimer to the throne of England, in *2 Henry IV* the role of Northumberland, in *Henry V* the confiscation of church property and the role of the Dauphin. *The Merry Wives* confirms the tendency by its introduction of Shallow in the first act and its neglect of him in the sequent action. By contrast the plays of the first tetralogy have a far more direct approach to their plots, and those of Shakespeare's full maturity in subtle ways build up expectations which prepare for the central conflicts. It almost looks as if Shakespeare, in the period from *King John* to *Henry V*, was particularly given to indirect approaches; and since the tendency is so general in the history plays of the period one has to wonder whether he deliberately chose this way of coming in at a tangent to his main business. He may, for instance, have been looking at character and theme in the opening scenes rather than planning intrigue, and been concerned to place his protagonists before us in revealing attitudes. From this point of view the openings of *Richard II* and *1 Henry IV* are quite functional, while that of *2 Henry IV* is relatively weak in that it portrays a person whose main contribution to the plot is to be reported dead in Act IV. On the other hand, though Bolingbroke may be portrayed vividly enough in the beginning of *Richard II*, there is not much focus on his character in the remainder of the play, and the conversation between Gaunt and the Duchess of Gloucester in Scene ii remains hard to fit into the play as a dramatic whole. *1 Henry IV* more or less begins and ends with Hotspur and could almost be regarded as his tragedy. But though the expository presentation of this temperamental Percy is highly relevant, the same does not apply to the discussion of Mortimer's claim to the throne which also receives a good deal of attention in the opening scenes.

It seems clear that Shakespeare's changes of direction cannot all have featured in preconceived designs. They bring about too many confusions and loose ends. One refuses to think that he fumbled in the opening scenes of these history plays, not knowing where he was going. But he may sometimes have started out at too leisurely a pace and allowed his introductory matter to get out of hand. In some cases – the importance of Gloucester in the opening of *Richard II* and of Mortimer in that of *1 Henry IV* are probably the best examples – he seems to have begun with an original conception of characters and conflicts only to find himself after a while too much at variance with his sources and constrained to yield to the authority of history. In this respect the chronicles obviously limited his freedom of invention to a much greater extent than did the sources for the non-historical plays. But if this explanation is valid it would indicate that Shakespeare did not always completely digest his chronicle material before he began to write. He would occasionally read – or reread – the chronicles piecemeal as he worked and check them for confirmation of his story line from time to time. Difficulties would then be dealt with as they arose. Some difficulties, of course, were caused by the use of two or more sources which did not agree among themselves, or of sources which were internally inconsistent. Hall and Holinshed did not always see eye to eye, and both were compilers who sometimes embodied contradictory views and information in their accounts. *Woodstock* and *The Famous Victories* sometimes differed from the chronicles.

Even apart from the chronicles, however, Shakespeare may have felt now and again that he was heading wrong, or getting stuck, and decided to change his plans. Or, more likely perhaps, he was caught up by fresh inspiration and carried away by unforeseen interests as he advanced. *Richard II* is a good example of an increasing involvement in a particular aspect of character and theme leading to a neglect of aspects which at first were more central. In spite of the unconformity which mars the structure few critics would regret its shift of interest. For Shakespeare as he matured clearly developed a flexibility of intent and a readiness to adopt the better option or welcome the emergent inspiration which in many cases preserved vitality where otherwise there might have been cold perfection. But with regard to the histories of the second period, i.e. of the middle and late nineties, it is worth observing that when, for whatever reason, he changed his plans he did not bother to go back and alter the opening scenes to conform with his new design. The faults remain.

The faultiest plays, if the superlative can be used in the geological sense, are the two *Henry IV*s. As I maintain, leaning on Harold Jenkins, there was here a yeasting of ideas and material which necessitated a division and partial duplication of the plot. I also maintain that there occurred a considerable rearrangement of scenes already composed or planned at the time of the division. Thus Falstaff's first meeting with Shallow was moved from Part I to Part II, where it fits in rather badly, though the maladjustment is disguised by the further meetings with which the action is supplemented. Part I relies on Part II for the fulfilment of some of its main expectations: King Henry's crusade, the succession of Hal, and the rejection of Falstaff. And Part II has an inconsistent picture of the prince, not only in relation to the ending of Part I but as he is seen (or surprisingly ignored) by the king. Somewhere and somehow in the process of rearrangement two or three scenes may have been lost as well: it is strange that we do not see Hal hitting the Lord Chief Justice since the incident is several times referred to, and it is stranger still that we do not witness Falstaff's borrowing of money from Shallow, since his impecuniosity and cadging form a major motif in the comic plot of *2 Henry IV*. Part I is greatly superior to Part II, but all in all the two plays have a festive abandonment which reduces their un-conformities, those of each separately or of the two together, to relative insignificance. One can hardly be surprised that Shakespeare felt no great need to tidy up meticulously.

While the advent of new ideas and attitudes during the process of composition probably accounts for most of the larger unconformities, some of them seem to be due to revision or to the addition of material to an already completed play. *Henry V*, in particular, seems to have been quite extensively revised. It is reasonable to suppose that Falstaff at one time accompanied the king to France but was revised out of the play for external or internal reasons. We now have only his death, which is irrelevant to the action, and his retainers going off without a captain. Fluellen and Pistol appear in episodes where Falstaff would have been more appropriate. Moreover, the Dauphin seems to be a late addition and to have assumed some of the part which originally belonged to Bourbon. He surprisingly appears at Agincourt after King Philip has expressly forbidden him to leave Rouen; but Shakespeare failed to follow up the opportunity he thus provided for himself of staging an encounter between the Dauphin and King Harry. Canterbury's oration in the parliament scene may have been inserted, rather superfluously, into the finished play to please a courtly audience. The night scenes in the camp at Agincourt exhibit signs of interpolation. And finally the choruses may have been added to stir the groundlings and to ornament performances in the public theatre. One wonders whether the author's apparent ambivalence in his attitude to Harry may also to some extent have been the result of revision.

Minor discrepancies which may be due to revision are to be found in practically all the other plays. Thus Montague replaces Salisbury in *3 Henry VI* without entirely removing the traces of Salisbury's presence. Four or more ghosts were probably added to *Richard III*, uttering curses which fail to work, and Stanley's role may have been expanded, giving rise to confused nomenclature (Derby for Stanley) and an unexpected and somewhat pointless appearance in Richmond's tent. The banishment scene of *Richard II* probably represents a revision of a similar scene in an earlier version, and the reactions of Bolingbroke and Gaunt and the behaviour of Aumerle have not been fully assimilated.

1 Henry IV is a special case, as I have already indicated. The additions which were probably made to the early Talbot play trail loose ends and lead up to solutions only in the *Contention* plays. Thus the quarrel of Winchester and Gloucester comes to a head in *2 Henry VI*, as does that of York and Somerset and the affair of Margaret and Suffolk. The fusion of the two plots is also imperfect in that the war plot does not support the assertion that losses in France are due to dissension at home. There is a duplication of the brawl between Gloucester's and Winchester's men, apparently to make their feud a matter of national concern, and Winchester in the first brawl retains the cardinalship which he may have had all along in the Talbot play, though he has to buy it with bribes in what seem to be the additional scenes. Whether revision at any stage led to an inconsistent presentation of Joan of Arc is impossible to decide, but it is at least legitimate to suppose that a more charitable view of the Maid supervened on her vilification in the youthful patriotic play.

Revision would naturally lead to a number of passages appearing in double versions, such as the two brawls in *1 Henry VI* and Talbot's farewell scenes in Act IV, or Canterbury's speeches to Ely and the king in *Henry V*. Shakespeare did not necessarily wish to replace one version by another in such cases. He may have wanted to keep both, or he may not have cared. But undoubtedly in many instances inconsistencies may be eliminated if two similar passages are regarded as alternatives and one or the other omitted. In such places one may suspect that the author failed to make his excisions clear enough or else that his editors in their eagerness to include as much as possible of the master's writings conflated everything that they found reasonably legible. This also applies to passages where Shakespeare may have hesitated in the original composition and tried out different solutions. Such hesitation or change of mind would provide a very satisfactory explanation of the inordinate length of the second wooing scene in *Richard III*, or the Constable's and Grandpré's parallel contemptuous descriptions of the English army in *Henry V*, or of Buckingham's contradictory farewell speeches in *Henry VIII*. It is even conceivable that the author sometimes intended different versions for different uses, e.g. for court performance and for the public theatre, that this accounts for some of the differences between quarto and Folio texts, and that what has come down to us is occasionally a combination of two distinct but equally authentic manuscripts. Other authors, of course, may have interfered with Shakespeare's works, adapting them for their own ends, and it will no doubt remain impossible to sort out all such alien contributions from genuine Shakespeare. But this does not invalidate the general principle of the possibility of authorial alternatives.

I have touched on the question of continuity between the plays in my introductory chapter and we have found frequent discrepancies especially between the plays which one would expect to be linked most closely, i.e. the plays of the *Henry VI* trilogy and the two parts of *Henry IV*. That efforts were made to see the whole historical cycle as a unified sequence is evident, and the epilogue of *Henry V* actually points back to the misfortunes depicted in the early *Henry VI* plays in defiance of the ending of the play itself. But there is nothing anywhere in the series like the continuous action and conservation of character of a truly two-part play like, say, *Promos and Cassandra*. Nor is there more than a very general thematic unity binding them together. The curse on the house of Lancaster is naturally most prominent in the second tetralogy, but Mortimer in *1 Henry VI* reminds us that the Yorkist claim goes back to Richard II, and the legitimacy of Henry VI is disputed as well as that of Henry IV. What is not insisted on anywhere except perhaps in Harry's self-righteous prayer before Agincourt is the sense of a supernatural scheme of retribution and penance, and the Tudor myth so dear to many critics hardly comes into evidence till the end of *Richard III*. The plays were worked out as separate dramatic units; and certain details, like the elimination of Salisbury from *3 Henry VI*, indicate that the separation was widened rather than narrowed in later revision.

From all this there emerges the picture of a dramatist who had a sharp eye for dramatic material, a tremendous creative impulse, an almost superhuman understanding of the human condition, and an intuitive feeling for the shapes of large and complex actions, but who did not work strictly in accordance with preconceived plans and did so less and less as he acquired practice. He often hesitated and sometimes ran into perplexities, and he was quite capable of making structural alterations while his plots were growing. He also revised his manuscripts, sometimes quite extensively. And he left behind a trail of abandoned ideas, imperfect fusions, and alternative readings.

The ultimate problem in connection with the unconformities of Shakespeare's plays is therefore the degree of success with which he disguised, transcended, or exploited them. I have indicated from time to time my general view that most of the irregularities we have discovered are such as can be overlooked by a reader or spectator intent on enjoyment, or such as can be made to vanish in production. Shakespeare's wisdom is awe-inspiring, his passion breath-taking, his laughter side-splitting, his mastery of words and of his dramatic medium unsurpassed whichever way one looks at his plays. But he is not faultless, in any sense of the word, nor can his faults always be ignored. In a much-admired play like *Henry V*, for instance, there is much that leaves one dissatisfied. Many critics have disliked the portrait of a royal prig. The introduction of the Dauphin is, if not a half-hearted, at least a half-realised affair. And Canterbury's disquisition on the Salic law is left hanging in the air, a boredom to a modern audience if recited in full. Even in the best of the history plays, *Richard III*, *Richard II*, and *1 Henry IV*, there are faults which cannot easily be overlooked.

I contend that the inconsistencies, contradictions, broken developments and other irregularities are actually there and have to be recognised. Their existence is not a matter of surmise, and it is disingenuous to explain them more or less on principle as deliberate sophistications. In looking for their causes one naturally must resort to hypothesis, and in particular cases one may hypothesise wrongly. But the cumulative evidence points over-whelmingly to the general probability of explanations such as those which have been put forward in the course of this study: changes of mind, new inspiration, fusion of old and new material, reliance on sources, excision, addition, revision, and, in minor things, carelessness.

To recognise the faults is not to disintegrate the plays but to see them more truly for what they are and to appreciate more fully the powers of intellect and imagination which hold us in spite of all. Perhaps we should be thankful that Shakespeare was not too pedantic in perfecting his plots and bringing all details in each play into accord with a basic design. He would hardly have had time to write thirty-seven plays; or to develop an understanding of human nature which made his last history play, unlike his first, much more remarkable for its wisdom than for its plot structure.

Notes

ABBREVIATIONS
Titles of Shakespeare's plays and of periodicals have been abbreviated in standard or easily decipherable forms. Note particularly:

SS   *Shakespeare Survey*
SSt   *Shakespeare Studies*
SQ   *Shakespeare Quarterly*
ES   *English Studies* (Lisse)
ELR   *English Literary Renaissance*

Chapter 1   Introduction

1. A. P. Rossiter, *Angel with Horns*, ed. Graham Storey (1961) p. 23.
2. M. R. Ridley, *Shakespeare's Plays: A Commentary* (1937; repr. 1957) p. 46.
3. Peter Bilton has analysed the dramatist's control of audience responses throughout the plays of the canon. See his *Commentary and Control in Shakespeare's Plays* (1974). See also E. A. J. Honigmann, *Shakespeare: Seven Tragedies* (1976).
4. Herbert S. Weil, Jr., at the International Shakespeare Conference at Stratford-upon-Avon, 1978.
5. See his 'Anticipation and Foreboding in Shakespeare's Early Histories', *SS*, 6 (1953), and 'Shakespeare's Art of Preparation' in *Shakespeare's Dramatic Art* (1972).
6. The closing lines of the scene, spoken by Winchester, are rendered thus in the Folio:

> The King from Eltam I intend to send,
> And sit at chiefest Sterne of publique Weale.

I accept the usual emendation of 'send' to 'steal', making the two lines a rhyming couplet, but this is not essential to my argument.
7. Introduction to the Arden *MM* (1965; 1976) p. xxiv.
8. Coleridge lists the 'Independence of the interest on the plot' and the 'Independence of the interest on *the story* as the groundwork of the plot' as characteristics of Shakespeare's plays. See T. Hawkes (ed.), *Coleridge on Shakespeare* (Penguin 1969) pp. 115–16.
9. T. W. Craik at the International Shakespeare Conference at Stratford-upon-Avon, 1978. I do not wish to accuse Professor Craik of uncritical adulation, however.
10. A rather special case of belief in authorial infallibility is that of W. J. Lawrence. In *Shakespeare's Workshop* (1928) he amply recognises the many blemishes of Shakespeare's play-texts as we have them and instances a number of inconsistencies and absurdities. But he puts them practically all down to tinkering by others and is especially caustic on the subject of court performances.

11. Emrys Jones, *The Origins of Shakespeare* (1977) pp. 134–9.

12. Karl P. Wentersdorf, 'The Conspiracy of Silence in *Henry V*', *SQ*, 27.3 (Summer 1976) 264–87. Wentersdorf points out that the Earl of Cambridge, alone of the conspirators, does cryptically hint at a political motive for his treason.

13. R. B. Bennett, 'Prince Hal's Crisis of Timing in the Tavern Scene of *Henry IV, Part I*', *Cahiers élisabéthains*, 13 (1978) 15–23.

14. J. R. Price, '*King John* and Problematic Art', *SQ*, xxi.1 (1970) 25–8.

15. *SQ*, xv.2 (1964) 1–10.

16. The session offered papers by Richard Levin on 'The Delapsing of Shakespeare' and by T. J. B. Spencer on 'When Homer Nods: Shakespeare's Artistic Lapses'. See D. Bevington and J. L. Halio (eds), *Shakespeare: Pattern of Excelling Nature* (1978).

17. Robert Ornstein, *A Kingdom for a Stage* (1972) p. 153.

18. E. M. W. Tillyard, *Shakespeare's History Plays* (1944; Peregrine Books 1962); Lily B. Campbell, *Shakespeare's "Histories" / Mirrors of Elizabethan Policy* (1947; University paperbacks 1964). Tillyard explains the Tudor myth and uses this term for it, pp. 59–61.

19. Tillyard, pp. 147, 149.

20. Tillyard, p. 61.

21. Irving Ribner, *The English History Play in the Age of Shakespeare* (1957); M. M. Reese, *The Cease of Majesty* (1961). See esp. Ribner, pp. 108–9.

22. In *Shakespeare from "Richard II" to "Henry V"*. The anti-Tillyard school is surveyed (and repudiated) by Robert P. Merrix in 'Shakespeare's Histories and The New Bardolators', *SEL*, xix.2 (1979) [179]–196.

23. A. L. French, 'Who Deposed Richard the Second?', *Essays in Criticism*, xvii (1967) 411–33; 'Joan of Arc and *Henry VI*', *ES*, xlix.5 (1968) 425–9; 'The World of Richard III', *SSt*, iv (1968) 25–39; ' "Henry VI" and the Ghost of Richard II', *ES*, [l], Anglo-American Supplement, xxxvii–xliii; 'The Mills of God and Shakespeare's Early History Plays', *ES* 55.4 (1974) 313–24.

    See also J. P. Brockbank, 'The Frame of Disorder – "Henry VI" ', in *Early Shakespeare* (Stratford-upon-Avon Studies 3, 1961; repr. 1967) pp. 72–99, esp. p. 98.

24. Ornstein's first chapter is especially important. The remainder is uneven, with an over-emphasis on psychological interpretation. Ornstein shares a general reluctance to enter into any kind of speculation about the processes which concluded with the printing of the Folio texts in 1623.

25. Tillyard, p. 99.

26. Ibid., pp. 320–1.

27. Ribner, p. 66.

28. Ribner, pp. 110, 160, 191.

29. Ornstein, pp. 6, 31.

30. Wilders, *The Lost Garden* (1978) pp. 1–10.

31. Wilders, p. 9.

32. Rossiter, *Angel with Horns*, pp. 20–2. John Russell Brown has an interesting comparison of the structure of Shakespeare's comedies with that of the histories. See his *Shakespeare and His Comedies* (1957) ch. II: 'Experiments in Comedy'. 'It would be hard', he says, 'to find two other series of plays which developed so much in step with each other' (p. 42).

33. Leo Kirschbaum, 'The Authorship of *1 Henry VI*', *PMLA*, lxvii (1952) p. 813. The variety of the history plays has also been commented on by Ribner, Ornstein, Wilders, and by Clifford Leech in 'The Unity of *2 Henry IV*', *SS*, 6 (1953).

34. In his Introduction to the New Cambridge edition of *R2* (1939), Dover Wilson suggested that Shakespeare used a source play now lost and that 'His unknown predecessor, soaked in the history of England, had read the chroniclers for him and had digested what they had to say upon the downfall of Richard II into a play-book ready to his revising hand' (1976 repr., p. lxxv). This theory has been amply repudiated, one of its earliest opponents being Tillyard, who wished 'to strengthen the ideas of an educated Shakespeare, and of a poet more rather than less like Dante and Milton in massiveness of intellect and powers of reflection' (*Shakespeare's History Plays*, p. 321). See also Emrys Jones, *The Origins of Shakespeare*.
35. E.g. by Tillyard, p. 163 and passim.

Chapter 2   The Whole Contention – One Play into Two

1. To this may be added the fact that Henslowe's Diary for 3 Mar. 1592 (1591 o.s.) mentions a 'ne' (presumably 'new') 'harey the vj', very likely Shakespeare's *1H6* (though this is controversial), whereas *2H6* and *3H6* are generally thought to have been written before 1592.
2. See *2H6*, I.i.92–3. IV.ix.4; *3H6*, I.i.112, III.i.76; *R3*, II.iii.17.
3. See Tillyard, *Shakespeare's History Plays*, pp. 161–2; Cairncross, Arden *1H6*, p. li. I am not impressed by the 'compelling arguments' for the priority of *1H6* marshalled by Hanspeter Born in his essay on 'The Date of *2, 3 Henry VI*' (*SQ* 25.3, 323–34). Born bases his conclusion on his own and others' opinion of Shakespeare's growing artistry and insight through the three *H6* plays in their F order, but, as will be seen, I can find little justification for this opinion. Among the authorities cited by Born are Hazelton Spencer, D. M. Ricks, M. M. Reese, and H. T. Price. On one point I do agree with Born, as will also be seen: that Shakespeare 'found the material for [his] planned second part to be so copious that he was forced to split it up into two plays' (p. 331).
4. Here and in the following, the quarto titles with modernised spelling and capitalisation denote the authentic texts represented by the *2–3H6* of the Folio, not the mutilated versions published in 1594–5 under those titles.
5. Act and scene divisions are not marked in either the Q or the F versions of *2–3H6* except for F's *Actus Primus. Scæna Prima* in both plays, but the conventional divisions are useful.
6. There are other repeated lines in the play, too:

    II.iii.37:   Thou setter up and plucker down of kings,
    III.iii.157: Proud setter up and puller down of kings!

    IV.v.16:   Now, brother of Gloucester, Lord Hastings, and the rest,
    IV.vii.1:   Now, brother Richard. Lord Hastings, and the rest,

    There is also a close similarity between the lines of York and Edward at I.iv.177–8 and II.iii.40–1:

    > Open thy gates of mercy, gracious God!
    > My soul flies through these wounds to seek out Thee.

    > Yet that Thy brazen gates of heaven may ope,
    > And give sweet passage to my sinful soul!

Two lines, at II.iv.12–13, are practically repeated from *2H6*, v.ii.14–15:

> *2H6: York.* Hold, Warwick! seek thee out some other chase,
> For I myself must hunt this deer to death.

> *3H6: Rich.* Nay, Warwick, single out some other chase;
> For I myself will hunt this wolf to death.

Q, for whatever reason, has none of these repetitions.

There is another close similarity between the lines in which Richard reports the 'brother's' (or Salisbury's) death at Towton (II.iii.14–22) and those in which Somerset reports the death of Montague at Barnet (v.ii.40–7); and Warwick in both contexts declares 'I will not [or: would not] fly.' Compare especially:

> II.iii.17–19:   And in the very pangs of death he cried,
>   Like to a dismal clangor heard from far,
>   'Warwick, revenge! Brother, revenge my death!'

> v.ii.41–4:   And to the latest gasp cried out for Warwick,
>   And said, 'Commend me to my valiant brother.'
>   And more he would have said; and more he spoke,
>   Which sounded like a cannon in a vault

In this case Q is more repetitious than F in its wording and anticipates or repeats F readings as well as its own.

Cumulatively, the repetitions suggest that Shakespeare was writing rapidly and a little carelessly and therefore repeating his own lines, though some of the repetitions may be deliberate.

7. Compare IV.viii, where Warwick apparently travels from London to Coventry in the time it takes Edward to break into the palace. Occasionally it may be useful to suppose that Shakespeare intended *two* scenes even if the stage is not emptied in between.

8. 'He still had half a play to write and he continued dutifully on his way, but he seems to be losing interest' (M. M. Reese, *The Cease of Majesty*, p. 198). Reese thinks Shakespeare was beginning 'to tire of the chronicle form, with its mechanical motivation, and to concern himself rather with the human problems of kingship' (ibid., p. 199).

9. The 'Edward IV' given at Stratford-upon-Avon in 1963 as the middle part of the 'Wars of the Roses' trilogy was adapted by Peter Hall and John Barton from the last two acts of *2H6* (after the death of Suffolk) and *3H6*. In 1681 and 1723 there were performances of looser adaptations by Crowne and Cibber respectively, apparently drawing on much the same portions of *2-3H6* as Hall's and Barton's 'Edward IV'. And in 1923 'Robert Atkins at the Old Vic produced *1 Henry VI* combined with "the first half of Part II" on 9 January, followed on 12 February with the rest of the play together with Part III' (see C.B.Y.'s note on 'The Stage History of *King Henry VI*' in the New Cambridge edition, pp. xl–xliv). The plays have obviously invited new divisions.

10. Hall does not specifically mention Northumberland as a 'captain' on the queen's side till we get to the preparations leading up to the battle of Towton, but speaks in general terms of 'all the Lordes of the Northe parte' and 'her Northren people'. Shakespeare singles out Northumberland and makes him prominent in the Parliament House scene and at the capture and torture of the Duke of York but seems to forget him after the parley before Towton. The historical Northumberland was killed at Towton.

11. Rossiter finds 'a sharp geological fault' in II.v of *3H6* (the molehill at Towton), where Shakespeare begins to show 'a steady preference for . . . the "ritualistic method"' ('The Structure of Richard the Third', *Durham University Journal*, XXXI (1938) p. 49). I see the molehill episode more as an interlude in *3H6* than as a new beginning.

12. Arden *2H6*, pp. l–li. See also Herschel Baker in his introduction to the Riverside edition of *1–3H6*: 'Part 2 is like its predecessor in its linear, episodic structure, but it is much more soundly built. For one thing, the lightly sketched but vivid episodes with which the play is dotted [. . .] are [. . .] not merely anecdotal but organic to the plot. For another, all the complicated strands of intrigue converge upon the rise of Richard, Duke of York, whose career gives shape and movement to the play' (op. cit., p. 590). Cairncross cites E. K. Chambers for a contrary opinion. See also Ribner, *The English History Play*, p. 99: 'it is almost inevitable that all three of the *Henry VI* plays should be episodic in structure; scenes are poorly related to one another, and there is little central unity to hold each play together.' This in spite of what Ribner says on the same page about 'the three plays as a unified trilogy'.

13. Both Q and F stage directions give Salisbury and Warwick an entry at the beginning of the scene. Q also has an exit for them, with the king, at l.222. It might be advisable for modern editors to adopt this Q S.D.

14. Since four people speak for the murder it is surprising to find York saying 'now we three have spoken it' (l.280). If one of the four was not always directly involved in the murder conspiracy, it would have to be York. The play clearly lays the chief guilt on Suffolk, the cardinal, and the queen.

    In the Q dialogue, the queen draws Suffolk, Buckingham, York, and Somerset into a huddle to 'consult of proud Duke Humphries fall', but however this is to be understood (and it may be simply an instance of confused reporting) Buckingham and Somerset are given no words to speak. The F text leaves us to infer that Buckingham and Somerset stand apart while the other four conspire, until the arrival of the post from Ireland.

15. New Cambr. *2H6*, pp. xlvii–xlviii. Wilson's assumption, however, is that Shakespeare revised an earlier play by Greene, an assumption which I do not share.

16. At III.i.121–3 York charges the Protector with devising 'strange tortures for offenders'. This speech must have been accidentally misassigned, either by the author or in the process of transmission. It should surely belong either to the cardinal, as in Q, or more likely to Buckingham, who is otherwise silent. York has already had his say, characteristically blaming Gloucester for the loss of France, and both the cardinal and Buckingham have previously charged the Protector with cruelty. Gloucester's reply, in the F version, also seems to presuppose a speech by Buckingham: 'Sharp Buckingham unburthens with his tongue / The envious load that lies upon his heart.' Buckingham does remain silent, however, between III.i.187 and IV.iv.7. In F he is not even entrusted with the levying of troops for York's Irish campaign, for which he is made responsible in Q. Instead, Suffolk is given this task. Q, but not F, has an entry for Buckingham at III.ii.13. He must be supposed to be present in this scene, although he does not speak.

17. At II.i.71 Edward calls him 'The flower of Europe for his chivalry'.

18. Reese, *The Cease of Majesty*, p. 181.

19. Clifford's oratory is similarly commented on by the king in *3H6*, II.ii.43.

20. See, however, Bullough: 'To a reader of the sources on the contrary it seems an astonishing *tour de force* in its handling of sprawling, recalcitrant material.' (*Sources*, III, p. 167.)

21. It looks as if Salisbury's brother (or son) Falconbridge was also in the original scene and that his part (including a speech at I.i.216) was given to Montague along with

Salisbury's. Cairncross, on insufficient grounds it seems to me, assigns all of Montague's speeches in I.i to Falconbridge (see Arden *3H6*, pp. xxi–xxii and notes to I.i.14 and I.ii.S.D.).

According to Hall, John Nevill was not created Lord Montague till after the battle of Towton and the coronation of Edward (when Edward's brothers were made dukes). Montague appears correctly as Warwick's brother in Acts IV–V, and his appearances in these acts probably belong to Shakespeare's original version of the play. When his part was pushed forward into Act I he was also introduced with Warwick in II.i. The awkwardness of his appearance there (he is silent throughout and only mentioned by Warwick after 72 lines) is a sufficient indication that he was added after the scene was first finished.

Q's revision is in places more consistent than F's. At I.i. 245 F reads '*Warwick* is Chancelor, and the Lord of Callice', where the original line was probably '*Salisbury* is Chancelor, *Warwick* Lord of Callice', which would have been historically correct (the Arden edition gets this the wrong way round). Q omits the line. In I.ii Q has Edward address his 'cosen *Montague*', which is correct. York, too, twice speaks to his 'cosen *Montague*', again correctly enough according to the usage of the time. F, however, has not corrected the 'brother' by which York and Montague address each other in the 1623 text.

Q has retained Richard's evidently original description of the death of *Salisbury* at Towton (II.iii). F makes him glorify an unidentified 'brother' of Warwick, who in the context of the extant play can only be *Montague*. Thus in F Montague seems to die first at Towton and then at Barnet. In Hall it is a bastard brother of Warwick who is killed before the battle of Towton. Cairncross suggests that Shakespeare may have confused 'the Bastard of Salisbury' with the old earl, but this is underestimating his intelligence. It seems more likely that Shakespeare or some unknown reviser fell back on the brother when he eliminated the father, not seeing that the brother would be understood as Montague.

If we restore Salisbury to his original part in Acts I–II it will be seen that Shakespeare got him out of the way before the battle of Wakefield by having York send him to London (I.ii.55–61), and then brought him to Towton to die. In Hall's account he was captured at Wakefield and subsequently beheaded 'with all the other prisoners', whereupon Margaret 'sent all their heddes, and the dukes head of Yorke, to be set upon poles, over the gate of the citie of Yorke'. Perhaps Shakespeare wanted to concentrate exclusively on the fate of York.

The only mention of Salisbury in the extant F *3H6* is Warwick's puzzling reference to his death 'by the house of York' at III.iii.186–7.

22. There are five plodding lines after what seems to be the closing flourish of IV.iii which introduce this last contradiction. They have all the appearance of being added – hardly by Shakespeare – after the scene was first written. They are not in Q.

23. Edward adds not only a new character but a new concern to *The True Tragedy*. Gwyn Williams argues that Shakespeare thought of him as Margaret's natural son by Suffolk ('Suffolk and Margaret', *SQ*, 25.3.310–22). But Shakespeare may have deliberately left him out of *2H6* to prevent our connecting him with Suffolk. If we still think we are meant to see him as a bastard it would make Henry's resignation of the succession to York and his heirs more acceptable, but this is hardly what Shakespeare wants, and we would have to do a lot of reading between the lines.

24. 'His metamorphosis into cunning conspirator seems a sudden radical alteration of character'; 'when Richard abruptly turns Machiavel, he develops a *sangfroid* that makes

York seem by contrast a slave of passion' (Ornstein, *A Kingdom for a Stage*, p. 58). Ornstein quotes lines 154–71 of Richard's soliloquy in iii.ii and remarks that 'the welling of hatred in these lines astounds because nothing in the earlier portrayal of Richard hints of this tormented sense of abnormality and inferiority. Twice his enemies sneer at his deformity without provoking his wrath' (p. 59).

25. Brockbank, 'The Frame of Disorder – "Henry VI" ' in *Early Shakespeare*, Stratford-upon-Avon Studies 3 (1961; 1967) p. 93.

26. The germ of *R2* may have lain in this scene. But it is interesting to notice that the problem of the right to adopt an heir is not broached either in *R2* or *H4*. The emphasis there is on the problem of voluntary abdication or deposition by force.

27. This speech may seem out of character as coming from the peace-loving Henry, but it must be remembered that he has not yet looked into the horrors of civil war. There is after all *some* development of character in *3H6*.

28. I find Philip Brockbank's statement unassailable: 'As it is, the plays of *Henry VI* are not, as it were, haunted by the ghost of Richard II, and the catastrophes of the civil wars are not laid to Bolingbroke's charge; the catastrophic virtue of Henry and the catastrophic evil of Richard are not an inescapable inheritance from the distant past but are generated by the happenings we are made to witness' (*Early Shakespeare*, p. 98). This view is argued at greater length and with some force by A. L. French in ' "Henry VI" and the Ghost of Richard II' (*ES*, Anglo-American Supplement 1969, xxxvii–xliii). See also Ribner, *The English History Play*, pp. 108–10.

  In 1974 French went so far as to doubt whether Justice reigns in the Yorkist plays at all: 'if Justice reigns in these plays, if the mills of God grind slow but grind exceeding fine, then that Justice – and that God – are incomprehensible to human minds. It is in this way that the tetralogy is so devastatingly subversive: starting off from a world of simple, heroic patriotism, embodied in Talbot and others, it moves towards a final world in which morality has ceased to have any meaning at all – where death has become totally capricious, striking down the innocent and sparing the guilty and sometimes, for no obvious reason, doing the reverse' ('The Mills of God and Shakespeare's Early History Plays', *ES*, 55.4 (1974) 313–24. See p. 323).

29. In i.i.107–9 and 136 the appeal to right by conquest is made by King Henry. The argument is also used by Oxford in iii.iii.81–90.

30. Michael Quinn has an interesting discussion of 'Providence in Shakespeare's Yorkist Plays' in *SQ*, x.l (Winter 1959) 45–52. According to Quinn, Shakespeare in these plays tends to show how events develop by their own logic of cause and effect rather than by the arbitrary direction of providence or fortune.

31. For a full discussion of Shakespeare's use of oaths and perjury in the first tetralogy see Faye L. Kelly, 'Oaths in Shakespeare's *Henry VI* Plays', *SQ*, xxiv.4 (Autumn 1973) 357–71.

32. While *2H6* has had a number of separate productions, I have no information that *3H6* has been produced independently. See C.B.Y. on 'The Stage History of *King Henry VI*', New Cambr., *3H6*.

Chapter 3   Treachery and Dissension – Two Plays into One

1. E. M. W. Tillyard, *Shakespeare's History Plays* (Peregrine, 1962) pp. 161–73; P. Alexander, *Shakespeare's Henry VI and Richard III* (1929) pp. 189–92; H. T. Price, *Construction in Shakespeare* (1951) pp. 24–37; L. Kirschbaum, 'The Authorship of

1 Henry VI', *PMLA* LXVII (1952) 809–22; G. Bullough, *Sources*, III (1960) pp. 34–5; J. P. Brockbank, 'The Frame of Disorder – "Henry VI"' in *Early Shakespeare* (Stratford-upon-Avon Studies 3), esp. p. 72; A. S. Cairncross, Introduction to the Arden *1H6* (1962) pp. li–lii; A. W. Pollard, *The Foundations of Shakespeare's Text* (1923); W. W. Greg, *The Shakespeare First Folio* (1955) pp. 185–6; E. K. Chambers, *William Shakespeare* (1930) vol. 1, pp. 289–93; J. Dover Wilson, Introduction to the New Cambridge *1H6* (1952) pp. ix–l.

2. Op. cit., pp. 25, 26, 35.

3. Ibid., p. 28.

4. See note 1 above.

5. Don M. Ricks, *Shakespeare's Emergent Form / A Study of the Structure of the Henry VI Plays* (1968) p. 99.

6. Ibid., p. 63.

7. *Early Shakespeare*, p. 78.

8. Emrys Jones misses this point when he explains the Countess episode as a comment on theatrical illusion: 'By means of this invented incident, . . . Shakespeare is alluding to the nature of the imaginative work he is engaged in as the author of a new kind of history play' (*The Origins of Shakespeare*, pp. 143–9).

9. The rhythm of defeat and victory is repeated *four* times if we begin with the first news of revolt and include Salisbury's repulse of the French attack in I.ii ('they are beaten back by the English with great loss'). But these opening events are not really dramatised.

10. *Construction in Shakespeare*, p. 34. Brockbank calls it a 'false peace' (*Early Shakespeare*, p. 80) and R. Ornstein thinks 'the concluding ceremonies of peace and concord are sham' (*A Kingdom for a Stage*, p. 40).

11. P. Bilton, *Commentary and Control in Shakespeare's Plays*, p. 24.

12. See e.g. H. T. Price: 'In the end the disunion and treachery resulting from the weakness of the King cause the loss of France' (*Construction in Shakespeare*, p. 25); A. Cairncross: 'The theme of the play is the loss of France, and the ruin of England' (Arden *1H6*, p. xlix); and M. M. Reese: 'It is primarily a play about the French wars, showing how Talbot . . . lost the English provinces in France . . .' (*The Cease of Majesty*, p. 168).
The 'fatal prophecy' quoted by Exeter in III.i.198–9

> That Henry born at Monmouth should win all,
> And Henry born at Windsor should lose all:

is not fulfilled until we get to *2H6*; nor has it any reference in the context to anything preceding the reign of Henry V. It is not true that *1H6* 'develops the general theme of Hall – the retribution on Henry VI for the original sin of his grandfather' (Cairncross, Arden ed., p. xlii). Even old Mortimer does not speak of the murder of Richard II. This subject with its attendant ideas of guilt and retribution only just begins to be developed in *The Contention* and *R3* and is not fully considered till *H4* and *H5*. See also Bullough, *Sources*, III, pp. 36–7 and my previous chapter (p. 36) with note 28.

13. Cf. Chambers, *W.S.*, I, pp. 290–1.

14. Ibid.

15. Tillyard, *Shakespeare's History Plays*, p. 149. Bullough (*Sources*, III, pp. 24–5) reminds us of the topicality in 1591–2 of scenes dealing with English military exploits in France, and this would certainly provide a good reason for a revival of an old Talbot play but hardly provides a basis for a dating of its composition.

16. Ribner, *The English History Play*, pp. 97–9. See also Greg, op. cit., pp. 185–6.

17. New Cambr. *1H6*, pp. xi–xii.

18. Arden *1H6*, note to I.i.39.
19. Including Dover Wilson, in spite of, or perhaps even because of, his theory of composite authorship – see his Introduction to the New Cambridge ed., pp. xiv–xv and Born, 'The Date of *2, 3 Henry VI*', *SQ*, 25.3 (1974) 323–34. Born has marshalled the evidence for the identification of *1H6* with Henslowe's 'harey the vj', but it is hard to accept his theory of the continuous composition by Shakespeare of *1–3 H6* in that order.
20. See *Sources*, III, pp. 24, 34. Marcus Mincoff offers an interesting but perhaps unnecessarily elaborate theory of a fairly continuous process of composition which nevertheless reveals stages in Shakespeare's growing confidence and traces of changes in design in the course of writing: see 'The Composition of *Henry VI, Part I*', *SQ*, 16.4 (1965) 279–87. I am in general sympathy with Mincoff's approach but find a much clearer distinction than he does between early parts of the play and later additions.
21. The subject was already there in Shakespeare's main source. Brockbank quotes from Holinshed, writing on the loss of a group of towns in 1451: 'Everie daie was looking for aid, but none came. And whie? Even bicause the divelish division that reigned in England, so incombred the heads of the noble men there, that the honor of the realme was cleerelie forgotten.' (Hol., p. 228) (*Early Shakespeare*, p. 77.)
22. There is nothing in Joan's own words in I.ii to make us doubt the sincerity of her piety and patriotism; and in her speech to Burgundy in III.iii she is allowed to present the French view of the war with eloquence and genuine feeling, which cannot be entirely cancelled out by the sarcasm of her final remark: 'Done like a Frenchman! – turn and turn again.' See also Brockbank. *Early Shakespeare*, p. 80. Brockbank points out that Shakespeare's inconsistent presentation of Joan goes back to Holinshed. But as A. L. French remarks, 'So odd and out of key with what has gone before is the third scene of Act V, when Joan enters and starts raising evil spirits, that we can only wonder whether there was not an abrupt change of intention on Shakespeare's part' ('Joan of Arc and *Henry VI*', *ES*, XLIX, 5, p. 427).
23. There are layers within layers as well, if we wish to analyse closely. Thus the three scenes featuring Talbot and his son (IV.v, vi, vii) are all for the most part in stilted rhymed verse and seemingly belong to the original play. But they are repetitious. Of Scenes v and vi Dover Wilson observes: 'Not only is the action almost identical (the father urging the son to save himself by flight; the son refusing to desert his father; both going forward into battle resolved to die together), but the two speakers repeat the same arguments, even at times in nearly the same words!' (New Cambr., p. xlv). The verbal similarities in lines like 'Fly, to revenge my death if I be slain', 'Fly, to revenge my death when I am dead' are only distinguished by the relative inelegance of the latter line. Scene vi also shares some verbal similarities with Scene vii ('Where is John Talbot?' / 'O, where's young Talbot?'; 'Thou Icarus' / 'My Icarus'). But vi and vii give very different accounts of the battle. According to Scene vi, John fights the Dauphin and is wounded by Orleans but saved by his father. In Scene vii the father is saved by the son, and John encounters Joan, who is not mentioned in vi. In scene vi Talbot complains of the Regent only, in vii the Dauphin holds both York and Somerset responsible for the French victory. Scene vi seems particularly primitive, and contains archaisms like 'well I wot' and 'die with mickle age'. I am sceptical of Dover Wilson's hypothesis that IV.v is Shakespeare's revision of IV.vi, the latter by Greene. But I do find it likely that IV.vi was meant to be cancelled.
24. Reese, *The Cease of Majesty*, p. 170n.
25. In the letter from Burgundy delivered by Falstaff to King Henry in IV.i, Burgundy says

he has 'join'd with Charles, the rightful King of France', but this is only an assertion of Charles's right, not of his having been crowned.

It is odd that Shakespeare should have Charles crowned at Rheims before the coming of Joan of Arc, since it was probably as well known in Shakespeare's day as it is in ours (thanks to Bernard Shaw perhaps) that she was instrumental in bringing about this event. In any case Hall and Holinshed place the coronation of Charles just before the capture of Joan by the English.

26. Shakespeare often has three citizens, three soldiers, three servants, etc. but not three messengers, though there are often two in quick succession and once, in *R3*, four.

27. I have followed the F pointing in placing a comma after 'Since arms avail not' instead of the semicolon of the Arden edition, so as to link this statement with 'now that Henry's dead'.

28. It is interesting to notice that the two lines in IV.vii which mention the failure of York and Somerset to bring rescue to Talbot (ll.33–4) are the only blank verse lines in the middle of 48 lines of rhymed verse.

29. See Arden ed., note to v.i.28ff. Mincoff thinks III.i 'was almost certainly intended as a substitute for' I.iii, 'which would provide a bad headache for the producer, and indeed simply could not have been played together with v.i'. See *SQ*, 16.4 (1965) p. 286.

30. After I.i we find Exeter speaking at the end of III.i, at IV.i.134 and the end of IV.i, at v.i.28–33, and at v.v.46–7.

31. I suspect that the passage in v.iii beginning with Reignier's line 'Welcome, brave Earl, into our territories' and a little later calling Suffolk 'deputy' to King Henry was at some point intended as a separate scene in which Suffolk was betrothed *pro forma* to Margaret *after* having won King Henry's consent. The present arrangement is obviously more economical, if less realistic.

32. New Cambr. ed., p. x.

33. I can only express surprise at Kirschbaum's defence of these rhymed scenes, which seems entirely insensitive to the badness of much of the verse. See *PMLA*, LXVII (1952) pp. 821–2.

Chapter 4 Plots and Prophecies – *King Richard the Third*

(The New Penguin *Richard III*, ed. E. A. J. Honigmann (1968) has been used for quotations and references.)

1. M. Neill, 'Shakespeare's Halle of Mirrors: Play, Politics, and Psychology in *Richard III*', *SSt.*, VIII (1975) p. 99.

2. Ribner, *The English History Play in the Age of Shakespeare* (1957) pp. 117–20. See also A. P.Rossiter, 'The Structure of Richard the Third', *Durham University Journal*, XXXI (1938) 44–75; and 'Angel with Horns: The Unity of Richard III' in *Angel with Horns* (1961) 1–21. In the former essay Rossiter analyses *R3* in terms of a 'ritualistic method', which is first introduced, he thinks, in II.v of *3H6* and there marks a new departure. In 'Angel with Horns' he sees *R3* as 'a symphonic structure . . . with first and second subjects and some Wagnerian *Leitmotifs*' (p. 7).

3. Reese, *The Cease of Majesty*, p. 208.

4. Rossiter, 'The Structure of Richard the Third' (see n. 2); Clemen, 'Anticipation and Foreboding in Shakespeare's Early Histories', *SS*, 6 (1953) 25–35.

5. This statement perhaps needs a slight qualification. Richard is at least made to *appear* secretive about his intentions in marrying Lady Anne and for a long time he successfully conceals his nightmares. See p. 63.

6. Richard threatens revenge on Rivers, *Dorset*, and Grey in the F text, but Dorset is replaced by Vaughan when it comes to the execution of this revenge. Q has 'Ryuers, Vaughan, Gray' in the first place, too.

7. Buckingham is the only person present in the cursing scene besides Richard who remains seemingly unaffected at first, to Margaret's annoyance. After his sceptical remarks it is surely wrong to attribute the speech 'My hair doth stand an end to hear her curses' to Buckingham, as the New Penguin edition does, following F. Q gives it correctly to Hastings.

8. He does not say that he foretold his death on All Souls' Day, however, as Honigmann thinks – see New Penguin *R3*, p. 18.

9. *SS*, 6, p. 27.

10. A. L. French thinks the curses in *R3* do not all 'come *entirely* true' and that the point of this is to show that there is no absolute reign of Justice in the world of the history plays. See 'The Mills of God and Shakespeare's Early History Plays', *ES*, 55, 4 (Aug. 1974) 313–24, esp. pp. 321–3.

11. Margaret in both the Q and F texts curses Rivers, Dorset, and Hastings for being 'standers-by' when her son 'was stabbed with bloody daggers' (I.iii.209–11), but in the execution scene at Pomfret Grey makes it clear that he, and not Dorset, was meant; and in IV.iv.68–9, Hastings, Rivers, Vaughan, and Grey are called 'the beholders of this frantic play' (i.e. of the stabbing of Edward). In Shakespeare's *3H6* none of them are standers-by, though Hall says that Dorset and Hastings took part in the murder of Edward. Shakespeare evidently wanted Dorset to be quite a young man in *R3* and replaced the older Dorset by Grey. He must have failed to do so at I.iii.209, and there would seem to be a good case here for emendation.

It should be clear from I.iii.254–9 that Margaret only scolds Dorset and does not specifically curse him. He is included, however, in the general curse on Elizabeth's children ('Long mayst thou live to wail thy children's death', l.203), as Elizabeth remembers in IV.i.43–6. It is from this curse that he escapes.

12. Compare the two other places where the word 'despair' occurs in *R3*:

> *Anne.* Fouler than heart can think thee, thou canst make
>   No excuse current but to hang thyself.
> *Richard.* By such despair I should accuse myself.
> *Anne.* And by despairing shalt thou stand excused
>   For doing worthy vengeance on thyself
>   That didst unworthy slaughter upon others.   (I.ii.83–8)

> *Queen Elizabeth.* I'll join with black despair against my soul
>   And to myself become an enemy.   (II.ii.36–7)

Compare also the three occurrences in *Lear*: IV.vi.33; V.iii.192; V.iii.255.

13. There are a number of good reasons for transferring these lines. They occur in a passage in V.iii, ll.205–16 as numbered in the New Penguin edition, but here quoted from the first quarto:

> 205 Me thought the soules of all that I had murtherd,
>   Came to my tent, and euery one did threat,
>   To morrows vengeance on the head of Richard.
>   *Enter Ratcliffe.*
> *Rat.* My Lord.

> *King.* Zoundes, who is there?
> 210   *Rat.* Ratcliffe, my Lord, tis I, the earlie village cocke,
> Hath twise done salutation to the morne,
> Your friendes are vp, and buckle on their armor.
> *King.* O Ratcliffe, I haue dreamd a fearefull dreame,
> What thinkst thou, will our friendes proue all true?
> 215   *Rat.* No doubt my Lord.
> *King.* O Ratcliffe, I fear, I feare.
> 216   *Rat.* Nay good my Lord, be not afraid of shadowes.

The following peculiarities may be noted: 1. The first three lines of this passage come abruptly and oddly at the end of Richard's soliloquy on starting out of his dream. One would expect Richard to identify his dream at the beginning (i.e. after 'Soft! I did but dream.') rather than at the end of the soliloquy. And if the lines are meant for information this can hardly be intended for the audience, supposing they have already seen and heard the ghosts. 2. The questionable lines as printed in F correspond in substantial details with the *first* quarto version, whereas they disagree with the *third* quarto from which, for the most part, the scene in the F text was pretty mechanically set. This certainly indicates a disturbance of *some* kind. 3. Lines 213–15 are omitted in F, in spite of its care in reproducing Q3 elsewhere. Most likely the compositor's eye jumped from the 'O Ratcliffe' of line 213 to the identical phrase three lines down, but the omission could be deliberate. At any rate it leaves Ratcliffe's exhortation 'be not afraid of shadowes' in line 216 without a point of reference. 4. Richmond describes his dream to his friends in the morning. He uses words which parallel those at the end of Richard's soliloquy:

> The sweetest sleep, and fairest-boding dreams
> That ever entered in a drowsy head
> Have I since your departure had, my lords.
> Methought their souls whose bodies Richard murdered
> Came to my tent and cried on victory.
> I promise you my heart is very jocund
> In the remembrance of so fair a dream.

This suggests that Richard's words, too, should be addressed to an interlocutor. Hall tells how the king 'recyted and declared to hys famylyer frendes in the morenynge hys wonderfull visyon and terrible dreame'. Both Richard and Richmond would then describe their dreams sufficiently to their friends to make the spectacle of the ghosts unnecessary, and the play is long enough without it. Even so, Shakespeare may have felt that he wanted this scene of combined Senecan eeriness and groundling entertainment, and it undeniably goes unobtrusively enough with the formalism of the play as a whole. (Clarence's dream, of course, is only described, but this is a different case, since Clarence is not a main character.)

The reason for the anomalies in the transmitted texts could be untidiness in the manuscript which was used by the Q compositor. Concerning the relationship of this manuscript to the copy for F see my *Memorial Transmission and Quarto Copy in 'Richard III'* (Oslo, 1970).

14. The Duchess of York in her last words to Richard calls on 'the little souls of Edward's children' to

> Whisper the spirits of thine enemies
> And promise them success and victory!   (IV.iv.192–4)

And Buckingham, on his way to execution, invokes the souls of

> Hastings, and Edward's children, Grey and Rivers,
> Holy King Henry and thy fair son Edward,
> Vaughan, and all that have miscarried
> By underhand corrupted foul injustice,

to mock his own destruction (v.i.3–9). He makes no specific mention of Clarence, Anne or, naturally, of himself.

15. The repetition looks like a memorial error in Q copied by F, which was here set from Q3. The lines perhaps more naturally belong to Anne than to Clarence, since she once, in the first wooing scene, herself pointed a sword at Richard and let it fall. This would make Clarence's lines a case of anticipation. But the repetition could also be a sign that Anne's appearance was an afterthought.

16. Reese, op. cit., p. 212. Cf. Ribner, p. 122: 'His [Richmond's] personality is deliberately underdeveloped . . .; he is instrument rather than actor.' And A. L. French: 'artistically speaking, Shakespeare was intent upon making Richmond as much of a cipher as possible' ('The World of Richard III', *SSt.*, IV (1968) p. 31).

17. An extreme example of attempts to prove the wooing scene psychologically probable is Donald R. Shupe's 'The Wooing of Lady Anne: A Psychological Inquiry', *SQ*, 29, 1 (Winter 1978) 28–36.

18. Tillyard, *Shakespeare's History Plays*, p. 204; Ribner, p. 118; New Penguin *R3*, p. 30.

19. Reese, p. 223; French, *SSt.* IV, pp. 25, 33–6.

20. There is no foundation in the play or the *H6* plays for the assertion that 'Richard woos Anne because Clarence has expropriated Anne's wealth, which Richard hopes to gain by doing away with Clarence and marrying her'. (*Shakespeare Newsletter*, Sep. 1971, review of Denzell S. Smith, 'The Credibility of the Wooing of Anne in *Richard III*', *PLL*, 7.2 (Spring 1971) 199–202.)

21. Cf. *3H6*, v.vi.71–3:

> I came into the world with my legs forward.
> Had I not reason, think ye, to make haste
> And seek their ruin that usurp'd our right?

Honigmann (p. 24) speaks of Richard's 'suddenness', which is another aspect of the same quality.

22. This apparently is the view taken by Louis E. Dollarhide in an article entitled 'Two Unassimilated Movements of Richard III: An Interpretation' (*Mississippi Quarterly*, XIV (1960) 40–6). Taking a cue from A. P. Rossiter, Dollarhide thinks that 'In writing *Richard III*, Shakespeare was evidently trying to do two things – first, construct a fable on a structure of curses and related emotive figures; and, second, present the portrait of "a witty king" . . .'. Dollarhide thinks that Shakespeare awkwardly and inconsistently brought the 'witty king' motif to a climax in Richard's successful wooing of Elizabeth when he had already set Richard on a declining course in the curses plot. Stephen L. Tanner reports this view (I am indebted to his report) and attacks it in his

own interpretation of the second wooing scene, 'Richard III versus Elizabeth' (*SQ*, XXIV.4 (1973) 468–72). Tanner contends that in giving Elizabeth the upper hand in the wit combat Shakespeare obviously meant to show that Richard was continuing his fatal descent. There is thus an unbroken downward movement from the third scene of Act IV on. I personally see no difficulty in combining a sense of Richard's declining power – both politically and mentally – with a recognition of his hard-won victory over Elizabeth in argument. He has not yet been finally defeated. And if Elizabeth's submission seems sudden this kind of quick yielding after long persuasion is far from unique in Shakespeare. It is more worrying that we hear nothing of Elizabeth's subsequent change of mind before Stanley sends word to Richmond 'that the Queen hath heartily consented / He [Richmond] should espouse Elizabeth her daughter' (IV.v.7–8 – these lines, incidentally, are misinterpreted by Tanner).

23. It cannot be ruled out that the reason why the F editors (or compositors) used Q3 as copy for two extended passages in *R3* was that the Q version for some reason contained speeches which were not in the manuscript to which they had access. We know that in one place it contained twenty lines of dialogue (the 'clock passage') which at any rate did not get into F, whether or not they were in the manuscript copy.

24. Margaret was left out by Cibber and in our own time by Olivier, though this, of course does not prove her superfluous.

25. 'Lord Hastings was to her for his delivery' is the Q reading. F reads 'Lord Hastings was, for her delivery' and the New Penguin 'Lord Hastings was for his delivery'.

26. See New Penguin *R3*, p. 15. Geoffrey Bullough, following G. B. Churchill and Dover Wilson, gives reasons for thinking *The True Tragedie* preceded *R3* – see *Sources*, III, pp. 238–9. In any case, 'Shores wife, King Edward the fourths Concubine' has her own complaint in the *Mirror for Magistrates*. Contemporary interest in Jane Shore is also attested by her appearance in the two parts of Heywood's *Edward IV* (1594?).

   Honigmann recognises the importance attributed to Jane Shore in the early scenes of *R3* but thinks she becomes mainly 'a moral touchstone' and concludes rather oddly that 'her function . . . is the same as that of the invisible Falstaff in *Henry V*' (New Penguin *R3*, pp. 41–2).

27. *Sources*, III, p. 239.

28. New Penguin *R3*, p. 18.

29. In *The True Tragedie* (Sc. xxi) Dorset is at least enquired after by Queen Elizabeth after the battle of Bosworth, and Richmond informs her that he had to remain in France as a pledge for the men provided by the French king.

30. Tillyard, pp. 199–200. See Reese, p. 224: 'a play which . . . is only a complement to *Henry VI*.' And French, *SSt.* IV, p. 25: 'if it is acted by itself, a great many references which are only meaningful in the light of *Henry VI* are baffling and have to be excised.'

31. New Penguin *R3*, pp.43–4.

32. The queen's reference to the Countess of Richmond in I.iii. 20–4, since that person does not appear in the play, can only serve to point out that she is Stanley's wife and to remind us of the existence of her son. Richmond himself is not mentioned till IV.i.42, when Dorset is advised to fly to him, but in the following scene Richard becomes concerned with Richmond and his name is mentioned seven times in quick succession and again three times in IV.iii.

   As for Stanley being an afterthought in I.iii as I suggest, the best indications are (a) that he is not brought off the stage again although he has no speeches and can have no part in the quarrelling and cursing that follow, and (b) that he is an unlikely person to bring news of the king's health to the queen. So, for that matter, is Buckingham, who takes over as spokesman for the two lords and also tells the queen that the king has called a meeting of the opposing factions at court to 'make atonement' between them. It turns out only a moment later (i.iii.62–8) that the queen knows more about this meeting than Buckingham. On top of these indications it is interesting to notice that the entry of Buckingham and Stanley is announced with the words (spoken by Grey), 'Here comes the Lord of Buckingham & Derby.' This is the F version. Q1 has both the verb and the noun in the plural ('Here come the Lords') whereas Q3–6 have 'Here comes the Lords'.

It seems likely that the muddle of Stanley and Derby in speech headings and stage directions later in the play is due to his first, erroneous, appearance as Derby. In *The True Tragedie*, Stanley remains Stanley throughout.

33. The change from Sir William Stanley to Lord Stanley may be counted as a discrepancy. Another has been pointed out in note 11: there are no 'standers-by' other than King Edward and his brothers and Queen Margaret during the killing of Prince Edward in *3H6*. In *3H6* it is King Edward who first stabs the prince. Richard recalls this once in the later play, when he tells Lady Anne, 'I did not kill your husband' and claims that he was 'slain by Edward's hands' (i.ii.91–2). At iv.iv.63 Margaret reminds the Duchess of York, 'Thy Edward he is dead, that killed my Edward'. But elsewhere in *R3* the blame for the murder of the prince is laid entirely on Richard. He himself admits to it in his soliloquy in i.ii. King Edward is made to appear relatively blameless in *R3*.

At i.iii.186 we are told, after the murder of Rutland has been brought up, that 'Northumberland, then present, wept to see it'. But in *3H6* Northumberland is not present at the slaying of Rutland but weeps to see the suffering of York (i.iv.169–71). In *R3* Richard claims that Elizabeth and her husband Grey 'were factious for the house of Lancaster' and that Grey was slain 'in Margaret's battle at Saint Albans' (i.iii.126–9), whereas in *3H6* Edward tells his brother that 'in quarrel of the house of York / The worthy gentleman did lose his life' (iii.ii.6–7).

In addition to the small *internal* inconsistencies in *R3* pointed out in note 11 above, it may be mentioned that Ratcliffe in the F version and Catesby in the Q version are present in two places simultaneously (see my *Iniurious Impostors and 'Richard III'* (Oslo, 1964, p. 22). And Margaret in recapitulating her mockery of Queen Elizabeth in iv.iv.82–91 remembers more than she ever said in the cursing scene in i.iii.196–208. Finally, Richmond's order to the Earl of Pembroke to see him in his tent 'by the second hour in the morning' (v.iii.31–2) is not followed up.

34. John Palmer sees the change in Richard taking place at an earlier time and fails to notice that Richard remains loyal not only to his father but to his brother Edward until the latter's marriage to Lady Elizabeth Grey. See his *Political Characters of Shakespeare* (1945) pp. 68–9. Rossiter, concentrating on the dramatic method of the early history plays, finds the most remarkable 'fault' in *3H6*, ii.v – see note 2 above.

Chapter 5   The Troublesome Theme of *King John*

(The new Arden *King John* edited by E. A. J. Honigmann (1954; repr. 1973) has been used for quotations and references. It should be noticed that its act and scene divisions differ from F and also occasionally from those traditionally adopted by other editors.)

1. See the Arden *KJ*, p. xix; *The Riverside Shakespeare* (1974) pp. 50, 765; New Penguin *KJ*, p. 10.

2. Blanche's parentage is not explicitly mentioned in the play, though her claim to the succession is referred to at III.iii.142 and v.ii.93–4.

3. See also Pembroke's remark on hearing of Arthur's death: 'That blood which ow'd the breadth of all this isle / Three foot of it doth hold' (IV.ii.99–100).

4. See for instance Honigmann's note to II.i.182. Smallwood (New Penguin ed.) points to 'the strong suggestion of John's bastardy in [Constance's] next speech' (i.e. lines 184–90), but his note to II.i.125 indicates that he thinks Constance is just returning abuse for abuse. It seems unlikely to me that Constance intends (or that Shakespeare intended) any reference to Eleanor's infidelity in her *first* marriage.

   As for Constance's infidelity and Arthur's bastardy, there may be another veiled allusion when King Philip tells King John that there are 'well-born bloods' on the French side 'to contradict his claim' and Faulconbridge interrupts, 'Some bastards too' (II.i.278–80).

5. '*Lewis*' and '*Lew.*' in three speech headings and '*King Lewis*' once in the dialogue of F in the scene corresponding to the Arden II.i are patently a mistake for (King) Philip, and editors (i.a. Dover Wilson and Smallwood) are right in emending accordingly. I do not share Wilson's view of Shakespeare's 'uncertainty about the names of historical persons' (New Cambr. *KJ*, p. xliv) or Smallwood's of his lacking concern 'with precise historical identity' (Penguin p. 353), but in other respects concur with their explanations. There is nothing very surprising about this authorial slip.

6. E.g. Dover Wilson p. xlii and Honigmann pp. l–li. In this case Shakespeare may have taken a wrong hint from *The Troublesome Raigne*, where, in the passage corresponding to the beginning of II.i. of *KJ*, Arthur links John's brother, meaning Richard, with John's nephew, meaning himself, and Lymoges remarks as if still referring to Richard:

   > Why *Arthur* heres his spoyle that now is gon,
   > Who when he livde outrode his Brother *John*:

7. I take it to be firmly enough established that *The Troublesome Raigne* preceded *KJ* and refer to the arguments of Dover Wilson (pp. xvii–xxxiv) and Smallwood (pp. 365–74). It will hardly be disputed that *TR* was written by a less gifted or less mature playwright than was *KJ* and I find it impossible to believe that such a lesser playwright would have been able to avoid verbal echoes from an earlier play or even close repetition to the extent that the author of *KJ* avoided them.

8. Bullough, *Sources*, IV, pp. 26, 86.

9. But see also the quotation from H. Swinburne, *Briefe Treatise of Testaments* (1590) given in Honigmann's note to I.i.124.

10. Except figuratively in a few instances, as I point out below.

11. See especially the speeches of Blanche and Constance in III.i.136–42 and the exchange of King Philip and Pandulph in III.i.188–9.

12. Thus Smallwood declares (p. 9) that 'Shakespeare places the largely unhistorical figure of the Bastard boldly in the centre of the political action. He also lures the audience into forgetting that John was succeeded by Henry III, while the dramatic focus falls with increasing certainty on the Bastard.'

13. See especially II.i.70. Philip may be saying something similar in II.i.276.

14. This is certainly Smallwood's opinion – see his ed., p. 21.

15. J. C. Van de Water, 'The Bastard in *King John*', *SQ*, XI.2, 137–46. J. L. Simmons repeats the idea that 'in the last two acts the Bastard comes much closer to epitomizing the loyal follower than he does the regal leader' (Van de Water, p. 144), but I find his attempt to refute the view that the Bastard changes and the view that he 'is entirely

outside the structure of the play' unconvincing. (See 'Shakespeare's *King John* and Its Source: Coherence, Pattern, and Vision', *Tulane Studies in English*, XVII (1969) 53–72, esp. pp. 69–70.)

16. Op. cit., pp. 143–4.

17. G. Boklund, 'The Troublesome Ending of *King John*', *Studia neophilologica*, XL (1968) 175–84; see p. 183. In fairness to Van de Water I must add that she does not think the Bastard essential to the action of the play in spite of his activity and eloquence.

18. New Penguin *KJ*, pp. 37–8.

19. Bullough, *Sources*, IV, p. 131.

20. Nomenclature in speech headings often goes by pages in F, suggesting editorial and/or compositorial responsibility. On the other hand, the French king is mistakenly called Lewis both in speech headings and in the dialogue in F, where the author would seem responsible (see n. 5). I find Dover Wilson's arguments for the common identity of the two Huberts (pp. xlv–xlvii) quite unconvincing.

21. *TR* gives no proper name to the Citizen who speaks for Angiers.

22. Aldis Wright, according to Dover Wilson (p. xlix), 'was apparently the first to perceive [the] true significance' of this passage, but the explanation seems fairly obvious, and I fail to be persuaded by Honigmann (p. xli) that Constance's delayed response is 'part of Shakespeare's standard "frenzy technique"'.

   In *TR* Shakespeare would have found only King Philip's invitation to Constance, 'Despaire not yet, come *Constance*, goe with me,' followed by their exits.

23. This being so, there is sufficient explanation within the play for John's wish for a second coronation, though his reference to reasons already given and his promise of further confidences on the subject may lead us to suspect that something may have been omitted from the received text, since we are made to expect information that is after all withheld.

24. J. R. Price is very likely right when he finds a deliberate ambiguity in Shakespeare's portrayal of John, as long as he means in the character and not the author's point of view. But I cannot share his enthusiasm for the ambiguity in the other characters. See '*King John* and Problematic Art', *SQ*, XXI, 1 (Winter 1970) 25–8.

Chapter 6   King Richard's Guilt and the Poetry of Kingship

1. Wells, Introduction to the New Penguin *R2*, p. 9.

2. See e.g. Dover Wilson, Introduction to the New Cambridge *R2*, p. xiii ('*Richard II* ought to be played throughout as ritual'); and Tillyard, *Shakespeare's History Plays*, pp. 244–52 (Shakespeare made 'the ceremonial or ritual form of writing [. . .] the very essence of the play').

3. See Wilson's Introduction, pp. xi–xii (esp. xii, n. 1) xiv, lxv.

4. But hardly at III.ii.122 as Dover Wilson surmises. See his note to this line.

5. The Q stage direction for v.iv, '*Exeunt. Manet sir Pierce Exton, &c.*', can only be explained as a remnant of an earlier and possibly more complete version in which Exton actually overheard Bolingbroke's wish to be rid of Richard. This being so, it is legitimate to guess that there may also have been other scenes which are now lost, e.g. clarifying the circumstances of Bagot's reappearance and the accusation of Aumerle.

6. See esp. A. P. Rossiter's chapter on *R2* in *Angel with Horns*. Ribner finds that 'The dependence of *Richard II* upon *Woodstock* has been amply demonstrated by Rossiter' and that it is 'everywhere apparent' 'that Shakespeare knew both *Edward II* and *Woodstock*

when he came to write his *Richard II*' (*The English History Play*, p. 145). Bullough, too, believes 'that *Woodstock* preceded *Richard II* and slightly affected [Shakespeare's] handling of the reign' (*Sources*, III, p. 358).

7. There is textual evidence for the king's uneasiness, but obviously this uneasiness can be demonstrated visually on the stage even in excess of textual authority. Some critics, too, go beyond the textual evidence in emphasising the extent to which the king himself stands openly accused in the first scene and is himself aware of it. Thus John Palmer, with deliberate but surely misapplied anachronism, declares that 'In accusing Mowbray, Bolingbroke is covertly attacking the King's government. He is playing the party game of His Majesty's Opposition, using the gestures of the period. Mowbray, of course, knows what Bolingbroke is driving at. So does everybody else' (*Political Characters of Shakespeare*, p. 122). Palmer interprets the first act of *R2* and the political conflict of the play in the light of the chronicle sources. In Holinshed's narrative, Hereford, in his accusations against Norfolk, touches the king more closely than in Shakespeare: 'he hath caused to die and to be murdered your right deere vncle, the duke of Glocester, sonne to king Edward . . .', and we are told that 'The king herewith waxed angrie'. Palmer's analysis of the underlying motives of the dispute between Bolingbroke and Mowbray is otherwise illuminating. Larry S. Champion ('The Function of Mowbray: Shakespeare's Maturing Artistry in *Richard II*', *SQ*, XXVI.1, 3–7) also realises the importance of the king's involvement in the murder charge and his awareness of this involvement. But I find Champion's attempt to prove that the king becomes furious with Mowbray for bringing the issue into the open unconvincing.

8. See especially the conversation between Northumberland, Willoughby, and Ross at the end of II.i.

9. This is in accordance with *Woodstock*. Holinshed on the contrary (following Hall) sees the Duke of Gloucester as a mischievous opponent of King Richard who deserved what he got.

10. Bullough, *Sources*, III, pp. 386–7.

11. Mowbray is banished and forgotten on insufficient grounds, as it would seem from the last part of the play, when the responsibility for the murder of Gloucester is transferred from Mowbray to Aumerle. The effect, at least retrospectively, is a feeling that the character was overemphasised in the opening scenes.

12. *SQ*, 29.1 (Winter 1978) 5–19. I am in general sympathy with Barkan's essay in so far as it 'runs against the tide of a good deal of criticism tending to see *Richard II* as extremely unified', but I cannot accept some of his more specific arguments, and in particular I think he is wide of the mark in his concluding assertions about King Richard, e.g. that he 'could not or would not get at the truth about Gloucester'.

13. One critic ingeniously disposes of the whole problem by suggesting that Aumerle becomes Richard's scapegoat and assumes his guilt, so that Richard 'can come to the deposition virtually an innocent man'. See Warren J. MacIsaac, 'The Three Cousins in *Richard II*', *SQ*, XXII, 2 (1971) 137–46.

14. Schoenbaum, ' "Richard II" and the Realities of Power', *SS*, 28 (1975) p. 13.

15. Rossiter, *Angel with Horns*, p. 28.

16. *SQ*, 29.4 (1971) 337–44. In an earlier article, 'Who Deposed Richard II?' (*Ess. in Cr.*, XVII, 1967, pp. 411–33), French suggested that Shakespeare first 'started to write about a Richard who abdicated rather than being deposed', then changed his mind, and adopted the official view of Richard as a king unlawfully deposed. The result was the ambiguous action and the confusing portrait of the king which we find in the play. I find little to recommend this particular unconformity theory.

17. Traversi, *Shakespeare from 'Richard II' to 'Henry V'*, p. 15.
18. Op. cit., pp. lxvii–lxviii.
19. New Arden *R2*, pp. lxiv–lxxi.
20. Bullough, *Sources*, III, pp. 378–9.
21. Empson, 'Falstaff and Mr. Dover Wilson', *Kenyon Review* XV.2 (Spring 1953) 213–62.
22. New Penguin *R2*, p. 18.
23. Campbell, *Shakespeare's "Histories"*, p. 200.
24. Reese, *The Cease of Majesty*, p. 161.
25. The right of the king to nominate his heir is pointedly discussed by King Henry VI and Richard of York in the first scene of *3H6*.
26. See especially IV.i.240–2. The first hint of this kind of presumption in Richard comes from Bolingbroke on being sentenced to banishment: 'Your will be done', perhaps ironically echoing the Lord's Prayer (I.iii.144).
27. For a comparison of attitudes to ambition in Shakespeare and Marlowe see my essay 'Two Aspects of Ambition in Elizabethan Tragedy: *Doctor Faustus* and *Macbeth*', *English Studies*, L.3 (June 1969) 235–48.
28. Cf. the words 'ambition' and 'pride' in Richard's reflections at V.v.18, 22.
29. In Shakespeare's play the stopping of the combat is not, as Palmer has it, 'a considered act of state'. Nor, surely, is 'the whole scene [. . .] in the nature of a practical joke' (*Political Characters of Shakespeare*, pp. 130–1).
30. In I.i.126–41 Mowbray answers Bolingbroke's accusations with convincing details, and his confession to having laid an ambush for John of Gaunt's life, for which he has been forgiven, adds to the impression of sincerity. Compare, too, Richard's farewell words to the combatants in the lists. It is almost as if he hopes Bolingbroke will be killed, while in Mowbray's eye he sees 'virtue with valour' (I.iii.98). See also Palmer, p. 130.
31. As R. F. Hill points out, 'Froissart and Holinshed unequivocally state that Bolingbroke was recalled by the enemies of Richard to seize the throne' ('Dramatic Techniques and Interpretation in "Richard II"', *Early Shakespeare*, pp. 101–21).
    Northumberland's defection from Richard is demonstrated again, in spite of his formal declarations, by small touches like his omission of the royal title in II.iii.6 and his failure to kneel in the royal presence at III.iii.72–3. A great deal is communicated by indirection in this play.
32. Cf. Ribner, 'Richard's deposition emerges dramatically as the result of his own character, rather than of the antagonism of Bolingbroke' (*The English History Play*, p. 164). Sengupta says of Bolingbroke that 'Shakespeare presents him in this play as a man who seizes the crown but is no usurper because his ambition grows with his opportunities and the crown is to him more a gift than a prize won by force or diplomacy' (*Shakespeare's Historical Plays*, p. 124). On the other hand, whatever Bolingbroke may feel, Richard with his dying breath reclaims his kingship:

> Exton, thy fierce hand
> Hath with the king's blood stain'd the king's own land.

We cannot entirely acquit Bolingbroke of usurpation.
33. Aumerle's abortive conspiracy serves the purpose of emphasising York's integrity and Bolingbroke's magnanimity but little else, unless we wish to add comic relief. Since the first conspiracy against Henry IV is so easily put down it does not, at this early stage of his reign, do much to suggest the insecurity of the usurper's tenure, and we have to wait for the *Henry IV* plays if we wish to see it as part of a larger pattern.

Note, however, the absence of York and Aumerle from *H4* (York is only mentioned in passing in *1H4*, I.iii.245.)

Palmer is hardly right in saying that 'Shakespeare's presentation of Aumerle's conspiracy has yet another dramatic purpose. It supplies the crowning motive for [Bolingbroke's] instigation of Exton to the murder of Richard' (*Political Characters of Shakespeare*, pp. 172–3). If this connection was ever made in the play it has now been lost.

34. The phrase 'sacred state' is used by Richard about his own condition in IV.i.209. The word 'sacred' is used eight times in *R2* and nine times in all the other English history plays (including *KJ* and *H8*) together. It does not occur in the *H4* plays, where Bolingbroke is back in a questionable position.

Other examples of the somewhat ambiguous transfer of divine sanction from Richard to Bolingbroke are to be found in York's account in v.ii of Bolingbroke's entry into London 'Whilst all tongues cried "God save thee, Bolingbroke!"' and 'Jesu preserve thee! Welcome, Bolingbroke!'; and in York's own declaration in the same scene:

> But heaven hath a hand in these events,
> To whose high will we bound our calm contents.
> To Bolingbroke are we sworn subjects now,
> Whose state and honour I for aye allow.

It should be noticed, too, that Shakespeare does not introduce Mortimer's claim to the succession to complicate Bolingbroke's position, though this claim becomes important in *1H4* and again in *1H6*, and we thus lose a link between the plays. On the contrary, Richard 'with willing soul' adopts Bolingbroke as his heir (IV.i.108–9).

35. The Tudor myth may have been pushed into the background in the later plays when it came to writing them, but its appearance in *R2* cannot be dismissed. The prophetic voice in that play which remains most significant is not that of Gaunt condemning the king but of Carlisle warning the nobles assembled in parliament of the bloodshed that will follow for generations upon the crowning of Bolingbroke. Holinshed blames the Duke of Hereford (Bolingbroke) for wanting 'moderation and loyaltie in his dooings, for the which,' he says, 'both he himselfe and his lineall race were scourged afterwards, as a dire punishment unto rebellious subjects' (Bullough, III, p. 409).

36. Arden *R2*, p. lxviii.

Chapter 7   Down-trod Mortimer and Plump Jack

1. In his introduction to the Arden edition, A. R. Humphreys paraphrases the opening lines of *1H4*: 'the King and nation are shaken and wan with care, and frighted peace pants out short-winded accents of new broils' (p. lviii). But the meaning of Shakespeare's 'time for frighted peace to pant' is obviously that peace can now get his (her?) breath back; and the 'new' broils', it is important to note, are not domestic but 'To be commenc'd in stronds afar remote'. Edward Dering avoided the possibility of misunderstanding these lines by altering 'new broiles' to 'sweete rest' and crossing out the following line, so as to read simply 'And breath short-winded accents of sweete rest'. There *is* a brief interval of peace, or so the king thinks.

2. *1H4*, III.ii.4–11; *2H4*, III.i.65–78; *2H4*, IV.v.183–91, 218.

3. Dering actually expands the first crusade announcement, on what authority it is hard

to say. Hardin Craig thought that 'the Dering version may be older than the earliest quarto of the Henry IV plays' and represents 'a manuscript of *Henry IV* when it was one play and not two' ('The Dering Version of Shakespeare's *Henry IV*', *PQ*, 35, 1956, pp. 218–19). My own theory, based partly on the sheet gatherings of Dering's manuscript, is that Dering intended at first to transcribe only Part I. When he went on to add some of Part II the little that he added could conceivably have come from an early draft of *Henry IV*.

Derek Traversi thinks that 'when the Jerusalem of the king's living thoughts is transferred from the Holy Land to the Westminster chamber in which he is destined to die [it] confers upon his life, as he takes leave of it, a sense of ironic fatality' (*Shakespeare from 'Richard II' to 'Henry V'*, p. 155). Without rejecting this interpretation I still see Henry's death in 'Jerusalem' as a consummation, in dramatic and symbolic terms, of his original wish.

4. Actually *1H4* does not convey much sense of the carnage which Carlisle prophesies – rather of the chivalric opposition of two brave champions. There is a grimmer realism in *2H4*. But Shakespeare was probably looking back to his first tetralogy rather than forward to the unwritten *H4* and *H5* when he wrote the prophecy. In this sense it is true to say that the *H6* plays and *R3* embody the Tudor myth. They were made to do so retrospectively.

5. Arden *1H4*, p. xxv.

6. According to II.iii.25–8 (Hotspur's soliloquy), York should have been at Shrewsbury, too. But he is not mentioned in Mortimer's muster of the rebels in the Bangor scene, nor does he give a reason for his non-appearance. Sprague says the introduction of York in a single, dispensable, scene in *1H4* 'is a chief reason . . . for thinking that the dramatist was already looking beyond the limits of a single play' ('Shakespeare's Unnecessary Characters', *SS*, 20, 1967, pp. 78–9). This is begging the question: *when* was *2H4* planned as a separate play?

7. Campbell, *Shakespeare's 'Histories'*, pp. 232–3. Henry refused to ransom Mortimer as Queen Elizabeth refused 'to rescue Mary from her incarceration by the Scots before her escape and flight to England'.

8. Professor Hugh Dickinson made much the same point back in 1961, though he thought it was Henry's guilt in the death of Richard that had to be muted for Hal's sake rather than his doubtful legitimacy. See 'The Reformation of Prince Hal', *SQ*, 12, 1 (Winter 1961) 33–46.

9. There are promises of Falstaff's reform, too, though it never happens. See esp. *1H4*, I.ii.92–5; II.ii.15–24; III.iii. 4–23; v.iv.162–4. The only change that comes over him is for the worse, as he grows in vanity after his exploits at Shrewsbury.

10. I.ii.190–212. A. G. Gross thinks the soliloquy is a conflation of two different versions and that after he first wrote the main part of it Shakespeare 'changed his mind about the design of the play' in the way indicated by Harold Jenkins (see below) and therefore wished to remove the promise of an early reformation. Thus 'lines 1–9 and 14–23 represent the original version, and lines 10–13 ("If all the yeere . . . rare accidents") the revision. Unfortunately, the compositor printed both' ('The Text of Hal's First Soliloquy', *Eng. Miscellany*, XVIII (1967) 49–54). The theory is not entirely implausible, since there does seem to be an incompatibility between lines 10–13 and the rest, but I cannot agree with Gross that with the supposed original soliloquy omitted there is no further promise of reform in *1H4*.

11. There are spokesmen for opposed views in the same number of *SQ*: XIX.1 (Winter 1968). David Berkeley and Donald Eidson hold that Hal is in no need of education – he

is always basically himself and only biding his time to show it: 'Blood will tell.' ('The Theme of *Henry IV*, *Part 1*, pp. 25–31.) S. P. Zitner, on the other hand, maintains that Hal is being educated all along. ('Anon, Anon: or, a Mirror for a Magistrate', pp. 63–70.) In neither of these articles is Hal considered as genuinely debauched, but see e.g. John Palmer's view in *Political Characters of Shakespeare*, pp. 180–249.

12. 'Give him as much as will make him a royal man, and send him back again to my mother' (*1H4*, II.iv.286–7). Robert B. Bennett sees Hal's turning away of the king's messenger as a 'crisis of timing', a missed opportunity deep with consequences ('Prince Hal's Crisis of Timing', *Cahiers élisabéthains* 13 (1978) 15–23). It is also much more than a crisis of timing, a gross insult.

13. Sengupta, *Shakespeare's Historical Plays*, pp. 136–8.

14. Wilson, Introduction to the New Cambridge *1H4*, pp. xi–xiii. See also *The Fortunes of Falstaff*, p. 64, and Tillyard, *Shakespeare's History Plays*, p. 265. Sengupta sees the two parts of *H4* as a single structural unit with Falstaff at the centre (*Shakespeare's Historical Plays*, pp. 127–9).

   To Dover Wilson's complementary pairing Traversi adds the idea of self-conquest as a main theme for the second part: 'Having asserted himself as a modern prince in the exercise of the chivalrous virtues, . . . Hal is now faced with the more arduous necessity of subduing his own will, of making himself the instrument of a conception of justice which transcends all personal considerations' (*Shakespeare from 'Richard II' to 'Henry V'*, see esp. pp. 7, 108).

   Sherman H. Hawkins marshals a great deal of erudition to prove that 'Prince Hal's education must encompass all four kingly virtues. These divide with pleasing symmetry: temperance and fortitude in Part I, justice and wisdom in Part II.' I cannot find anything like this neat patterning in the plays. See Hawkins, 'Virtue and Kingship in Shakespeare's *Henry IV*', *ELR*, 5.3 (Autumn 1975) 313–43.

15. Ribner, *The English History Play*, p. 171. Hunter, '*Henry IV* and the Elizabethan Two-part Play', *RES*, new series v (1954) 236–48.

16. Arden *1H4*, p. xxviii.

17. *Sources*, IV, pp. 159–60.

18. H. Edward Cain thinks *1H4* complete in itself and *2H4* simply an addition. See 'Further Light on the Relation of *1* and *2 Henry IV*', *SQ*, III.1 (Jan. 1952) 21–38. There are too many signs of redistribution of material to make this theory plausible.

19. Richard David, 'Shakespeare's History Plays / Epic or Drama', *SS*, 6 (1953) 129–39, see p. 137. David thinks '*2 Henry IV* has pot-boiler written all over it'.

20. Dover Wilson finds relics of 'the L. C. Justice plot' in *1H4*, I.ii.63–4, 83–6, and III.ii.32–3. See his introduction to the New Cambridge *1H4*, p. xii.

21. There is a Lincolnshire place name (Stamford fair) in III.ii and there are Gloucestershire names in v.i, iii. Shakespeare may have begun to alter the Gloucestershire names to suit the new context in Part II and failed to follow suit in Act v.

22. Wilson, *The Fortunes of Falstaff*, p. 89.

23. Traversi, *Shakespeare from 'Richard II' to 'Henry V'*, pp. 136–8.

24. James Black points out that 'Hal's rejoinder to Falstaff at Shrewsbury in *Part 1*', 'Why, thou owest God a death', is echoed by Feeble in Part 2: 'A man can die but once, we owe God a death.' ('Counterfeits of Soldiership in *Henry IV*', *SQ*, XXIV.4 (Autumn 1973) p. 381). This could be another indication that the material for one play was divided into two.

25. Compare Falstaff's 'I do remember him at Clement's Inn' at III.ii.302–3. There are also inconsistencies about the number of recruits in this scene, of the kind one is

tempted to blame on theatrical adaptation. There are supposed to be 'half a dozen sufficient men' for Falstaff to inspect, but only five are named. He can have four but apparently leaves with only three. This last disparity, of course, may be accounted for by the bribes received in lieu of conscription.

26. At the end of II.iv, where Peto is probably a mistake for Poins. Dering has Poins.

27. There is also a letter for 'old mistress Ursula' whom Falstaff has 'weekly sworn to marry since [he] perceived the first white hair of [his] chin'. Her identity is not explained.

    Falstaff's letters are obviously requests for money, as we can tell not only from the context but from his final salutation in the letter to the prince: 'Thine by yea and no – which is as much as to say, as thou usest him' (II.ii.124–5). They might well be parodies of the prince's missives in *1H4*.

28. Probably the first part is somewhat less self-contained than the second. It does not bring the history of King Henry IV to a satisfactory conclusion and leaves Falstaff with kudos rather than the ignominy he deserves. The Archbishop's mobilisation in IV.iv definitely points to a continuation. But the second part begins with a scene – Northumberland receiving reports from Shrewsbury – which is purely transitional, and it introduces Falstaff with a reputation derived from his exploits in the first part.

29. Edgar T. Schell thinks the speech in which 'King Henry prophesies the anarchy to follow upon the accession of his son' is a purely rhetorical structure designed 'to serve the needs of the play's dramatic structure': 'language must effect here what action cannot: it must make of Hal momentarily a prodigal through whose reformation the play is brought into dramatic focus' ('Prince Hal's Second "Reformation"', *SQ*, 21, 1 (Winter 1970) 11–16). I see this as an attempt to turn an accident of composition into a subtlety of invention.

30. Clarence has an entry in the SD for *H5*, I.ii. J. H. Walter's note for this SD in the Arden edition says that he does not appear elsewhere in the play. This is a mistake: Clarence is addressed by the king at v.ii.84. In the quarto he also has a speaking part at Agincourt.

31. Jenkins, *The Structural Problem in Shakespeare's 'Henry the Fourth'*, p. 24.

32. As Humphreys points out in his footnote for III.i.66, the king is wrong not only about this Warwick being a Nevil but about his being present when Richard prophesied against Northumberland. This is one of the minor discrepancies between *H4* and the earlier plays.

33. Lord Bardolph's part in *2H4* is also a bit problematic. Judging by I.iii, he might have been designed for a larger part, as the rebel who is sceptical of success. But he doesn't appear again. Possibly the prominence of the other Bardolph made it difficult to go on using him. Humphreys thinks Lord Bardolph's part in I.i 'may originally have been Umfrevile's' – see his notes to I.i.34 and I.iii.81 in the Arden edition.

    The quarto *2H4* of 1600, followed e.g. by the modern Riverside edition, includes Lord Bardolph in the SD for the Gaultree Forest encounter (IV.i), which must be wrong. A man of his standing could not be completely ignored in the dialogue if he were present. His absence from the rebel army after he has been seen in council with the other leaders is insufficiently explained and reminds one of Mortimer's unexplained absence from Shrewsbury.

34. Traversi, *Shakespeare from 'Richard II' to 'Henry V'*, pp. 111–12.

Chapter 8   The Disunity of *King Henry V*

1. J. H. Walter (ed.), the Arden *H5*, Introduction, p. xi.

2. Walter follows Dover Wilson in thinking the reference is to the Curtain Theatre, see his note to Prologue, line 13.

3. See e.g. Dover Wilson in the New Cambridge *H5*, pp. 113–14.

4. On Shakespeare's omission of any 'hand-to-hand combats between leading figures on the two sides' see C. H. Hobday, 'Imagery and Irony in "Henry V" ', *SS*, 21 (1968) 112.

5. Bullough, *Sources*, IV, p. 382. Elizabethans may have had a general impression that the Dauphin was always the virtual ruler of France. Compare Shakespeare's *1H6* and *KJ*.

6. Bullough, *Sources*, IV, p. 320.

7. Ibid., p. 330.

8. Q *H5* is one of the indubitably 'bad quartos' and almost certainly compiled from memory of the play as performed on the stage. The Q version probably had only one bishop. The initial stage direction for its opening scene, i.e. the parliament or council scene, gives an entry to '2. Bishops', but there is no reason to suppose that more than one of them is represented by the '*Bi.*' of the speech headings, so the stage direction could be derived from a written source.

9. It is tempting to speculate that there may have been one version of the play for the public stage and one adapted for performance at court, in which case Q would represent the court version and F possibly a conflation of both. This would mean that the choruses, which are not in Q, were for 'οι πολλοι, which would be not unnatural, although G. P. Jones thinks they were written for performance at court (see his '*Henry V*: The Chorus and the Audience', *SS*, 31 (1978) 93–104, esp. pp. 95ff). W. J. Lawrence (*Shakespeare's Workshop*, 1928) thinks it was mainly court adaptations of the play which fell into the printers' hands.

10. The phrase 'some certain dukedoms' looks like an incomplete echo of Canterbury's lines in I.i.87–8, where he speaks of Henry's 'true titles to some certain dukedoms, / And generally to the crown and seat of France'.

11. Exeter's embassy in *H5* parallels the return of the Archbishop of Bourges to France in *FV*. Bourges is the bearer of answers first to King Charles then to the Dauphin which correspond to Exeter's messages. Bourges reports that Henry 'is alreadie landed', Exeter that 'he is footed in this land already'. Both the anonymous author of *FV* and Shakespeare may have been partly thinking of the mission of Henry's pursuivant at arms Antelope which is mentioned by Hall and Holinshed. Antelope was dispatched from Southampton as the king was about to embark, but Hall and Holinshed differ as to Henry's motive in sending him.

12. In *1H4* the hostess is married to 'an honest man' (III.iii.91 and 118) while in *2H4* she is a widow and asserts that Falstaff has sworn to marry her (II.i.68, 80, 89–90). Both Mistress Quickly and Doll Tearsheet quarrel violently with Pistol in *2H4* (II.iv), and though Doll seems to know him the hostess does not. In v.iv, we learn that Pistol has killed a man on account of Doll, and the hostess, apparently, is also held responsible. So there has at least been some association between Pistol and the two women, but hardly of the kind to prepare us for a marriage between Pistol and Mistress Quickly. Nor is there much support for this liaison in *The Merry Wives*, II.ii.130–2, though some editors have seen a connection.

13. As Dover Wilson has pointed out (New Cambridge *H5*, p. 115), there is no question here of a mere careless substitution of Doll for Nell. It is Doll who is said by Pistol to be in the spital at II.i.74–7.

14. See the New Cambr. *H5*, pp. 114–15.

15. Arden *H5*, pp. xxxvii–xxxviii.

16. Pistol's information, 'for I shall sutler be / Unto the camp, and profits will accrue', does not come till near the end of the scene where the three rogues speak of going to France, and Gower's explanation concerning Pistol – 'Why, 'tis a gull, a fool, a rogue, that now and then goes to the wars to grace himself at his return into London under the form of a soldier.' – comes long afterwards, in III.vi.

17. Arden *H5*, p. xxxvii.

18. The boy's soliloquy may be an addition to the original scene as Walter thinks, 'probably to prepare the audience for the deaths of Bardolph and Nym' (Arden, p. xxxvii). Notice that he threatens to leave the service of the three thieves, but when we see him again in IV.iv he seems to be still serving Pistol. In *2H4* the boy was Falstaff's page, and in *H5* at II.i.81 he still speaks of Falstaff as 'my master'. It was probably Falstaff who first took him to France.

19. New Cambridge *H5*, p. 115, See also Wilson's *The Fortunes of Falstaff*, pp. 124–5.

20. Arden *H5*, p. xxxix.

21. Ribner, *The English History Play in the Age of Shakespeare*, p. 182.

22. One comic scene is left undeveloped and one is muddled, and Fluellen is concerned in both. His quarrel with Macmorris in III.ii leads to nothing in spite of the latter's horrible threat to cut off Fluellen's head. (Both Macmorris and Jamy, incidentally, appear only in this one scene.) In the glove episode of IV.vii the king first tells Williams to fetch Gower, then asks Fluellen, who has been listening, to do the same. He also asks Fluellen if he knows Gower, though Fluellen has just spoken in praise of the English captain. Gower, of course, is not wanted: it is all a clumsy device to make Williams challenge Fluellen.

23. By G. W. Williams in a paper read at the International Shakespeare Conference at Stratford-upon-Avon, August 1978. See also Peter Bilton, *Commentary and Control in Shakespeare's Plays* (1974).

24. Cf. H. C. Goddard: 'Through the Choruses, the playwright gives us the popular idea of his hero. In the play, the poet tells the truth about him' (*The Meaning of Shakespeare* (1951) p. 218). Goddard sees the difference as intentional and functional.

25. Anthony S. Brennan thinks the contradictions introduced by the Chorus deliberate, part of 'a contrast of attitudes which illuminates a structure of ideas regulating the play'. See 'That Within Which Passes Show: The Function of the Chorus in *Henry V*', *PQ*, 58.1 (Winter 1979) 40–51. This does not explain the factual discrepancies and lack of correlation between the choruses and the play proper, however.

   John Wilders finds the happy ending ironical in the light of the epilogue and what the audience knew about the son of Harry and Katharine. See *The Lost Garden*, pp. 44–5. This would presuppose a much tighter integration of the choruses with the play than what we actually find.

26. New Cambr. *H5*, p. 113.

27. This may be true to some extent of the quarto text as well, though it is less apparent there because so much has been lost through abridgment and memorial transmission. Some of the passages which should have been omitted may have been simply overlooked, e.g. the King of France's order to the Dauphin to stay in Rouen. See also n. 9 above.

28. Salisbury is praised by both Exeter and Bedford (by Clarence in Q) after his first exit, yet he has only these two brief appearances and we never learn what becomes of him.

29. See New Cambr. *H5*, p. 116.

30. The time is mentioned by the chorus. The time references in the Agincourt scenes are well co-ordinated. Rossiter finds a similar careful use of 'the time-references by which the audience are moved imaginatively through the night before Bosworth . . . such as

would only be put in by a dramatist who knew quite well what he was about'. He sees 'the only complete parallel to this careful treatment of time . . . in *Faustus*'. ('The Structure of Richard the Third', *Durham Univ. Journal*, XXXI (1938) p. 70.)

31. Wilson lists the most prominent critics who have written in dislike or admiration of Harry in his Introduction to the New Cambr. *H5*, p. xv, n. 2.
32. Tillyard, *Shakespeare's History Plays*, pp. 306–8.
33. Palmer, *Political Characters of Shakespeare*, pp. 218–19, 247.
34. Battenhouse, '*Henry V* as Heroic Comedy' in R. Hosley (ed.), *Essays on Shakespeare and Elizabethan Drama* (1963) pp. 163–82. See p. 168.
35. C. H. Hobday, 'Imagery and Irony in "Henry V"', *SS*, 21 (1968) 107–13; William Babula, 'Whatever Happened to Prince Hal? An Essay on "Henry V"', *SS* 30 (1977) 47–59; Andrew Gurr, ' "Henry V" and the Bees' Commonwealth', *SS* 30 (1977) 6–72.
36. Hobday, op. cit., p. 109.
37. There is further irony for those who know *2H4* in the fact that war has already been considered before the action of *H5* begins, and Henry is grasping at any excuse he can find for it. This of course is not the only time Henry is illogical or hypocritical. Many critics have found his arguments in the debate with the three soldiers both faulty and disingenuous. See e.g. Palmer, op. cit., pp. 237–40.
38. A more frequent word in *H4* is 'greatness'. It occurs seven times in each of the two parts of *H4* and five times in *H5*.
39. Holinshed must take some of the blame for Harry's pervasive piety, but Shakespeare chose to use this bias in Holinshed.
40. Cf. Battenhouse, op. cit., p. 172. See also Samuel Daniel's *Civile Wars*, bk. 3, stanza 127 (here quoted from Campbell, *Shakespeare's "Histories"*, p. 243, n.):

> And since my death my purpose doth preuent
> Touching this sacred warre I tooke in hand,
> (An action wherewithall my soule had ment
> T'appease my God, and reconcile my land)
> To thee is left to finish my intent,
> Who to be safe must never idly stand;
> But some great actions entertaine thou still
> To hold their mindes who else will practise ill.

41. There can be no doubt that this is a case of bribery and corruption, and Hall confirms the impression conveyed by the play itself:

> The cause of this offre semed to some of the wise prelates nether decente nor conuenient, for thei well forsawe and perfightly knewe that if the commõs perceiued that thei by reward or offre of money would resist their request & peticion, that thei stirred & moued with a fury wold not onely rayle and despise theim as corruptours of Princes and enemies of publique wealthe, but would so crye and call on the kyng and his temporall lordes that thei were like to lese bothe worke and oyle, cost and liuyng: (fo.xxxv^v)

Dover Wilson seems to be completely blinded by his patriotic enthusiasm for the play when he declares that there is 'not a hint of a bribe on the Archbishop's part, still less of his provoking the King to war in order to protect Church property!' (New Cambr. *H5*, p. xxii). Similarly Palmer, 'There is no suggestion that these amiable priests are in the least to blame for their very natural alarm at the prospect of having to contribute a thousand pounds by the year to the King's coffers' (*Political Characters*, p. 219). There is more involved than the contribution to the king's coffers anyway: Palmer does not mention the 'hundred almshouses right well supplied'. Ornstein similarly thinks 'there is nothing devious in Canterbury's relation with the King and nothing that smacks of hypocrisy in his patriotic fervour' (*A Kingdom for a Stage*, p. 179).

42. Cf. Battenhouse, op. cit., p. 179.

43. *Political Characters*, p. 185. See also Palmer's complete chapter on 'Henry of Monmouth', pp. 180–249. Sengupta has an attractive but rather simplistic view of Henry V as 'a man of action who is uncritical about his own assumptions' (*Shakespeare's Historical Plays*, p. 141).

44. Tillyard, *Shakespeare's History Plays*, p. 281.

45. See the conflicting explanations of his reform given by the two bishops, quoted above. In his meeting with his brothers and the Lord Chief Justice after his father's death Harry himself admits, 'The tide of blood in me / Hath proudly flow'd in vanity till now' (*2H4*, v.ii.129–30). And in his speech to the Dauphin's messengers he makes the surprising statement:

> We never valu'd this poor seat of England;
> And therefore, living hence, did give ourself
> To barbarous licence;

Both these statements indicate that his reform was sudden and unpremeditated.

46. Ornstein may be right in his view of *H5* that 'Little in it is perfunctory or indifferent'; but he goes on: 'it has none of the muddles and contradictions of *King John*, none of the lapses of inspiration that are obvious in other History Plays', and this is clearly unacceptable (op. cit., p. 175).

47. New Cambr., *H5*, p. lv.

48. The Gilbert Talbot who fought at Agincourt was the elder brother of the John Talbot who occurs in *H6*, but Shakespeare obviously tried to include names in Harry's battle oration which would sound familiar and evoke patriotic responses. It is surprising, perhaps, that in the Folio version Harry mentions Warwick, Talbot, and Salisbury, who have insignificant or non-existent parts in the play, while he leaves out Erpingham, Westmoreland, Suffolk, and York, though the two latter die in the battle. The quarto omits Talbot and Salisbury and includes Clarence and York in Harry's oration. It has no Westmoreland. Historically neither Bedford, nor Warwick, nor Westmoreland was present at Agincourt.

The Bedford of *H5* and *H6* is John of Lancaster in *H4*. While links between *H5* and the *H4* plays are relatively weak as far as *dramatis personae* are concerned the links with *H6* seem to have been deliberately strengthened.

Chapter 9 All Is True, or the Honest Chronicler

1. The pageantry has been emphasised by e.g. G. Wilson Knight in *The Crown of Life* (1947), Irving Ribner in *The English History Play in the Age of Shakespeare* (1957), and John D. Cox in '*Henry VIII* and the Masque', *ELH*, 45 (1978) 390–409; the mythic elements by e.g. Howard Felperin in 'Shakespeare's *Henry VIII*: History as Myth', *SEL*, 6 (1966) 225–46, and Ronald Berman in '*King Henry the Eighth*: History and

Romance', *ES*, 48, 2 (1967) 112–21; the looseness of plot by e.g. Ribner, op. cit., and A. R. Humphreys in his Introduction to the New Penguin *H8* (1971).

2. Op. cit., p. 290.
3. Cf. Lee Bliss: 'This is a rather bleak picture of an England where double-dealing seems the norm rather than the exception, where the king's "pleasure" may be derived from appetite but is understood as law, and where men hardly dare discuss – much less act upon – matters of national concern' ('The Wheel of Fortune and the Maiden Phoenix of Shakespeare's *King Henry the Eighth*', *ELH* 42 (1975) 1–25. See p. 10).
4. Op. cit., pp. 245–6.
5. See R. A. Foakes, Introduction to the New Arden *H8* (1957, UP 1968) p. xlix. Foakes particularly refers to Hardin Craig's *An Interpretation of Shakespeare* (1948).
6. Felperin, pp. 243–4.
7. Frederick O. Waage, 'Henry VIII and the Crisis of the English History Play', *SSt*, 8 (1975) 297–309; see p. 297 and cf. Lee Bliss, op. cit., esp. p. 19.
8. Berman, op. cit., p. 118.
9. New Penguin *H8*, p. 19. Humphreys (p. 18) allies himself with Aldis Wright and David Nichol Smith and quotes Wright's opinion of *H8*: 'without plot, without development, without any character on which the interest can be concentrated throughout.'
10. A. R. Humphreys in the main defends the division of the play between Shakespeare and Fletcher suggested by James Spedding in 1850 – see the New Penguin *H8*, pp. 21ff. He also provides a useful critical list of the main contenders for and against the collaboration theory pp. 50–4. To the supporters of collaboration may be added Cyrus Hoy and to the defenders of Shakespeare's sole authorship Irving Ribner, Howard Felperin, H. M. Richmond, and Lee Bliss.
11. Ribner, p. 291. See also Humphreys, New Penguin *H8*, pp. 35–9.
12. R. A. Law, 'The Double Authorship of *Henry VIII*', *SP*, 56 (1959) 471–88. See p. 488.
13. Spedding is quoted by Foakes, Arden *H8*, p. xlvii; Law, op. cit., p. 486; Waage, op. cit., p. 297.
14. Foakes, Arden *H8*, p. xlviii. Foakes does not endorse this view but refers it to a number of adverse critics of the play's structure whom he lists in a footnote: W. A. Wright, D. Nichol Smith, A. A. Parker, Eugene M. Waith, and R. Boyle.
15. Buckingham's valedictory speeches in II.i are inconsistent (see my introductory chapter and pp. 155–6 below) but not so as to create any major problems outside that scene.
16. See especially I.ii.132–5 and II.iv.168–79. It is interesting to notice that the question of legitimacy, so much at the centre of the early plays, is also present in *H8*. The links with *KJ* are especially strong in this respect.
17. See v.i.129–33. The king now admits that 'such things have been done'.
18. Arden *H8*, p. lii.
19. G. Wilson Knight, *The Crown of Life*, p. 306.
20. Arden *H8*, pp. liii–liv.
21. Knight, pp. 334–6.
22. Arden *H8*, p. lviii.
23. See note 3 above.
24. Bliss, op. cit., p. 20.
25. Knight, pp. 306–15.
26. Arden *H8*, pp. lxi, lxiii. Cf. Bullough, *Sources*, IV, p. 448.
27. Henry's daughter Mary is mentioned by the king in II.iv.172–9 and by Katherine in IV.ii.131–8.

28. That human individuals could be both good and bad at the same time was always a part of Shakespeare's psychological and moral insight. That they could be greatly good and greatly bad at the same time was demonstrated in *R2*. A more penetrating character analysis is found in *Julius Cæsar*. To quote Geoffrey Bullough (*Sources*, v, p. 57):

> what Shakespeare learned from Plutarch was to represent more clearly than before the paradoxes of human motive, the mixture of good and evil in the same person. [. . .] In *Julius Cæsar* the dramatist achieves a somewhat detached tolerance in his attitude towards historical figures, and at the same time a critical attitude towards politics and those who take part in it.

    At least one critic has also found a psychological relativism in *Julius Cæsar* similar to that which I find to be central in *H8*: see Rene E. Fortin, '*Julius Cæsar*: An Experiment in Point of View', *SQ*, XIX.4 (Autumn 1968) 341–7.
29. For Katherine's judgment of Henry see also Bliss, op. cit., p. 11.
30. Buckingham's warning against false friends may even be seen to be directed against the king. Wolsey's famous last words ('. . . he would not in mine age / Have left me naked to mine enemies') are certainly a veiled accusation of the king for his ingratitude. And Katherine cannot entirely conceal her bitterness. Is there a little of Webster's political radicalism in Shakespeare's last play?
31. See also Bliss, op. cit., pp. 5–6: 'Shakespeare capitalizes on the inconsistencies of the chronicles and with them enhances his use of multiple sympathetic perspectives.'
32. Humphreys, Penguin *H8*, p. 8: 'The title as Wotton cites it – *All is True* – was perhaps an alternative to that using the King's name, and meant to draw attention, as the Prologue also does, to the play's unusual care to be historically authentic.' Contrast Felperin's view, op. cit., p. 227: '*Henry VIII* departs from history, that is, from Holinshed, more radically than any of the earlier dramas – so much so, that the subtitle of the play, "All Is True", makes one wonder whether Shakespeare is not ironically hinting that we revise our conventional notions of historical truth, even of mimetic truth itself.'
33. Bliss, op. cit., p. 3.
34. There remains an anti-foreign bias which finds an explicit outlet in the proclamation against French manners in I.iii. It must be supposed that the proclamation is issued by the king and is designed to set him in a favourable light. It has no other dramatic significance.

Bibliography

Alexander, P., *Shakespeare's Henry VI and Richard III* (Cambridge University Press, 1929).

Babula, W., 'Whatever Happened to Prince Hal?: An Essay on "Henry V"', *SS*, 30 (1977) 6–72.

Baker, H., Introductions to the English history plays, *The Riverside Shakespeare* (Boston: Houghton Mifflin, 1974).

Barkan, L., 'The Theatrical Consistency Of *Richard II*', *SQ*, 29.1 (Winter 1978) [5]–19.

Battenhouse, R. W., '*Henry V* as Heroic Comedy', in R. Hosley (ed.), *Essays on Shakespeare and Elizabethan Drama* (Routledge, 1963).

Bennett, R. B., 'Prince Hal's Crisis of Timing in the Tavern Scene of *Henry IV, Part I*', *Cahiers élisabéthains*, 13 (Apr. 1978) 15–23.

Berkeley, D. and D. Eidson, 'The Theme of *Henry IV, Part 1*', *SQ*, XIX.1 (Winter 1968) [25]–31.

Berman, R., '*King Henry the Eighth*: History and Romance', *ES*, XLVIII.3 (Apr. 1967) 112–21.

Bevington, D. and J. L. Halio (eds), *Shakespeare: Pattern of Excelling Nature* (Newark, N.J.: University of Delaware Press, 1978).

Bilton, P., *Commentary and Control in Shakespeare's Plays* (Oslo: Universitetsforlaget; N.Y.: Humanities Press, 1974).

Black, J., 'Counterfeits of Soldiership in *Henry IV*', *SQ*, XXIV.4 (Autumn 1973) [372]–82.

Bliss, L., 'The Wheel of Fortune and the Maiden Phoenix of Shakespeare's *King Henry the Eighth*', *ELH*, 42 (1975) 1–25.

Boklund, G., 'The Troublesome Ending of *King John*', *Studia neophilologica*, XL (Uppsala, 1968), 175–84.

Born, H., 'The Date of *2,3 Henry VI*', *SQ*, XXV.3 (Summer 1974) [323]–34.

Brennan, A. S., 'That Within Which Passes Show: The Function of the Chorus in *Henry V*', *PQ*, 58.1 (Winter 1979) 40–51.

Brockbank, J. P., 'The Frame of Disorder – "*Henry VI*"', in *Early Shakespeare* (see below).

Brown, J. R., *Shakespeare and His Comedies* (Methuen, 1957).

Bullough, G., *Narrative and Dramatic Sources of Shakespeare*, vols III–V (Routledge; N.Y.: Columbia University Press, 1960, 1962, 1964).

Cairncross, A. S. (ed.), *King Henry VI, Parts I, II, III*, The Arden Shakespeare (Methuen, 1962, 1957, 1964; University Paperbacks, 1969).

Campbell, L. B., *Shakespeare's "Histories": Mirrors of Elizabethan Policy* (San Marino: Huntington Library, 1947; Methuen, University Paperback, 1964).

Chambers, E. K., *William Shakespeare*, vols I–II (Clarendon Press, 1930).

Champion, L. S., 'The Function of Mowbray: Shakespeare's Maturing Artistry in *Richard II*', *SQ*, XXVI.1 (Winter 1975) [3]–7.

Clemen, W., *Shakespeare's Dramatic Art* (Methuen, 1972).

———, 'Anticipation and Foreboding in Shakespeare's Early Histories', *SS*, 6 (1953) 25–35.

Coleridge, S. T., see Hawkes.

Cox, J. D., '*Henry VIII* and the Masque', *ELH*, 45 (1978) 390–409.

Craig, H., *An Interpretation of Shakespeare* (New York: Dryden Press, 1948).

———, 'The Dering Version of Shakespeare's *Henry IV*', *PQ*, 35.2 (1956) 218–19.

David, R., 'Shakespeare's History Plays: Epic or Drama', *SS*, 6 (1953) 129–39.

Dickinson, H., 'The Reformation of Prince Hal', *SQ*, XII.1 (Winter 1961) [33]–46.

Dollarhide, L. E., 'Two Unassimilated Movements of Richard III: An Interpretation', *Mississippi Quarterly*, XIV.1 (Winter 1960/61) 40–6.

Early Shakespeare, Stratford-upon-Avon Studies 3 (Edward Arnold, 1961, 1967).

Eidson, D., see Berkeley.

Empson, W., 'Falstaff and Mr. Dover Wilson', *Kenyon Review*, XV.2 (Spring 1953) 213–62.

Evans, G. B. (ed.), *The Riverside Shakespeare* (Boston, Mass.: Houghton Mifflin, 1974).

Felperin, H., 'Shakespeare's *Henry VIII*: History as Myth', *SEL*, VI.2 (Spring 1966) [225]–46.

Foakes, R. A. (ed.), *King Henry VIII*, The Arden Shakespeare (Methuen, 1957; University Paperback 1968).

Fortin, R. E., '*Julius Cæsar*: An Experiment in Point of View', *SQ*, XIX.4 (Autumn 1968) [341]–7.

French, A. L., 'Who Deposed Richard the Second?', *Essays in Criticism*, XVII (1967) 411–33.

———, 'Joan of Arc and *Henry VI*', *ES*, XLIX.5 (Oct. 1968) 425–9.

_____, 'The World of Richard III', *SSt*, IV (1968) 25–39.

_____, ' ''Henry VI'' and the Ghost of Richard II', *ES*, [L], Anglo–American Supplement (1969) xxxvii–xliii.

_____, 'The Mills of God and Shakespeare's Early History Plays', *ES*, 55.4 (Aug. 1974) 313–24.

Goddard, H. C., *The Meaning of Shakespeare* (University of Chicago Press, 1951).

Greg, W. W., *The Shakespeare First Folio* (Oxford: Clarendon Press, 1955).

Gross, A. G., 'The Text of Hal's First Soliloquy', *English Miscellany*, XVIII (1967) 49–54.

Gurr, A., ' ''Henry V'' and the Bees' Commonwealth', *SS*, 30 (1977) 6–72.

Hall, E., *The Union of the Two Noble and Illustrate Famelies of Lancastre & Yorke* (London, 1548; University Microfilms). See also Bullough.

Harbage, A., 'Shakespeare and the Myth of Perfection', *SQ*, xv.2 (Spring 1964) [1]–10.

Hawkes, T. (ed.), *Coleridge on Shakespeare* (Penguin Books, 1969).

Hawkins, S. H., 'Virtue and Kingship in Shakespeare's *Henry IV*', *ELR*, 5.3 (Autumn 1975) 313–43.

Hill, R. F., 'Dramatic Techniques and Interpretation in ''Richard II'' ', in *Early Shakespeare* (see above).

Hobday, C. H., 'Imagery and Irony in ''Henry V'' ', *SS*, 21 (1968) 107–13.

Holinshed, R., *The Third volume of Chronicles* (London, 1587; University Microfilms). See also Bullough.

Honigmann, E. A. J., *Shakespeare: Seven Tragedies* (Macmillan, 1976).

_____ (ed.), *King John*, The Arden Shakespeare (Methuen, 1957; University Paperback, 1967).

_____ (ed.), *King Richard the Third* (Penguin Books, 1968).

Hosley, R. (ed.), *Essays on Shakespeare and Elizabethan Drama* (Routledge, 1963).

Humphreys, A. R. (ed.), *The First Part of King Henry IV*, *The Second Part of King Henry IV*, The Arden Shakespeare (Methuen, 1960, 1966; School and Paperback edns 1961, 1967).

_____ (ed.), *King Henry the Eighth* (Penguin Books, 1971).

Hunter, G. K., '*Henry IV* and the Elizabethan Two-part Play', *RES*, new series v (1954) 236–48.

Jenkins, H., *The Structural Problem in Shakespeare's ''Henry the Fourth''* (Methuen, 1956).

Jones, E., *The Origins of Shakespeare* (Clarendon Press, 1977).

Jones, G. P., '*Henry V*: The Chorus and the Audience', *SS*, 31 (1978) 93–104.

Kelly, F. L., 'Oaths in Shakespeare's *Henry VI* Plays', *SQ*, xxiv.4 (Autumn 1973) [357]–71.

Kirschbaum, L., 'The Authorship of *1 Henry VI*', *PMLA*, lxvii.5 (Sept. 1952) 809–22.

Knight, G. W., *The Crown of Life* (Oxford University Press, 1947; Methuen, University Paperback, 1965).

Law, R. A., 'The Double Authorship of *Henry VIII*', *SP*, 56 (1959) 471–88.

Lawrence, W. J., *Shakespeare's Workshop* (Blackwell, 1928).

Lever, J. W. (ed.), *Measure for Measure*, The Arden Shakespeare (Methuen, 1965; University Paperback, 1967).

Levin, R., 'The Delapsing of Shakespeare', in *Shakespeare: Pattern of Excelling Nature* (see Bevington).

Leech, C., 'The Unity of *2 Henry IV*', *SS*, 6 (1953) 16–24.

MacIsaac, W. J., 'The Three Cousins in *Richard II*', *SQ*, xxii.2 (Spring 1971) [137]–46.

Merrix, R. P., 'Shakespeare's Histories and The New Bardolators', *SEL*, xix.2 (Spring 1979) [179]–96.

Mincoff, M., 'The Composition of *Henry VI, Part I*', *SQ*, xvi.4 (Autumn 1965) [279]–87.

Muir, K. (ed.), *The Tragedy of King Richard the Second*, The Signet Classic Shakespeare (N.Y.: New American Library, 1963).

Neill, M., Shakespeare's Halle of Mirrors: Play, Politics, and Psychology in *Richard III*', *SSt*, viii (1975) 99–129.

Ornstein, R., *A Kingdom for a Stage* (Harvard University Press, 1972).

Palmer, J., *Political Characters of Shakespeare* (Macmillan, 1945).

Pollard, A. W., *The Foundations of Shakespeare's Text* (Oxford University Press, 1923).

Price, H. T., 'Construction in Shakespeare', *University of Michigan Contributions in Modern Philology*, no. 17 (1951).

Price, J. R., '*King John* and Problematic Art', *SQ*, xxi.1 (Winter 1970) [25]–8.

Quinn, M., 'Providence in Shakespeare's Yorkist Plays', *SQ*, x.1 (Winter 1959) [45]–52.

Rees, J., *Shakespeare and the Story* (Athlone Press of the University of London, 1978).

Reese, M. M., *The Cease of Majesty: A Study of Shakespeare's History Plays* (Edward Arnold, 1961).

Ribner, I., *The English History Play in the Age of Shakespeare* (Princeton University Press, 1957).

Ricks, D. M., *Shakespeare's Emergent Form: A Study of the Structure of the Henry VI Plays* (Utah State University Press, 1968).

Ridley, M. R., *Shakespeare's Plays: A Commentary* (Dent, 1937, repr. 1957).

Rossiter, A. P., *Angel with Horns*, ed. G. Storey (Longman, 1961).

——, 'The Structure of Richard the Third', *Durham University Journal*, XXXI (1938) 44–75.

Schell, E. T., 'Prince Hal's Second "Reformation" ', *SQ*, XXI.1 (Winter 1970) [11]–16.

Schoenbaum, S., ' "Richard II" and the Realities of Power', *SS*, 28 (1975) 1–13.

Sen Gupta, S. C., *Shakespeare's Historical Plays* (Oxford University Press, 1964).

Shupe, D. R., 'The Wooing of Lady Anne: A Psychological Inquiry', *SQ*, 29.1 (Winter 1978) [28]–36.

Simmons, J. L., 'Shakespeare's *King John* and its Source: Coherence, Pattern, and Vision', *Tulane Studies in English*, XVII (1969) 53–72.

Smallwood, R. L. (ed.), *King John* (Penguin Books, 1974).

Smidt, K., *Iniurious Impostors and "Richard III"* (Oslo: Norwegian Universities Press, 1964).

——, *Memorial Transmission and Quarto Copy in "Richard III"* (Oslo: Universitetsforlaget; N.Y.: Humanities Press, 1970).

——, 'Two Aspects of Ambition in Elizabethan Tragedy: *Doctor Faustus* and *Macbeth*', *ES*, L.3 (June 1969) 235–48.

Spencer, T. J. B., 'When Homer Nods: Shakespeare's Artistic Lapses', in *Shakespeare: Pattern of Excelling Nature* (see Bevington).

——, 'Shakespeare's Careless Art', in M. Crane (ed.), *Shakespeare's Art: Seven Essays* (University of Chicago Press, 1973).

Sprague, A. C., 'Shakespeare's Unnecessary Characters', *SS*, 20 (1967) 75–82.

Tanner, S. L., 'Richard III versus Elizabeth', *SQ*, XXIV.4 (Winter 1973) [468]–72.

Tillyard, E. M. W., *Shakespeare's History Plays* (Chatto & Windus, 1944; Penguin Books, 1962).

Traversi, D., *Shakespeare from "Richard II" to "Henry V"* (Hollis, 1957).

Ure, P. (ed.), *King Richard II*, The Arden Shakespeare (Methuen, 1956; Export Edition 1959, repr. 1962).

Van de Water, J. C., 'The Bastard in *King John*', *SQ*, XI.2 (Spring 1960) [137]–46.

Waage, F. C., '*Henry VIII* and the Crisis of the English History Play', *SSt*, VIII (1975) 297–309.

Walter, J. H. (ed.), *King Henry V*, The Arden Shakespeare (Methuen, 1954, repr. 1977).

Wells, S. (ed.), *King Richard the Second* (Penguin Books, 1969).

Wentersdorf, K. P., 'The Conspiracy of Silence in *Henry V*', *SQ*, 27.3 (Summer 1976) [264]–87.

Wilders, J., *The Lost Garden: A View of Shakespeare's English and Roman History Plays* (Macmillan, 1978).

Williams, G., 'Suffolk and Margaret', *SQ*, xxv.3 (Summer 1974) [310]–22.

Wilson, J. D. (ed.), *The Works of Shakespeare* (Cambridge University Press, 1921–62).

_____, *The Fortunes of Falstaff* (Cambridge University Press; N.Y.: Macmillan, 1944).

Young, C. B., 'The Stage History of *King Henry VI*', in Dover Wilson's edition of Part 1 (1952) and Part 3 (1952).

Zitner, S. P., 'Anon, Anon: or, a Mirror for a Magistrate', *SQ*, xix.1 (Winter 1968) [63]–70.

Index